MW00353088

Strangers to Relatives

*The Adoption and Naming of
Anthropologists in Native North America*

Edited by Sergei Kan

UNIVERSITY OF NEBRASKA PRESS

LINCOLN AND LONDON

"What's in a Name?
Becoming a Real Person in a Yup'ik Community"
by Ann Fienup-Riordan
was previously published in
*Hunting Tradition in a Changing World:
Yup'ik Lives in Alaska Today*,
ed. Ann Fienup-Riordan
(New Brunswick: Rutgers University Press, 2000)

© 2001 by the
University of Nebraska Press
All rights reserved
Manufactured in the
United States of America
∞

Library of Congress
Cataloging-in-Publication Data
Strangers to relatives :
the adoption and naming
of anthropologists
in Native North America /
edited by
Sergei Kan.
p. cm.
Includes bibliographical
references and index.
ISBN 0-8032-2746-9 (cl. : alk. paper) —
ISBN 0-8032-7797-0 (pbk. : alk. paper)
1. Indians of North America.
2. Ethnologists—North America.
3. Ethnology—Field work.
4. Adoption—North America.
5. Names, Indian—North America.
I. Kan, Sergei.
E98.A15 S77 2001   305.897'0072—dc21   00-061593

Contents

Strangers to Relatives

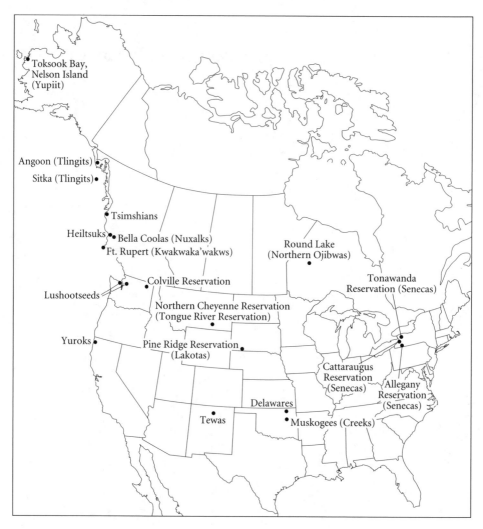

Primary Native communities and places discussed in the text

Editor's Introduction

The idea of this volume grew out of my own experience as an anthropologist who has been engaged since 1979 in ethnographic fieldwork among the Tlingits of southeastern Alaska and whose research has benefited greatly from my having been adopted by two Native families/matrilineages (see chapter 9). Although I have always considered my friendship with the individuals who adopted me and gave me Tlingit names, as well as close ties with a number of other Tlingit men and women, to be an important part of my professional and personal life and although I have often spoken about these relationships with my students, until recently I was reluctant to discuss them in the context of a professional meeting or write about them. Having been trained in history in Russia in the early 1970s and in symbolic/interpretive anthropology in the United States in the mid- to late 1970s, I resisted for a long time the turn toward reflexivity that has occurred in American anthropology in the past 20 years, especially in the 1990s (Clifford and Marcus 1986; Marcus and Fischer 1986; Behar and Gordon 1995; Behar 1996).

Despite my initial skepticism about the scholarly (rather than the literary) contribution of works that scrutinized the anthropologist-informant relationship (e.g., Read 1965; Powdermaker 1967; Briggs 1970; Rabinow 1977; Dumont 1978), I could not disagree with the notion that the personal background and history of the fieldworker—his or her "race," gender, ethnicity, religion, age, et cetera—as well as the nature of the fieldworker's relationship with his or her informants (consultants) inevitably affect both the fieldwork and the ethnographic text based on it (see also Okely and Callaway 1992).

Although I continue to oppose the notion promoted by some postmodernists that "ethnography has no other reality than a literary make-belief" (Okely 1992:3), I agree with the widespread view that much of our "data" are constructed in the context of a dialogue with our Native interlocutors. Hence it makes sense to explore the nature of the relationship between the participants in this dialogue (D. Tedlock 1979). As Okely (1992:2) points out, "A fundamental aspect of anthropology concerns the relationships between cultures and groups. The autobiography of the fieldworker anthropologist is neither a cultural vacuum, nor confined to the anthropologist's own culture, but is instead placed in a cross-cultural encounter. Fieldwork practice is always concerned with relationships. . . . The autobiographical experience of fieldwork requires the deconstruction of those relationships with the rigor demanded elsewhere in the discipline (cf. B. Tedlock 1992:xiii)." [1]

Having eventually caught the "reflexive bug," I began asking anthropologists who have done research among American Indians whether their experience resembled mine in any form. Several of them answered affirmatively and pointed out that Native Americans' adoption of anthropologists as relatives has been going on since the days of Lewis Henry Morgan. A number of colleagues expressed their surprise that such a common occurrence has never been the subject of a scholarly symposium or publication.[2] Inspired by this response, Thomas Buckley and I organized a session on the subject for the 1995 annual meeting of the American Anthropological Association. Given the audience's positive response, I decided to put together a collection of papers on the subject. All the participants in that session, including the discussant, Raymond D. Fogelson, are featured in this volume. In addition, I solicited papers from William Fenton, Elisabeth Tooker, Jay Miller, and Ann Fienup-Riordan.[3]

Although I did not intend to include papers covering every major Native American "culture area" or every major period in the history of American Indianist ethnology, the essays in this volume, which appear in a more or less chronological order, range from Tooker's account of Morgan's adoption by the Tonawanda Senecas in 1845 to Harkin's discussion of Boas's acquisition of a Kwakwaka'wakw name in

1894, and from Fenton's memoir about his adoption by the Hawk clan Senecas at Coldspring in 1934 to Ann Fienup-Riordan's account of the various names given to her over the years by various Yup'ik people and her continuing relationship with them. Hence the coverage is sufficiently broad, temporally and geographically, to allow some generalizations on the nature of the relationship between American Indians and American anthropologists.

It is important to note that, from the Indian point of view, there is nothing particularly unusual about adopting an anthropologist, especially someone who has spent a great deal of time in the community and shows an understanding of local cultural norms. Kinship, after all, has always been the central idiom of social relations in Native American societies (Miller 1992; Fogelson 1998).[4] As Straus pointed out in the oral presentation on which chapter 8 is based, "The process of turning strangers into relatives has been going on a long time in Indian Country. Anthropologists who have participated in this process are only a small part of a long history."

Using one well-researched example, that of the Sioux, we can see how important it was for Native Americans to transform strangers, usually seen as potentially dangerous, into kin "in order to have a means of dealing with them and a basis for trusting them" (DeMallie 1994:131) and, I might add, take better advantage of any potential benefits these newcomers could bring with them (see Harkin, chapter 2). This process created what Ella Deloria (1944:27) referred to as "social kinship," considered by her people as legitimate as genealogical kinship. But, as DeMallie (1994:132) points out, "In recounting genealogies, such 'adoptive' relationships are rarely mentioned; to point them out would imply some breach of faith or moral failing on the part of the one adopted." As long as the adopted former stranger spoke the local language and acted in accordance with local custom, he or she was not differentiated from those born into the local community (DeMallie 1994:130).

DeMallie's point is echoed by Gilbert McAllister's observation about the so-called fictive kinship in Kiowa-Apache society, made half a century earlier: "If a stranger coming into the group was to take any part in the communal life, he also almost of necessity fitted into the kinship pattern. If he did not become attached to some family, it is impossible to see how he could continue to exist. Captives were frequently incorporated into the tribe, and hence there probably is no such person as a 'pure' Kiowa-Apache. Everyone can trace relationships to Kiowa, Pawnee, Arapaho, Cheyenne and other tribes (1937:112)." [5]

Another well-known form of precontact adoption is that of the Iroquois and other Native American societies that replenished ranks decimated by warfare with men captured from enemy tribes. Women captured from these groups were also adopted and taken as wives by the captors; the children of these unions generally became full-fledged members of their fathers' nation (see Mishkin 1940; Lynch 1985; Richter 1992; Strong 1992; Fenton, chapter 3). [6] Among the rank-conscious peoples of the Northwest Coast, members of neighboring societies, especially aristocrats, were often adopted into local descent groups and given names-titles owned by the group (Drucker 1955; Harkin, chapter 2; Kan, chapter 9). [7] In addition, a Northwest Coast lineage (house) could adopt a member of a related kinship group in order to honor that person and/or strengthen itself. In moiety-based societies, like the Tlingits, such adoptions could take place only within the same moiety (see Kan, chapter 9) but as Jay Miller (personal communication) has recently reminded me, in times of dramatic social change (brought about by depopulation or colonialism), moieties could be rebalanced and in-marrying spouses given appropriate name and moiety affiliation. [8]

Adoption of strangers in precontact Native American societies was further encouraged by the widespread custom of addressing every individual in one's social universe (and often other-than-human persons and spirits as well) by kinship terms rather than by name (see, e.g., Eggan 1937; DeMallie 1994).

With the arrival of European explorers, fur traders, missionaries, government officials, and others, the old mechanism of turning outsiders into relatives was utilized as a means of socializing these persons and resolving the ambiguity of their status of stranger (Fenton, chapter 3; Harkin, chapter 2; Fogelson, commentary). The historical record is full of accounts of whites and other outsiders captured by Indians and socialized to become full-fledged members of the host community. [9] Although some of these "Indians by adoption" returned to their Euro-American world voluntarily or were forcibly retaken under the terms of treaties and agreements,[10] others remained with their captors and came to identify strongly with that culture.

Other forms of adoption existed as well—white fur traders married to Native American women or engaged in partnerships with Native American men were usually incorporated into local kinship systems and given indigenous names. Powerful Euro-American missionaries and government officials were sometimes adopted in the hope that this would induce them to treat their Indian adopters in a friendlier and more culturally appropriate manner (see, for example, Tanner 1956; Brown 1980; Anderson 1984; Lynch 1985; Bolt 1992). Finally, any outsider who became a trusted friend of a Native American person, family, or community was often adopted and named.[11]

Thus it is not surprising that the first anthropologists entering the Native American social universe were often made relatives as well. As Casagrande (1960a:xi) pointed out, "The relationship between the anthropologist and a key informant has many of the attributes of other kinds of primary relationships: between student and teacher, employee and employer, friends and relatives—as a matter of fact, it is often assimilated to the latter." And, given the centrality of kinship in Native American cultures, it is not surprising that the interaction between an ethnographer and the so-called key informant often encourages the latter to treat the former as a relative. Claire Farrer (1991, 1992, 1994), for example, has been conducting ethnographic research on a Mescalero Apache Reservation since the mid-1970s. After she had worked closely with one ritual specialist and holy man for some time, he and his family decided to adopt her. As Farrer (1994:236) explains, this was done "as a means of legitimizing the amount of time he and I were spending together. They were two choices: we could marry or become relatives. Bernard was already married, so we became relatives— I became a sister to Bernard and his siblings, while my daughter was niece to many and cousin to many more."

Motives for adopting ethnographers varied from pity or genuine affection to pragmatic calculation (an attempt to control an outsider who is being given some secret or sensitive information; see the Bella Coola adoption of McIlwraith described by Harkin in chapter 2 and a more recent case of the Tewa adoption of the Newberry Library scholars mentioned by Miller, chapter 6). One of the best documented early cases of an ethnographer being adopted by Native Americans was that of Frank Hamilton Cushing, probably the first American ethnologist to live for an extended period of time in an Indian community (see Pandey 1972; Gronewold 1972; J. Green 1979; Hinsley 1983). According to Cushing, he was taken in as a family member by the governor of the Zuni pueblo, who felt sorry for the small white man who had been left without provisions by his fellow expedition members, after he declared that he wanted to spend time among the Indians. Pandey, who has conducted fieldwork among the Zunis since the late 1960s, believes that, while pity may have played a role in the Zuni decision, there were more pragmatic reasons to adopt "Kushi," give him a Zuni name, and eventually make him a member of the powerful bow priesthood.[12] Having white missionaries, teachers, traders, and other non-Zunis in the pueblo, it was not surprising that a white man was made a bow priest. Besides being accustomed to them as part of everyday lives, the Zunis were also at times dependent upon their contacts with the outside world, especially various agencies of the federal government. In fact, Cushing was not the first white person to be offered this position, but he was the first to accept it. As a sign of his acceptance as a full member of their community, the Zunis tried repeatedly to persuade him to marry a local woman, an offer he politely refused (Pandey 1972:323–324).[13]

As has often been the case with the adoption of Euro-Americans into small but factionalized Indian communities, not everyone was pleased with Cushing's new status, especially his incorporation into the society of the bow priests, whose secrets he began to reveal in his publications. According to one of Pandey's informants, several prominent priests were killed not long after Cushing was made a bow priest, and some members of the community saw Cushing's admission to the society as the cause. There was also considerable opposition within the village to Cushing's drawing of sacred ceremonies, which he was able to overcome only through audacity, an ability to divide Zuni public opinion, and the help of his powerful "older brother," the governor (Gronewold 1972:42; Cushing in J. Green 1979:70–74).[14]

While Cushing was almost certainly guilty of revealing esoteric information about Zuni spirituality to the non-Zuni world, he also has been widely admired for writing some of the most accurate and sensitive accounts of Zuni culture. He repaid his hosts in proper Zuni fashion in 1882 by taking a group of them to the East Coast to obtain water from the "Ocean of the Sunrise" for sacred ceremonies. He also defended his adopted community from a land grab by an influential American politician and businessman (Gronewold 1972:42).

What is particularly interesting about Cushing's adoption is the Zuni insistence that he behave like a true Zuni. They demanded that he wear only Zuni clothing, eat only Zuni food, and have his ears pierced for the adoption ritual. They explained that adoption would make him rich in relatives (something most of the ethnographers discussed in this volume also experienced): "Little brother, you may be a Washington man, but it seems that you are very poor. Now, if you do as we tell you, and will only make your mind to be a Zuni, you shall be rich, for you shall have fathers and mothers, brothers and sisters, and the best food in the world" (J. Green 1979:68).

The notion that Indians sometimes had pragmatic reasons for adopting ethnographers seems to be illustrated by the Seneca adoption of Morgan and his friends from the Grand Order of the Iroquois. As Tooker points out in chapter 1, the 1840s were a difficult period for the Senecas. Aware of Morgan's interest in their society and maybe even his intention to write about them, they may have decided to recruit him as an ally, hoping to exchange an Iroquois name (which Morgan clearly fancied) and information about their life for favorable publicity and advocacy on their behalf (cf. Harkin, chapter 2, regarding the Bella Coola adoption and naming of Edward Sapir). At the same time, this act of giving something to a sympathetic member of the dominant society might also be interpreted as a symbolic statement of the fact that, despite American expectations, the Senecas were not ready to fade away.

Morgan's personal ties with Ely S. Parker, a member of an influential Seneca family, played an important role in his adoption. Friendship between an ethnographer and an individual Indian or Indian family is a common prerequisite for adoption. In many cases, those adopting an ethnographer care little about the research he or she is doing but are concerned with the ethnographer as a person. Thus friendship ties between Fenton and the Coldspring Senecas began long before he became a professional ethnographer and even long before he was born, when his paternal grandfather offered food and shelter to a destitute Indian family (Fenton, chapter 3). This is how William and Marla Powers (chapter 5) see their long-standing relationship with their Oglala kin, and this was the case with my own adoption by Charlotte Young, who saw me first and foremost as a compassionate friend and member of her congregation. This is still true for many of her children and grandchildren (Kan, chapter 9).

As Vine Deloria (1997:219), an old critic of our profession, has warned, "Anthros [*sic*] should not misinterpret the natural hospitality of Indians as an endorsement of anthropology or support for their work. Indians may like their work and admire their skills but only because they have first accepted the individual as a person." As chapters by Fenton, Straus, Black-Rogers, Powers and Powers, Miller, and Kan show, personal ties between an anthropologist and the person who has adopted him or her continue after the latter's death. And the anthropologist's spouse and children are often incorporated as relatives into the same family and given indigenous names (see Powers and Powers, chapter 5; Kan, chapter 9; Fienup-Riordan, chapter 10).[15]

At the same time, there is plenty of evidence to challenge Deloria's dismissal of the notion that at least some American Indians find ethnographic research to be of significant interest and value to them and their descendants (V. Deloria 1969, 1997).[16] Thus, Buckley's mentor and adopted senior relative, Harry Roberts, encouraged him to go to graduate school in anthropology "to set the record straight on the Yuroks" (Buckley, chapter 7). Similarly Mark Jacobs's strong desire to have accurate information on his culture compiled by an anthropologist led to our cooperation, which gradually evolved into friendship and culminated in his making me a member of his lineage and giving me his deceased brother's name (Kan, chapter 9).[17]

For better or for worse, anthropologists have sometimes been the only interested listeners with whom Indian elders could share their knowledge. While this was more common in the past, when younger Native Americans were discouraged by both the dominant society and sometimes by their own families from learning their mother tongue and traditional culture, it is still the case that an ethnographer often has more time to spend with an elder than this elder's family and friends. Thus on a couple of occasions in 1979–80 I felt rather uncomfortable during visits to some of my elderly Tlingit consultants and friends, when our conversations took place in the same room where the younger members of the family were watching television, paying little attention to the fascinating stories told by their father or grandmother.[18] In fact, I would argue that by spending long hours listening to an elder's stories and reminiscences, an ethnographer often becomes that person's surrogate younger sibling, child, or grandchild.

Occasionally an ethnographer's adoption appears to have been precipitated by a religious or visionary experience. Mitchell Redcloud Sr., for example, adopted Nancy Lurie (1972:160–161) in 1944, when he was dying of cancer in a Madison hospital. Although by that time Lurie had already established rapport with a number of other Winnebago (Ho-Chunk) elders, Redcloud's action had been prompted primarily by the fact that she had first appeared in his dream. Similarly, Farrer's Apache brother informed her that before she arrived on the reservation he had dreamed that someone was coming with whom he should work on recording things he knew about his people, their history, and language (Farrer 1992:82–83).

The act of making an anthropologist a part of one's family or clan (and sometimes community or tribe) can also be seen as an attempt to control his or her behavior as well as information about the local culture that the person would eventually make public (Harkin, chapter 2). From the Indian point of view, the adoptee should respect his or her new family and avoid embarrassing or hurting it in any way. While not all anthropologists (particularly in the past) lived up to these expectations, being adopted has certainly made many anthropologists more careful about the questions they ask and the data they publish.[19]

The initiative for establishing either a quasi-kinship relationship or a full-fledged adoption sometimes comes from the anthropologist himself (herself), who deliberately uses kinship terms in addressing informants. For example, Gilbert McAllister (1937:132–133) addressed his elderly Kiowa-Apache informant as "grandfather" to encourage the man to work with him.

At this point we should pause to reflect on a key question of whether the adoption and naming of anthropologists have been uniquely North American phenomena. While some anthropologists working outside North America have also been adopted and/or named by their local hosts,[20] a special closeness between Native Americans and those who have studied their culture seems to have existed in the past and, as the contributors to this volume demonstrate, continues to exist. In fact, as a number of historians of American anthropology have pointed out (Hinsley 1994; Lurie 1988; Fogelson 1985, 1999, commentary; Darnell 1998; Adams 1998:193–261), between the 1870s and the 1930s, American anthropology was synonymous with what Adams (1998: 255–256) calls "Indianology." In his words, "As a legacy of Indianology, Americans have tended to feel closer to their subjects and to identify with them more than have other anthropologists. This was partly a consequence of propinquity. Unlike Africans and Polynesians, the Indians did not live a world away from their investigators; sometimes they lived in the next county. Without undue expense they could be visited and studied during summer vacations, on weekend trips to the reservations, or even in a nearby city workplace."

This observation is certainly true for such early ethnographers as Morgan, who resided not far from the Seneca reservation, or Boas, who continued to undertake summer field trips to coastal British Columbia even in advanced age and was able to bring to New York City his key "informant" and collaborator, George Hunt (Berman 1996). As a number of the essays in this volume demonstrate, American ethnographers of today not only repeatedly visit "their" communities and families but often host Native American friends and adopted relatives in their own homes (Powers and Powers, chapter 5; Straus, chapter 8; Miller, chapter 6; Kan, chapter 9; Fienup-Riordan, chapter 10). Given this geographic propinquity of the ethnographers and their "subjects," it is not surprising that the former have often been incorporated into the kinship network of the latter. This possibility of long-term relationship of friendship and research cooperation plus an early development of literacy and Western schooling among Native North Americans have also resulted in the rise of *indigenous* ethnographers, which seems to have occurred somewhat earlier in Canada and the United States than elsewhere in the world.[21]

But geographic proximity has only been part of the story. As Adams (1998:256) points out, the relationship between American anthropologists and Native Americans has also been characterized by some sense of shared identity and shared experience. Despite significant status, class, and racial differences, the anthropologist and the Indian could identify with one another as fellow Americans or fellow Canadians at least in some contexts. Thus, for example, Mark Jacobs, a decorated and proud World War II veteran, shares my own patriotic feelings toward the United States as a key participant in the coalition that crushed Nazi Germany and militaristic Japan. This shared experience has also meant that American anthropologists have been more likely to experience a sense of guilt when confronted with the harsh reality of American Indian life. Not surprisingly, since the time of Morgan's involvement with the Senecas, North American ethnologists have been more likely than their European counterparts to engage in some form of "applied" or "action" anthropology or at least to offer some concrete help to "their own" Indian families and communities (see McNickle 1979; Kelley 1985; Lurie 1988).[22]

As the essays in this collection and other ethnographers' reports indicate, anthropologists' adoptions vary from informal (Straus, chapter 8; Miller, chapter 6; Farrer 1991, 1992, 1994) to very formal (Fenton, chapter 3; Kan, chapter 9). The nature of the adoption depends on both the social structure and ideology of the adoptive group and the nature of its relationship with the adoptee. Thus Briggs's 1970 adoption as a daughter by a Canadian Inuit family was very informal, since Inuit social structure is flexible and kinship group membership is relatively fluid (see Fienup-Riordan, chapter 10). The Tlingits, on the other hand, have a much less flexible social structure, wherein one's matrilineal group membership cannot be altered, and they tend to formally incorporate adopted Euro-Americans into a clan and give them a formal name-title. This act gives the adoptee a proper place and role in the ceremonial system (Kan, chapter 9; Miller 1984, chapter 6).

Similarly, some ethnographers are given a Native name and others are not, but the absence of a name does not necessarily indicate that the relationship is not a close one (cf. Fienup-Riordan, chapter 10). To understand why a name was or was not given to an adopted ethnographer, one would have to take the local community's social structure and naming system into consideration, as well as the nature of its relationship with the adoptee (cf. Miller, chapter 6).[23]

The final question to be addressed is the impact of adoptions on ethnographic research and the ethnographers' reactions to them. As a number of essays appearing here and as other accounts suggest, anthropologists often have a strong desire to be adopted. Some are motivated by pragmatism—they anticipate (often correctly) that this will facilitate their integration into the Native community and hence the field research itself. Thus Briggs (1970:20–21) arrived in a small Canadian Inuit community, having read accounts by several male ethnographers who had been adopted as "sons" by Inuit families and had traveled with them as members of their household. She too hoped to be adopted, and she even obtained a letter of introduction from Inuit missionary acquaintances describing her wish to her Native hosts.[24]

Others enter the field with romantic ideas about "living with the Indians" and being given an Indian name. These emotions are part of a long-standing American cultural mythology exemplified by James Fenimore Cooper's novels and films such as *Dances with Wolves* (R. Green 1988; Powers 1988; P. Deloria 1998; Straus, chapter 8). Some ethnographers have been motivated by a desire to legitimate themselves by becoming Indian in spirit if not in "blood." As Pauline Turner Strong pointed out to me (personal communication), "This kind of legitimization is generally connected with romanticism, and is directed toward a (popular) Euroamerican audience rather than to one's Indian relatives. Morgan is an example of this . . . as is Elsie Clews Parsons's use of her Hopi name on the title page of her *American Indian Lives*" (see Parsons 1922; see also Adams 1998 : 98 – 112, 193 – 261).

When I arrived in Alaska in 1979, in the aftermath of a devastating critique of anthropologists by Vine Deloria (1969), being adopted by a Native family was an indication of my being accepted as a person, one who was no longer seen as a meddling outsider (Kan, chapter 9). Whether they are intended that way or not, we perceive our adoptions as a validation of our research. I also believe that those of us who are the only children or who come from small families find the sudden acquisition of many affectionate and supportive relatives a psychologically satisfying experience that has nothing to do with a "wannabe complex." Some ethnographers, myself included, also experience what Bill and Marla Powers (chapter 5) describe as a "pleasurable feeling of belonging to another culture of choice" or at least a sense of having a good grasp of that culture's essential values and rules for proper social conduct.

While an ethnographer's status as an adopted member of the community being studied in many instances enhances his or her fieldwork, it also imposes some limitations. One is often forced to side with the adoptive family and see the local culture from its particular point of view.[25] We all recognize, of course, that ethnographers should try to avoid or at least minimize biasing their research, even though that is not always possible (see Black-Rogers, chapter 4; Straus, chapter 8; Powers and Powers, chapter 5; Kan, chapter 9). Whether or not an ethnographer feels that his or her responsibility to the adoptive family comes before a responsibility to anthropology (see Miller, chapter 6; Powers and Powers, chapter 5; Straus, chapter 8), an ethnographic account that is biased heavily in favor of the group being studied is deserving of criticism (cf. Boelscher 1985). At the same time, having experienced the warmth and generosity of one's adopted kin, an ethnographer (at least the modern-day one) is less likely to produce an account that deals *only* with impersonal social groups and categories and not real-life individuals.[26]

I would like to conclude this introduction with two observations. The first is borrowed from Straus (chapter 8), who points out that we should not treat our adopted status as a badge of honor and consider "unadopted" anthropologists as less fortunate and producing ethnographic work of lesser quality. Many of these scholars are first-rate ethnographers, whose writing about Native Americans is truly outstanding.[27] We should also keep in mind that some anthropologists might choose not to reveal their adopted status or Native American names because they or their adopters consider this inappropriate.[28] As the essays in this volume demonstrate, some of anthropologists are much more willing than others to provide the details of their adoption and discuss their relationship with their Native American relatives.[29]

My second observation has to do with the United States and Canadian governments' definition of who is and who is not an Indian. Because these bureaucratic definitions are the product of Western folk theories of kinship, they emphasize "blood" as the key symbol of kinship and "blood quantum" as the main criterion for defining membership in a Native American tribe. Since tribal membership in the postcontact era determines a person's access to certain limited (and often dwindling) resources, Indian communities have exhibited greater caution in adopting outsiders than their predecessors did in the precolonial era (see, for example, Snipp 1989:362–365; Strong and Van Winckle 1996). Thus, as DeMallie (1994:132–133) points out, "The [Sioux] use of blood as a metaphor for kinship may reflect American culture and the innovation of a system of inheritance based on genealogy that was imposed by the BIA [Bureau of Indian Affairs] and that has become an important focus of reservation life. Such an emphasis on genealogy was also bolstered by the introduction of stan-

dardized surnames around the turn of the century, another significant innovation fostered by the BIA." [30]

Given this bureaucratic legacy and the increasing Indian nationalism that has accompanied the new sovereignty movement (Bordewich
1996), I would expect resistance, especially from younger and more
militant Native Americans, against the adoption of Euro-Americans
in general and anthropologists in particular.[31] Despite this politiciza-
tion of the issue of adoption, however, non-Indians will almost certainly continue to be adopted by Native Americans.[32]

On the one hand, with the rising rates of Indian-white intermarriage, more and more non-Indian spouses have to be incorporated
into Native communities (Thornton 1998).[33] On the other hand, with
more American Indians studying, working, and residing outside reservations and tribal enclaves, the number of Indian-white friendships
will continue to grow, and so will the need to transform friendly
outsiders into relatives. Among them, I expect to find some ethnographers, especially if they continue to behave as respectful visitors,
patient listeners, and trusted allies toward the people whose history
and culture they study and if they are willing to adjust their research
agenda to their hosts' needs. As Jay Miller points out in chapter 6,
"Naming is foremost a recognition of common humanity and kinship.
Families name and rename their members, as do communities. By including someone neither born nor married into that family and community, naming indicates that that person is, in some sense, a kindred
spirit. Above all, it suggests that they conform to native ideals about
conduct and personality." He concludes, "In all, naming and adoption constitute a formal recognition of shared sentiments, along with
a way of rendering other humans manageable and trustworthy. In
close and caring societies where only your immediate kin can be fully
trusted, . . . you need all the relatives you can get."

NOTES

1. I should point out that while I find much of this reflexive writing by
   ethnographers valuable and interesting, I worry about an excessive
   preoccupation with one's own self which does seem to color the
   work of some anthropologists (see, e.g., Rabinow 1977; Behar 1996).

2. William Sturtevant, personal communication 1995. My perusal of

a substantial body of recent works dealing with ethnographic research revealed that while friendship between the anthropologist and his or her informant have been the subject of several collections (e.g., Casagrande 1960b; Kimball and Watson 1972; Grindal and Salamone 1995), adoption and naming of ethnographers by their native hosts has rarely been discussed, except very briefly. The absence of a separate volume on the subject is especially surprising, given the fact that by now most other aspects of the fieldwork experience (including sex and violence between the ethnographer and his or her informant) seem to have been scrutinized (see Kulick and Willson 1995; Nordstrom and Robben 1995; Markowitz and Ashkenazi 1999).

3. I would like to thank William Sturtevant for encouraging me to solicit papers from Fenton and Tooker. I would also like to express my gratitude to Thomas Buckley and especially Raymond Fogelson for their valuable advice and encouragement throughout this project. Pauline Turner Strong as well as the University of Nebraska Press's two anonymous readers deserve a special word of gratitude for their thoughtful comments on an earlier draft of this introduction. I should also point out that I did make a concerted effort to solicit papers from a number of Native American anthropologists, several of whom expressed strong support for this project. For various reasons, however, none of them were able to make a contribution to this collection.

4. The following characterization of Sioux kinship recently produced by DeMallie (1994:133) can easily be expanded to most American Indian cultures: "The kinship system itself provided the foundation for social unity and moral order. The norms of kinship were the most basic cultural structures patterning the social system; they formed a network that potentially embraced all members of society and related them as well to the sacred powers of the world at large."

5. Cf. DeMallie's statement that "although anthropologists generally relegate adoption to the category of fictive kin, for the Sioux, adoption constitutes genuine kinship" (1994:143).

6. In some Native American societies, such as the Iroquois, according to Shoemaker (1995:53–54), some consciousness of adoptive rela-

tions remained long after the adoption had taken place. (I would like to thank Pauline Turner Strong for reminding me of Shoemaker's point.)

7. George Hunt, Boas's chief research collaborator, represents a classic example of this process. His father was English, and his mother was a Tongass Tlingit. He nonetheless was adopted by the Kwakwaka'wakws and initiated into their secret ceremonial societies, eventually becoming an expert on their history and culture (see Berman 1996).

8. According to Jay Miller (personal communication), this is what happened in the 1980s and 1990s among the Skidegate Haidas.

9. The first American anthropologist to point out the importance of this phenomenon, which he labeled "transculturalization," was Irving Hallowell (1963). The scholarly literature on Indian captivity is extensive (see, for example, Axtell 1981). For some of the best recent works on this subject see Calloway 1992 and especially Strong 1992, 1999.

10. I would like to thank Jay Miller for reminding me of this phenomenon.

11. A classic example of this phenomenon was Nicholas Black Elk's adoption of the poet John G. Neihardt, whom he saw as a spiritual person destined to receive the great wisdom of the Lakota people. In a typical Sioux fashion, Black Elk conceptualized their relationship as a kinship-based one and hence addressed Neihardt as his son or nephew and gave him a Lakota name (DeMallie 1984:37–38).

12. Of course, it helped to have chosen to dwell with the governor, the pueblo's most powerful official; the latter came to like Cushing and began treating him as a younger brother, eventually adopting him into his clan.

13. Eventually Cushing brought his American wife to stay in the pueblo and when a baby girl was born there during her visit, she was given the woman's first name. This is an interesting example of a "reverse naming," which has occasionally occurred in the history of Indian relationships with anthropologists. For example, Alice

Fletcher adopted her longtime friend and scholarly collaborator, Francis La Flesche, an Omaha, as her son (Mark 1988).

14. In a typical Pueblo fashion, some Zunis accused Cushing of practicing witchcraft (Cushing in J. Green 1979:157–160). For a contemporary Zuni view of Cushing and his adventures at Zuni, see Hughte (1994).

15. Farrer (1994:39), who has for many years conducted ethnographic research among the Mescalero Apaches and has been informally adopted as a sister by a religious leader and traditionalist, reports that the latter used to reprimand her teenage daughter for culturally inappropriate behavior, saying, "You shame our whole family when you . . ." In fact, in some cases, it is not the anthropologist herself but her child who gets adopted. This was the case with Maureen Trudelle Schwarz's teenage daughter, who was adopted by her mother's Navajo hosts and closest friends into their clan in order to sponsor a puberty ceremony for the girl (Schwartz 1997:xv).

16. For another very critical perspective on American anthropologists' relationships with and treatment of American Indians, see Biolsi and Zimmerman (1997). For a much more balanced view, shared by this author, see Lurie (1988) and Adams (1998:243–258).

17. For similar examples from an earlier era in the history of American anthropology, see Casagrande's 1960 account of his and Robert Ritzenthaler's adoption by John Mink, an Ojibwe religious leader and traditionalist, and Lurie's 1972 description of her relationship with Mitchell Redcloud Sr., who adopted her as his daughter. Both events occurred in the early 1940s.

18. Some of the children and grandchildren of these elders have now become more interested in the traditional culture and have requested from me tape recordings I made of stories told by and interviews with their deceased senior relatives.

19. An anthropologist who betrays his adopted family's trust risks losing his adopted status. I am aware of at least one case when a certain anthropologist had his Native name and, by implication, his group membership formally taken away by the clan that had adopted him.

20. See, for example, essays in a volume edited by Grindal and Salamone (1995).

21. For the discussion of American Indian ethnographers and intellectuals see the essays in Liberty (1978) as well as Bailey (1995), Berman (1996), DeMallie (1999), Parks (1999), and Medicine (1999).

22. Of course, as a number of American anthropology's critics have pointed out, greater efforts to contribute to the well-being of Native Americans should have been made by those who have specialized in studying Indian cultures (V. Deloria 1969; Biolsi and Zimmerman 1997).

23. While some Native American societies bestow old inherited names on the ethnographer, others coin new ones that might reflect their feelings about the recipient. Occasionally such names may not be particularly flattering. Thus Alanson Skinner (1921), known for his persistent badgering of his Menominee friends and relatives by adoption (he was a nephew of several leading ritualists and was admitted into the Medicine Society) for sacred artifacts, was given the name Little Weasel, since this animal "never returns empty from the hunt."

24. It is interesting that Briggs (1970:21) was somewhat ashamed of her desire to be adopted, seeing it as "unprofessional." Lurie (1972: 160–161), another anthropologist of the older generation, also admits being embarrassed by her key informant's wish to adopt her and his confession about having seen her standing next to him in a dream. Of course, our current views about having to separate one's professional and personal identities and lives are quite different from these. Thus none of the participants in this volume seem to share Lurie's or Briggs's sentiments, with the exception of Black-Rogers (chapter 4), who initially did have some reservations about her adoption by the Round Lake Ojibwas.

25. In some cases being adopted could both enhance one's research and place one in a psychologically uncomfortable position. This is what happened to Briggs (1970) when her adopted Inuit family began to treat her as a young daughter to be bossed around.

26. With the genre of Native American biographies once again be-

coming popular in anthropology, a number of ethnographers have produced interesting accounts of their adopted relatives' lives (e.g., Blackman 1982; Cruikshank 1990). For an earlier work in this genre see an autobiography of a Winnebago (Ho-Chunk) woman, recorded and edited by Lurie (1961).

27. One such scholar is Peter Nabokov who, in fact, suggested the term "unadopted" to me by proposing to contribute a paper to this volume with the tongue-in-cheek title "The Loneliness of an Unadopted Ethnographer." Unfortunately, he could not find the time to write it.

28. I am grateful to Pauline Turner Strong for reminding me of this phenomenon.

29. Compare, for example, the essays by Miller or Powers and Powers with those by Buckley or Straus.

30. Cf. Straus's (1994:166) discussion of contemporary Northern Cheyenne kinship, in which she points out that among them adoption today no longer "makes full relatives out of aliens, since blood can be lost but never acquired."

31. See, for example, a highly partisan critique of DeMallie's understanding of Sioux kinship, as based primarily on culture and behavior rather than on blood, by a Sioux literary critic, Elizabeth Cook-Lynn (1996:94–95).

32. It is important to note that in the past some objections to the adoption of anthropologists and other non-Indian outsiders were also voiced by certain individual members or factions of Native communities where such an adoption was about to take place, especially when they feared that such an adoption would confer hunting and other rights on the adoptee. See, for example, the debate within the Allegany Seneca community, which arose at the time of Fenton's adoption into the Hawk clan (Fenton, chapter 3). Fenton's example also illustrates an interesting difference of opinion within a Native American community about the meaning of an outsider's adoption.

33. In recent years, indigenous nations in Canada and the United

States have finally been able to set up their own criteria for membership. Some of these nations, particularly the smaller ones which feel that their survival is under threat, have tried to make these criteria as well as the ones for residence on their reserve or reservation highly restrictive (see Snipp 1989; Thornton 1998).

REFERENCES

Adams, William Y. 1998. *The Philosophical Roots of Anthropology.* Stanford CA: Center for the Study of Language and Information.

Anderson, Gary C. 1984. *Kinsmen of Another Kind: Dakota-White Relations in the Upper Mississippi Valley, 1650–1862.* Lincoln: University of Nebraska Press.

Axtell, James. 1981. The White Indians of Colonial America. Chapter 7 of *The European and the Indian: Essays in the Ethnohistory of Colonial North America.* Oxford: Oxford University Press.

Bailey, Garrick, ed. 1995. *The Osage and the Invisible World: From the Works of Francis La Flesche.* Norman: University of Oklahoma Press.

Behar, Ruth. 1996. *The Vulnerable Observer: Anthropology That Breaks Your Heart.* Boston: Beacon Press.

Behar, Ruth, and Deborah A. Gordon, eds. 1995. *Women Writing Culture.* Berkeley: University of California Press.

Berman, Judith. 1996. "The Culture as It Appears to the Indian Himself": Boas, George Hunt, and the Methods of Ethnography. In *Volksgeist as Method and Ethic: Essays on Boasian Ethnography and the German Anthropological Tradition*, ed. George W. Stocking Jr., 215–256. Madison: University of Wisconsin Press.

Biolsi, Thomas, and Larry J. Zimmerman, eds. 1997. *Indians and Anthropologists: Vine Deloria Jr. and the Critique of Anthropology.* Tucson: University of Arizona Press.

Blackman, Margaret B. 1982. *During My Time: Florence Edenshaw Davidson, a Haida Woman.* Seattle: University of Washington Press.

Boelscher, Marianne. 1985. Review of *During My Time: Florence Eden-*

shaw Davidson, a Haida Woman, by Margaret Blackman. *Anthropos* 80:1–3.

Bolt, Clarence. 1992. *Thomas Crosby and the Tsimshian: Small Shoes for Feet Too Large*. Vancouver: University of British Columbia Press.

Bordewich, Fergus M. 1996. *Killing the White Man's Indian: Reinventing Native Americans at the End of the Twentieth Century*. New York: Doubleday.

Briggs, Jean L. 1970. *Never in Anger: Portrait of an Eskimo Family*. Cambridge: Harvard University Press.

Brown, Jennifer S. H. 1980. *Strangers in Blood: Fur Trade Company Families in Indian Country*. Vancouver: University of British Columbia Press.

Calloway, Colin. 1992. *North Country Captives: Selected Narratives of Indian Captivity from Vermont and New Hampshire*. Hanover NH: University Press of New England.

Casagrande, Joseph B. 1960a. Preface of *In the Company of Man*, ed. Joseph Casagrande, 9–16. New York: Harper.

———. 1960b. John Mink, Ojibwa Informant. In *In the Company of Man*, ed. Joseph Casagrande, 467–488. New York: Harper.

Clifford, James, and George E. Marcus, eds. 1986. *Writing Culture: The Poetics and Politics of Fieldwork*. Berkeley: University of California Press.

Cook-Lynn, Elizabeth. 1996. *Why I Can't Read Wallace Stegner and Other Essays: A Tribal Voice*. Madison: University of Wisconsin Press.

Cruikshank, Julie. 1990. *Life Lived like a Story: Life Stories of Three Yukon Native Elders*. Lincoln: University of Nebraska Press.

Darnell, Regna. 1998. *And Along Came Boas: Continuity and Revolution in Americanist Anthropology*. Philadelphia: John Benjamins.

———. 1999. Theorizing American Anthropology: Continuities from the B.A.E. to the Boasians. In *Theorizing the Americanist Tradition*, ed. Lisa Philips Valentine and Regna Darnell, 38–51. Toronto: University of Toronto Press.

Deloria, Ella. 1944. *Speaking of Indians*. New York: Friendship Press.

Deloria, Philip J. 1998. *Playing Indian*. New Haven: Yale University Press.

Deloria, Vine, Jr. 1969. *Custer Died for Your Sins: An Indian Manifesto*. New York: Avon.

―――. 1997. Conclusion: Anthros, Indians, and Planetary Reality. In *Indians and Anthropologists: Vine Deloria Jr. and the Critique of Anthropology*, ed. Thomas Biolsi and Larry J. Zimmerman, 209–221. Tucson: University of Arizona Press.

DeMallie, Raymond J. 1984. *The Sixth Grandfather: Black Elk's Teaching Given to John G. Neihardt*. Lincoln: University of Nebraska Press.

―――. 1994. Kinship and Biology in Sioux Culture. In *North American Indian Anthropology: Essays on Society and Culture*, ed. Raymond J. DeMallie and Alfonso Ortiz, 125–146. Norman: University of Oklahoma Press.

―――. 1999. "George Sword Wrote These": Lakota Culture as Lakota Text. In *Theorizing the Americanist Tradition*, ed. Lisa Philips Valentine and Regna Darnell, 245–258. Toronto: University of Toronto Press.

Drucker, Philip. 1955. *Indians of the Northwest Coast*. New York: American Museum of Natural History.

Dumont, Jean-Paul. 1978. *The Headman and I: Ambiguity and Ambivalence in the Fieldwork Experience*. Austin: University of Texas Press.

Eggan, Fred, ed. 1937. *Social Anthropology of North American Tribes*. Chicago: University of Chicago Press.

Farrer, Claire R. 1991. *Living Life's Circle: Mescalero Apache Cosmovision*. Albuquerque: University of New Mexico Press.

―――. 1992. Centering: Lessons Learned from Mescalero Apaches. In *The Naked Anthropologist: Tales from Around the World*, ed. Philip R. DeVita, 79–89. Belmont CA: Wadsworth.

————. 1994. *Thunder Rides a Black Horse: Mescalero Apaches and the Mythic Present*. Prospect Heights IL: Waveland Press.

Fogelson, Raymond D. 1985. Interpretations of the American Indian Psyche: Some Historical Notes. In *Social Contexts of American Ethnology, 1840–1984*, ed. June Helm, 4–27. Washington DC: American Anthropological Association.

————. 1998. Perspectives on Native American Identity. In *Studying Native America: Problems and Prospects*, ed. Russell Thornton, 40–59. Madison: University of Wisconsin Press.

————. 1999. Nationalism and the Americanist Tradition. In *Theorizing the Americanist Tradition*, ed. Lisa Philips Valentine and Regna Darnell, 75–83. Toronto: University of Toronto Press.

Green, Jesse, ed. 1979. *Zuni: Selected Writings of Frank Hamilton Cushing*. Lincoln: University of Nebraska Press.

Green, Rayna D. 1988. The Indian in Popular American Culture. In *History of Indian-White Relations*, ed. Wilcomb Washburn, 587–606. Vol. 4 of *Handbook of North American Indians*. Washington DC: Smithsonian Institution.

Grindal, Bruce, and Frank Salamone, eds. 1995. *Bridges to Humanity: Narratives on Anthropology and Friendship*. Prospect Heights IL: Waveland Press.

Gronewold, Sylvia. 1972. Did Frank Hamilton Cushing Go Native? In *Crossing Cultural Boundaries: The Anthropological Experience*, ed. Solon T. Kimball and James B. Watson, 33–50. San Francisco: Chandler.

Hallowell, A. Irving. 1963. American Indians, White and Black: The Phenomenon of Transculturalization. *Current Anthropology* 4: 519–531.

Hinsley, Curtis. 1983. Ethnographic Charisma and Scientific Routine: Cushing and Fewkes in the American Southwest, 1879–1893. In *Observers Observed: Essays on Ethnographic Fieldwork*, ed. George W. Stocking Jr., 13–52. Madison: University of Wisconsin Press.

————. 1994 [1981]. *The Smithsonian and the American Indian: Mak-*

ing a Moral Anthropology in Victorian America. Washington DC: Smithsonian Institution Press.

Hughte, Phil. 1994. *A Zuni Artist Looks at Frank Hamilton Cushing: Cartoons by Phil Hughte*. Zuni NM: A:shiwi A:wan Museum and Heritage Center.

Kelley, Lawrence C. 1985. Why Applied Anthropology Developed When It Did: A Commentary on People, Money, and Changing Times, 1930–1945. In *Social Contexts of American Ethnology, 1840–1984*, ed. June Helm, 122–138. Washington DC: American Anthropological Association.

Kulick, Don, and Margaret Willson, eds. 1995. *Taboo: Sex, Identity, and Erotic Subjectivity in Anthropological Fieldwork*. New York: Routledge.

Liberty, Margot, ed. 1978. *American Indian Intellectuals*. St. Paul MN: West.

Lurie, Nancy O., ed. 1961. *Mountain Wolf Woman, Sister of Crashing Thunder*. Ann Arbor: University of Michigan Press.

———. 1972. Two Dollars. In *Crossing Cultural Boundaries: The Anthropological Experience*, ed. Solon T. Kimball and James B. Watson, 151–163. San Francisco: Chandler.

———. 1988. Relations Between Indians and Anthropologists. In *History of Indian-White Relations*, ed. Wilcomb Washburn, 548–556. Vol. 4 of *Handbook of North American Indians*. Washington DC: Smithsonian Institution.

Lynch, James. 1985. The Iroquois Confederacy and the Adoption and Administration of Non-Iroquoian Individuals and Groups prior to 1756. *Man in the Northeast*, no. 30:83–99.

McAllister, Gilbert J. 1937. Kiowa-Apache Social Organization. In *Social Anthropology of North American Tribes*, ed. Fred Eggan, 99–169. Chicago: University of Chicago Press.

McNickle, D'Arcy. 1979. Anthropology and the Indian Reorganization Act. In *The Uses of Anthropology*, ed. Walter Goldschmidt, 51–78. Washington DC: American Anthropological Association.

Marcus, George E., and Michael M. J. Fischer. 1986. *Anthropology as Cultural Critique: An Experimental Moment in the Human Sciences*. Chicago: University of Chicago Press.

Mark, Joan. 1988. *A Stranger in Her Native Land: Alice Fletcher and the American Indians*. Lincoln: University of Nebraska Press.

Markowitz, Fran, and Michael Ashkenazi, eds. 1999. *Sex, Sexuality, and the Anthropologist*. Urbana: University of Illinois Press.

Medicine, Bea. 1999. Ella Cara Deloria: Early Lakota Ethnologist (Newly Discovered Novelist). In *Theorizing the Americanist Tradition*, ed. Lisa Philips Valentine and Regna Darnell, 259–267. Toronto: University of Toronto Press.

Miller, Jay. 1984. Feasting with the Southern Tsimshian. In *The Tsimshian: Images of the Past, Views for the Present*, ed. Margaret Seguin, 27–39. Vancouver: University of British Columbia Press.

———. 1992. A Kinship of Spirit. In *America in 1492*, ed. Alvin Josephy, 305–337. New York: Alfred A. Knopf.

Mishkin, Bernard. 1940. *Rank and Warfare among the Plains Indians*. New York: J. J. Augustin. Reprint, Lincoln: University of Nebraska Press, 1992.

Nordstrom, Carolyn, and Antonius C. G. M. Robben, eds. 1995. *Fieldwork under Fire: Contemporary Studies of Violence and Survival*. Berkeley: University of California Press.

Okely, Judith. 1992. Anthropology and Autobiography: Participatory Experience and Embodied Knowledge. In *Anthropology and Autobiography*, ed. Judith Okely and Helen Callaway, 1–28. London: Routledge.

Okely, Judith, and Helen Callaway, eds. 1992. *Anthropology and Autobiography*. London: Routledge.

Pandey, Triloki N. 1972. Anthropologists at Zuni. *Proceedings of the American Philosophical Society* 116(4):321–337.

Parks, Douglas R. 1999. James R. Murie and the Textual Documentation of Skiri Pawnee. In *Theorizing the Americanist Tradition*, ed. Lisa

Philips Valentine and Regna Darnell, 227–244. Toronto: University of Toronto Press.

Parsons, Elsie Clews, ed. 1922. *American Indian Life: By Several of Its Students.* New York: B. W. Huebsch.

Powdermaker, Hortense. 1967. *Stranger and Friend: The Way of an Anthropologist.* New York: W. W. Norton.

Powers, William K. 1988. The Indian Hobbyist Movement in North America. In *History of Indian-White Relations,* ed. Wilcomb Washburn, 557–561. Vol. 4 of *Handbook of North American Indians.* Washington DC: Smithsonian Institution.

Rabinow, Paul. 1977. *Reflections on Fieldwork in Morocco.* Berkeley: University of California Press.

Read, Kenneth E. 1965. *The High Valley.* New York: Scribner's.

Richter, Daniel K. 1992. *The Ordeal of the Longhouse: The Peoples of the Iroquois League in the Era of European Colonization.* Chapel Hill: University of North Carolina Press.

Schwarz, Maureen Trudelle. 1997. *Molded in the Image of Changing Woman: Navajo Views on the Human Body and Personhood.* Tucson: University of Arizona Press.

Shoemaker, Nancy. 1995. Kateri Tekakwitha's Tortuous Path to Sainthood. In *Negotiators of Change: Historical Perspectives on Native American Women,* ed. Nancy Shoemaker, 49–71. New York: Routledge.

Skinner, Alanson. 1921. Recollections of an Ethnologist among the Menomini Indians. *Wisconsin Archaeologist* 20:41–74.

Snipp, Matthew C. 1989. *American Indians: The First of This Land.* New York: Russell Sage.

Straus, Anne S. 1994. Northern Cheyenne Kinship Reconsidered. In *North American Indian Anthropology: Essays on Society and Culture,* ed. Raymond J. DeMallie and Alfonso Ortiz, 14–171. Norman: University of Oklahoma Press.

Strong, Pauline Turner. 1992. Captivity in White and Red: Convergent Practice and Colonial Representation on the British-American Frontier, 1606–1736. In *Crossing Cultures: Essays on the Displacement of Western Civilization*, ed. Daniel Segal, 33–104. Tucson: University of Arizona Press.

———. 1999. *Captive Selves, Captivating Others: The Politics and Poetics of Colonial American Captivity Narratives*. Boulder CO: Westview Press.

Strong, Pauline Turner, and Barrick Van Winckle. 1996. "Indian Blood": Reflections on the Reckoning and Refiguring of Native North American Identity. *Cultural Anthropology* 11(4):547–576.

Tanner, John. 1956 [1830]. *A Narrative of the Captivity and Adventures of John Tanner*. Minneapolis: Ross and Haines.

Tedlock, Barbara. 1992. *The Beautiful and the Dangerous: Encounters with the Zuni Indians*. New York: Viking.

Tedlock, Dennis. 1979. The Analogical Tradition and the Emergence of a Dialogical Anthropology. *Journal of Anthropological Research* 35:387–400.

Thornton, Russell. 1998. The Demography of Colonialism and "Old" and "New" Native Americans. In *Studying Native America: Problems and Prospects*, ed. Russell Thornton, 3–14. Madison: University of Wisconsin Press.

1

Lewis H. Morgan and the Senecas

Elisabeth Tooker

In 1851, Lewis H. Morgan published *League of the Ho-dé-no-sau-nee, or Iroquois*, an account of the culture and society of the six tribes of the Iroquois confederacy: Senecas, Cayugas, Onondagas, Oneidas, Mohawks, and Tuscaroras. As John Wesley Powell (1880:115) later remarked, this was "the first scientific account of an Indian tribe ever given to the world." It remains today the best single account of traditional Iroquois culture.

In recent years, it has sometimes been said that Morgan's interest in the Iroquois was sparked by the fight of the Tonawanda Senecas to regain their reservation, which had been sold under the so-called Compromise Treaty of 1842. Morgan's efforts in their behalf were successful, and in gratitude the Tonawanda Senecas adopted him. This opened the way for the research that he published in *League of the Iroquois*.

There is in this tale a moral for the novice fieldworker: If the researcher provides aid to the people he intends to study, he will be rewarded by access to the information he seeks. The story is, however, a convenient fable. Although Morgan did lend his efforts in the fight of the Tonawandas to regain their reservation, he was unsuccessful. The reservation was not brought back until 1857 by a treaty for which there is no evidence Morgan had any part. Although there is some evidence that the Tonawanda Senecas adopted Morgan partly because of his aid to them, the adoption came at the end of the research that resulted in his first major article on the Iroquois, "Letters on the Iroquois," published in the *American Review* in 1847. These "Letters" later formed a substantial portion of *League of the Iroquois.*

During Morgan's lifetime, anthropology emerged as a distinct discipline spurred by what is sometimes called the second era of exploration. The great aim was to map the peoples of the world, what were called "races," a word that encompassed not merely physical appearance but also customs, including language. By 1879 the subject was important enough for the first course in anthropology to be introduced at the University of Rochester, taught not by Morgan but by Joseph H. Gilmore, professor of rhetoric, logic, and English. Gilmore's interest in the subject may well have been spurred by university president Martin B. Anderson, who had a long and active interest in the subject (Tooker 1990:47). Two years later, in 1881, the year of Morgan's death, Edward B. Tylor's *Anthropology* was published. The following year, a course in anthropology was introduced at Bucknell University by its president, David J. Hill, who in 1885 published *Lecture Notes on Anthropology*. In 1886, the year he was appointed professor of American archaeology and linguistics at the University of Pennsylvania (thus becoming the first professor of anthropology in the United States), Daniel G. Brinton published two lengthy articles, one on anthropology and the other on ethnology in his *Iconographic Encyclopaedia*. By 1890, interest in teaching anthropology and in building natural history museums had progressed to the point that trained professionals were deemed necessary, and three graduate students were enrolled, two at Harvard and one at Clark University. With this development, two classes of anthropologists emerged, professional and amateur, and the men who had developed the discipline, Morgan among them, were relegated to the position of mere amateurs.

In the nineteenth century, anthropology was regarded as a part of natural history, a subject that attracted Morgan. His interest in the Iroquois specifically, however, had its roots in the circumstance of his birthplace—an area that had been the homeland of the Cayuga Indians until the state bought it in a series of treaties at the end of the eighteenth century. Born on November 21, 1818, on a farm in Scipio a few miles south of the village of Aurora on the east side of Cayuga Lake in upstate New York, Lewis Morgan was the fourth of eight children that Jedediah Morgan had by his second wife, Harriet Steele Smith. Until

Lewis was three, his family lived on land recently purchased by the state from the Cayuga Indians. In 1822, Jedediah purchased a house in the village of Aurora and moved his family there. He died in 1826, when Lewis was only eight.

Lewis Morgan grew up in Aurora, attending Cayuga Academy there. In 1838, he entered Union College as a junior. Graduating in 1840, he returned to Aurora, read law, and was admitted to the bar. In 1841 he delivered two lectures, both probably at Cayuga Academy: one on geology and one on the Grecian race. The following year he gave an address on temperance at Tupper's Corners, and in 1843 he wrote two more on the same subject, one delivered at both Genoa and Springport and the other at Scipio. He also published several articles in the *Knickerbocker* under the pen name "Aquarius." The first, dated November 1842 and published in January 1843, is an account of the Greek general Aristomenes the Messenian. Morgan compares the character of Aristomenes to that of Washington. The second, "Thoughts at Niagara," appeared in the September issue. In it, the features of the Canadian Falls are seen as an allegory for Great Britain and those of the American Falls as one for the United States. The third, "Mind or Instinct: An Inquiry Concerning the Manifestations of Mind in the Lower Orders of Animals," dated October 1843, was published in the November and December issues of the *Knickerbocker*. Morgan argues that "instinct" is a non-explanation and that all animals "think," that is, have a mind; this is an idea he developed further in *The American Beaver and His Works* (1868).

After college, Morgan joined a secret society called the Gordian Knot. It soon floundered, as such organizations of young men are apt to do, and in an effort to revitalize it, its members, perhaps at Morgan's suggestion, decided to reorganize it as an "Indian Society" modeled after that of the Iroquois confederacy. It came to be called the New Confederacy or the Grand Order of the Iroquois (GOI).

GOI chapter meetings featured initiation of new members, dancing in Indian costume, and refreshments. Each initiate took the name of a noted Indian. Morgan chose Schenandoah, the name of an Oneida chief best remembered for his friendship with the missionary Samuel Kirkland. It was a name he later used as a nom de plume in his "Letters on the Iroquois."

The decision of the members of the Gordian Knot to reorganize their fraternity into an "Indian society" was not an exceptional one. Ever since the founding of the Republic, and even before then, various organizations utilizing real and presumed Indian custom had been established, the Sons of Liberty being only one example. What distinguished the Grand Order of the Iroquois was the determination of its members, especially Morgan, to learn more about Indian history and culture. Such books as were available, among them B. B. Thatcher's *Indian Biography* (1832) and William L. Stone's biographies of Red Jacket (1841) and Joseph Brant (1838), contained virtually no information on the organization of the Iroquois League. If the Grand Order was to model its organization on that of the League, it would have to obtain such knowledge from the Indians themselves. The noted Onondaga chief Abram LaFort, who as a youth had received a white education, was made an honorary member of the order in January 1844, and members of the order may well have interviewed him. Possibly, too, they met Peter Wilson, a Cayuga, then a medical student at Geneva College. But it was Morgan's chance meeting with Ely S. Parker in an Albany bookstore in the spring of 1844 and his subsequent conversations with Jemmy Johnson and two other Tonawanda Seneca chiefs with Parker serving as interpreter that provided the order with the best ethnographic data they had obtained to that date.

That chance meeting in Albany brought together three remarkable men: Morgan, Parker, and Johnson. Parker later gained recognition as a civil engineer, aide to Ulysses S. Grant in the Civil War, and commissioner of Indian affairs in the Grant administration. A man at home in both white and Indian worlds, Parker was born in 1828 on the Tonawanda Reservation and attended the Baptist mission school there, receiving the English name Ely Stone, the name of a local Baptist elder instrumental in establishing the Tonawanda mission station. When about ten years old, he went to Canada, and returning home a few years later, he decided to become more fluent in English. He returned to the mission school, serving as interpreter at the school and the church until 1843, when he entered Yates Academy in Yates, Orleans County, some 15 miles north of the reservation. He was still a student there when Morgan met him the next year.

Parker and his great-uncle, Jemmy Johnson (Parker's "grandfather" in the Seneca system of kinship terminology), were members of a lineage of the Wolf clan that had produced a number of distinguished

Seneca leaders, among them the noted prerevolutionary chief Kayah-sota', the prophet Handsome Lake, the prominent chief Cornplanter, the then aged but still active Governor Blacksnake, and the famous orator Red Jacket. Jemmy Johnson had been born about 1774 at Cana-waugus, an important Indian village on the Genesee River near present Avon. After the American Revolution, a number of Iroquois who had been living in the Genesee valley moved further west. Johnson was among those who settled at the village Tonawanda on the great bend of Tonawanda Creek. A few years before his death in 1815, Handsome Lake, driven out of the Allegany settlement by some of his followers there, moved to Tonawanda, where he also had followers and relatives and where his mother had died and was buried.

About ten years after Handsome Lake's death, the women at Tonawanda asked Johnson to recall the life and teachings of the prophet at a council there. Handsome Lake's words were being forgotten and, consequently, the women believed, the people were falling into evil ways. They called on Johnson because he had often sat in council when his "grandfather," Handsome Lake, had spoken and he had been one of his aides or prompters.[1] The initial meeting at which Johnson recalled the life and teachings of the prophet proved so successful that it became an annual affair. Followers of the prophet came to Tonawanda each fall to hear Johnson's discourse, one delivered over the span of three or four mornings. A few years later, at a Six Nations council held at Tonawanda on September 4, 1830, seven months after Red Jacket's death, Johnson was raised up as Red Jacket's successor. He was given the medal Red Jacket had received in 1792 from George Washington while visiting Philadelphia, then the United States capital, as a member of an Indian delegation. Johnson never achieved the prominence Red Jacket had as a political leader. He was, however, one of the two leading chiefs at Tonawanda. The other was John Blacksmith, the only League chief then living at Tonawanda, After his death, his chiefly name-title, one that belongs to the Wolf clan, was given to Ely Parker.

The Tonawanda chiefs headed by Jemmy Johnson whom Morgan met in Albany were undoubtedly there to try to get the state to do what it could to restore to them their reservation, sold by the Compromise Treaty in 1842. The Tonawanda Reservation had been established in 1797 by the Treaty of Big Tree. By this treaty, the Senecas sold much of their land, reserving for their own use tracts where their principal settlements were then located: six small reservations along the Genesee River (Canawaugus, Big Tree, Little Beard's Town, Squawky Hill, Gardeau, and Caneadea) and four large ones, one on the Allegheny River, one on Cattaraugus Creek, one on Buffalo Creek, and the one on Tonawanda Creek.

Little Beard's Town was sold in 1803, and in 1826 by a treaty signed at Buffalo Creek the remaining Genesee reservations were sold along with over 70 percent of the Tonawanda Reservation (leaving only 12,800 acres), about 40 percent of the Buffalo Creek Reservation, and a lesser portion of the Cattaraugus Reservation. Pressure on the Senecas to sell their remaining lands increased in the 1830s, and by a treaty signed in 1838 (but so suspect it was not proclaimed by President Van Buren until 1840) the Senecas sold all of their reservations in New York State and agreed to move west. Objections to this blatantly fraudulent treaty were so intense that a new agreement, the Compromise Treaty, was signed in 1842. By this treaty only the Buffalo Creek and Tonawanda Reservations were sold: those living on them were to remove to the two reservations that were not sold, Cattaraugus and Allegany, or to lands reserved for them in Kansas. The Tonawanda Senecas objected to the treaty, stating that they had not agreed to it, and undertook what was to be a long battle to regain their reservation.

That the Tonawanda delegation was in Albany for a week that spring of 1844 permitted Morgan to interview them a number of times, and it is perhaps for this reason Morgan obtained as much information as he did. Then, too, the Tonawanda Senecas were not uninterested in having whites know about their political organization. They argued that the Compromise Treaty of 1842 was not binding on them as it was not agreed to in accordance with Iroquois custom. Morgan's interest in this organization, albeit that of the League and not that of the Senecas per se, may have seemed to them convergent with their own desire that whites understand the principles of their form of government.

At a meeting of the Aurora chapter of the order on April 17 after he had returned from Albany, Morgan gave a report on what he had learned from the Senecas as well as what he had found concerning the state's treaties with the Cayugas in two handwritten volumes of Indian treaties then in the Office of the Secretary of State.

A month and a half later, on June 7, Morgan gave an address to the chapter entitled "Vision of Kar-is-ta-gi-a, a Sachem of Cayuga." In this fanciful tale, Morgan recounts a vision that Steeltrap (Kar-is-ta-gi-a), leader of the Cayugas who had returned to their homeland on Cayuga Lake after the American Revolution, supposedly had about 90 years earlier. The images throughout are those fraught with special meaning to members of the chapter, among them Aurora, as it then was and how it had been before white man had settled there. The motif is also that of the order: the Iroquois having been destroyed, their customs are restored—especially their initiation rites, often held in a grove, of young warriors clothed in Indian costume—and their confederacy reinstituted. The *Knickerbocker* published this piece in its September issue, along with two pages of additional commentary that included a brief summary of information Morgan had obtained in Albany. It was Morgan's first publication on the Iroquois.

The "anniversary meetings" of the order, the yearly meeting of all the chapters of the order, were held in August during the week the public examination of Cayuga Academy students and graduation ceremonies took place. Many in the society had been students at the academy, and this popular public event provided a convenient occasion for the annual meeting of the order.

At its anniversary meeting in 1844, the order adopted a constitution that incorporated some information Morgan had obtained in Albany from Jemmy Johnson and Ely Parker. For example, Morgan reported (erroneously) that each of the six tribes of the League had eight clans,[2] what in this constitution became the framework for naming new chapters. The order's earlier plan had called for six chapters (Cayuga, Seneca, Onondaga, Oneida, Mohawk, and Tuscarora nations), but by allowing eight clans (or tribes) to each nation, the total number of possible chapters was raised to forty-eight. Under this new arrangement the Aurora chapter became the Wolf tribe of the Cayuga Nation. The next chapter to be organized in the former territory of the Cayuga Indians was to be called the Turtle tribe; the third chapter, the Hawk tribe of the Cayuga Nation; and so on until eight Cayuga Nation chapters had been established. The same system was to apply to the other nations.

At this anniversary meeting Morgan was elected Grand Tekarihogea of the Iroquois, the title given to the head of the order.[3] Late the same year (1844) Morgan moved to Rochester to establish a law practice, and he quickly established a chapter of the order there. He also made plans for the 1845 anniversary meeting, to be held again in Aurora in August. At that meeting, Henry R. Schoolcraft gave the address and William H. C. Hosmer read the poem.[4] A new constitution was adopted, and Morgan was reelected Grand Tekarihogea.

In late September, a council of the Six Nations was held at Tonawanda for the purpose of raising up new League chiefs to replace those who had died. It was the first such council held in some years and was undoubtedly scheduled to coincide with the council held each fall at Tonawanda at which Jemmy Johnson gave his annual address on the life and teachings of Handsome Lake, a meeting attended by delegations of followers of Handsome Lake from the various Iroquois reservations.

Morgan did not let the opportunity to attend pass, and he and two other members of the Rochester chapter went to Tonawanda with Ely Parker, then attending Cayuga Academy. They were joined there by a member of the Aurora chapter. It was Morgan's first field trip to the Tonawanda Reservation.

As have many later anthropologists, Morgan found that field observation corrected and expanded information gained by interview alone. On October 7, after he had returned from Tonawanda, Morgan wrote to Schoolcraft, reporting on what he and the others had done and seen, noting, "It would require more room than 20 letters would furnish to explain what we saw and heard, the mode of election and deposition, the lament for the dead, the wampum, the two sides of the council fire, etc. etc. and the other ceremonies connected with raising up sachems; also the dances, the preaching, and the feast. The fact is my head is so crammed with matters pertaining to the Iroquois that I intend for my own relief to set down immediately and write a series of essays upon the government and institutions of the Iroquois for publication. Perhaps I shall send them to [George H.] Colton [of the *American Review*]" (Morgan 1845). Then on November 7, 1846, he delivered "Notes on the Iroquois" to the Rochester chapter of the order.

By January 1846, the dispute between the Tonawanda Senecas and the Ogden Land Company still had not been resolved. The land company maintained that the Tonawanda Reservation land was theirs to sell; the Tonawanda Senecas insisted that the Compromise Treaty of 1842 was not binding on them and that the land company could not sell their lands. In their efforts the Tonawanda Senecas did not have the aid of the Quakers, who had done much in negotiating the Compromise Treaty and who now urged the Tonawandas to accept it. They did, however, have the support of a large number of local whites who were outraged at the actions of the Ogden Land Company. One such was John H. Martindale, district attorney of Genesee County since 1842, who more than any other white guided the legal strategy that eventually led to the "buying back" of the Tonawanda Reservation in 1857.

Late in 1845, the Grand Order of the Iroquois formally offered its assistance, which was accepted by the Tonawanda chiefs, and on January 7, 1846, at a meeting in Ithaca, members of the order drew up a petition and plans were made for Morgan to go to Washington. Morgan spent considerable time during the next three months gathering signatures on printed copies of the petition, making at least two trips up the Genesee valley and two to the Tonawanda and Buffalo Creek Reservations.

Then, on March 21, a mass meeting was held at the Genesee County courthouse in Batavia. A memorial and resolutions were drawn up, and Morgan was appointed to bear the proceedings of the meeting to the U.S. Senate.

Morgan left Aurora for Washington on April 3, stopping in New York City, where he delivered a slightly revised version of the paper on the government and institutions of the Iroquois that he had given to the Rochester chapter of the order in November.[5] Neither Morgan's nor Parker's lobbying efforts in Washington, were successful, however, and on August 6, the Senate Committee on Indian Affairs postponed further consideration of the matter until the next session.

The annual anniversary meeting was held as usual that August in Aurora. Ely Parker gave a speech; William H. C. Hosmer read a poem; and Morgan presented a paper on Indian trails, territories, and place-names. The poem and address featured at each anniversary meeting were read the following day: Alfred B. Street giving the poem and Giles F. Yates, the address. At this meeting, a new Grand Tekarihogea of the order was chosen, and the leadership was passed to those who would reorganize the order along the lines of a more conventional secret society. While retaining some Indian symbols, the order largely abandoned the attempt to model its organization after that of the Iroquois League.

His two terms as Grand Tekarihogea having ended, Morgan turned to completing his study of Iroquois government. He wrote George H. Colton, and having receiving an encouraging reply from him regarding publication of a series of articles in his *American Review*, Morgan expanded his earlier paper into a series of "Letters." On October 27, in the company of Charles T. Porter (his future brother-in-law) and Thomas Darling, he went to Tonawanda for a ten-day visit, one purpose being to check the first of these letters.[6] Ely Parker served as interpreter.

It was while he was on this trip that Morgan was adopted by the Tonawanda Senecas, along with Porter and Darling. As Parker indicates in the following account, which he sent to Morgan late in January 1847 (now in the Morgan Papers in the University of Rochester Library), the ceremony was held in the council house then located near Tonawanda Creek. This council house, or longhouse as it is now often called, was rectangular in plan, having benches along the walls—an arrangement that leaves the center open for the dances that are so prominent in Iroquois ritual. Custom dictates that women and children sit on the benches at one end of the longhouse, and men sit at the other end. For some of the dances, a bench or two benches are moved to the center of the longhouse to provide seating for the musicians. For other dances, the lead singer leads the dance, in some using a musical instrument. The "singing tools" employed are percussion instruments, used to keep time for the dancers. Principal among them are the horn rattle (made from a section of animal horn), the turtle rattle (made from a large snapping turtle, and played by pounding one of its edges on the bench), gourd rattle (made from a gourd), and the water drum (a small wooden keg with a leather head and water in the bottom). The dances themselves are circle dances, danced counterclockwise around the room, usually with the women dancing separately from the men.

Typically, Iroquois ceremonies begin with the Thanksgiving address, which returns thanks for the various beings (including plants, animals, water, sun, moon, and stars) on this earth and above—a speech not noted by Parker in his description. This is followed by the dances traditionally deemed appropriate to the occasion (in this case, also social dances, performed "for fun"). The ceremony concludes with the distribution of the feast, most prominently a soup.

Features of the speeches Parker records also contain familiar Iroquois themes: for example, the return of thanks to the Creator that "he has seen fit and proper to preserve our lives to be present" in the opening speech, the statements regarding the purpose for which the ceremony is held and what is to follow, and the use of the phrase "to be of one mind." The reference to a great tree whose roots extend to the four directions is one to the "great tree of peace," a common image for the Iroquois League.

Ely S. Parker's Report of the Adventures of Lewis H. Morgan, Charles T. Porter, and Thomas Darling at Tonawanda on Saturday, the 31st of October 1846

By common report we heard that on Wednesday previous to the Saturday above mentioned, three of our pale faced brothers had come to visit us in our forest homes, and had consequently taken lodgings at one of our cabins. Now it has happened to us Indians that we are not as famous as our white brothers in many respects. We are not as civilized and enlightened, and therefore we do not enjoy the benefits of the many improvements that are daily brought before the public for their use. We do not yet comprehend the mode of navigating the waters by steam and of annihilating space and time by the same method. We still retain many of the primitive customs of our fathers, and among them the art of navigating the waters, save that the wooden [boat] is substituted in place of the bark canoe. Now it was owing to this that a sad misfortune happened to our brothers or rather we may say to one, viz. our Darling. In the nature of things it was necessary that the Tonawanda Creek should be crossed, before we could unite hands as brothers. An attempt was accordingly made to cross the creek in an Indian canoe, but not being accustomed to the particular mode of managing it, from the Signs of the Times, it became evidently necessary that one of the crew should roll out in order to calm the troubled waters, and sooner than thought, poor Darling rolled out of the canoe, bag and baggage, and the Tonawanda Creek was happy to receive him into its watery bosom.

But we will not enlarge upon this topic. Suffice it to say that

Darling did not drown, but they all reached our quiet village without any further serious misfortune. The next day after their arrival I met with them and was very happy to welcome them among us. I soon ascertained that there had been some talk of initiating them regular Senecas. It seems that the request had been made by our brothers to one of our leading and influential men, and by Jemmy Johnson referred to the managers of all dancers. After full consultation, they answered that no reason existed why their request should not be granted, and that if the initiates were prepared the necessary ceremonies would be performed on Saturday, at the same time making them to understand that provision for a feast was to be supplied by them, in order to induce the people to attend. To all of which the initiates assented.

On Saturday the weather was extremely bad. In the morning it commenced raining and continued all day. Great fears were entertained that the gathering to witness the ceremonies would be but small. In the afternoon the initiates and myself repaired to the council house. Upon arrival we found that there were evident signs of a great and respectable audience. The feast had been all prepared during the day, and although it rained, it had a strong tendency in our favor, for it drove those who were out of doors into comfort and heat within. As soon as all the arrangements could be made, the initiates were directed to the seats on a wooden [bench] at one end of the council house. At this end were the men, at the other the women, and in the center were placed the kettles of soup etc. for the feast. The number of people [was] estimated at about 200 or 250.

Dennis Sky, alias Ho-ees-ta-hont (bell in his mouth) then made a short speech to the people. He commenced by saying, "Friends and relations. By previous arrangements we are now assembled in this our accustomed gathering place. The Great Spirit has seen fit and proper to preserve our lives to be present to witness the ceremonies of this occasion. Let us all be of one mind in acknowledging our gratitude to him for this great blessing. The ceremonies we are about to perform may be new to many of you. You have done right in coming to witness the scene. You are all aware that we have assembled for the benefit of our brothers, the Ho-de-no-son-nee. They are pale faces, members of that great community who are the oppressors of the Indian men. Many of you may think that the managers in this case have done wrong in complying with their request to become initiated as Senecas and be equal in standing as we in our tribes, but you must remember that they have told us that they are members of the Society of Hondenosonnee, who are banded together to relieve as far as lies in their power the sufferings and misfortunes of the few scattered remnants of Iroquois, who, we may justly say, lives now only from name and memory. You must remember also that already they have assisted us in opposing the nefarious designs of the Ogden Land Company. One of those present has been to Washington to see if we could not be relieved from the necessity of a removal from our lands. So far as we know they intend to be faithful to their word, to aid the oppressed Indian. Mothers, we urge upon you the necessity of observing strict decorum, while our brothers' benefit shall last. And you warriors, we hope that you may not treat illy the initiates, and we trust that you will do all in your power to make the ceremonies of the evening pleasing and entertaining. We hope that harmony and peace may exist between the minds of you all. We should be extremely ashamed if our brothers should go and publish the proceedings of this evening's meeting, and they be obliged to say that we could not keep peace among ourselves, but were constantly quarrelling one with another. We want that you should all respect not only your own selves, but also have some regard to the character and name of our nation. I am conscious that I speak not merely my own feeling and desires, but of every good and reflecting man now present. We are weak, for our power has been broken, and our white brothers are strong. We should therefore as the weaker party treat our stronger brothers with respect, but not humble ourselves to them as slaves."

Dennis Sky having resigned the floor, Jesse Spring alias Hasge-sa-oh (axe in his hand) arose and said, "Friends and relations. The duty has devolved upon me to announce to you the arrangement of the evening as determined upon by the managers. You are all aware for what we have assembled. A few days ago, some of our pale faced brothers came among us, and intimated to one of our leading men, their desire to become members of our nation by adoption. They no doubt knew the fact that, when anyone chooses to become a member of our nation by making an application to some of our leading and influential men, and providing for a feast which is always customary on such occasions as our inducement to bring the people together, [they ought] not to be scrupulous in adopting. The matter of adoption was referred to the managers and prompters, and they concluded that there was no reason why we should not adopt them. They accordingly stated to our brothers that they had agreed to grant their request, and so soon as the means wanted be furnished for assembling the people, the arrangements would be completed. The managers at the same time referred the giving of names to the chiefs. But in this we have been disappointed. The managers have this evening been informed that the chiefs have made no arrangements so far as this is concerned, and it now becomes the duty of the tribes [clans] to which they are respectively to belong to come forward and present their proper names. The people will observe into what tribe they are adopted by watching who it is that leads the initiate around the room. The managers desire to request the warriors to keep perfect order, and to lend their aid in making the evening performances interesting. The first dance in order will be the War dance, and the second the Grand Religious [Great Feather] dance as the proper accompaniments of the occasion. These also will be for the benefit of our brothers. When these are over, we shall have the privilege of having as many more as we choose. But whether we have any more or not we want all to behave with propriety and decency."

The dancers then withdrew to dress for the dance. But before they withdrew, the initiation ceremony was performed. L. H. Morgan was first led around the room by John Bigfire of the Hawk tribe. Morgan therefore became a Hawk. The leader sang a Thanksgiving song [Personal Chant] while the initiate went around the room, the warriors keeping time to the song by a low guttural sound. The women also kept time by clapping together their hands. The name given to Morgan was Da-ya-da-o-wo-ko; [it] signifies lies across.[7] Porter was then announced as the next person to be led around the room. The name was Da-ya-a-we; [it] signifies he is bringing or fetching. He was then also led around the room, the leader singing a Thanksgiving song. The leader was Isaac Shanks of the Wolf tribe. Consequently Porter became a Wolf de facto. The third and last person announced was Darling. The name given him was Ga-e-we-yo; [it] signifies religion, good news, or glad tidings. The leader sang a Thanksgiving song while leading him around the room, the warriors and women keeping time to the song. He was led by William Kennedy of the Deer tribe. Darling therefore came a Deer man to us. This closed the mere ceremony of initiation.

While the dancers were preparing for the great War dance, Jesse Spring announced to the people that to pass time, the managers had determined to have the Fish dance in which they requested all to participate. The singers were to be the best and the leader the first best. This is a dance in which both men and women take part. The singers facing one another take their seats on a long bench. One has a drum and the other a gourd rattle, with which they beat time to their songs. The dancers dance around the bench facing one another, and at certain periods in the song, the dancers change places, each turning around. The step is easy, consisting only in alternate stamping very lightly with the feet.

When this was concluded and the house had become somewhat still, we heard the thrilling and animating war whoop ring through the air, announcing to us that not only a trusty band of warriors but the dancers themselves were approaching to the place of meeting. Presently was heard a little drum and martial music Indian style. Now a swarthy band of warriors twelve in number presented themselves at the door of the lodge. Some were dressed in theatrical style, while others were painted and labored to look as grim and terrific as paint and coal could make them; others again were nearly naked. They were armed some with tomahawks, some with war clubs, while others with sticks only. The band of singers were four in number. They had between them two drums with which they beat time to their war song. The song commenced and the war whoop was sounded as a signal to commence the dance. As I heard the long shrill whoop and looked upon the motley group of warriors who had stript themselves for the dance, I could not avoid reflecting upon the changed condition of the Indian race. Once the savage yell and the painted band were the terror of the white man. Men, women, and children were alike victims to the unmitigated fury of the Indian. As the dancers played their warlike antics before me, with pleasure I thought of the time when my fathers were strong, when their arms were felt over half the American continent, when with joy they danced around the captive bound for the torture and the stake. Their warlike features have not changed, the same spirit burns within the bosoms of their children, and though now they have not a captive to torture at the stake, yet they can celebrate the adoption of their white brothers into their nation.

At this dance presents were made to the singers, dancers, and the women who prepared the feast. Presents consisted mostly of tobacco of which the Indians are very fond. It is customary for the dancers and spectators always to accompany their present with a short speech. This custom prevailed this evening. It is not possible for me to rehearse all the short speeches that were then made by men distinguished for their prowess and ability. A few short ones I will relate.[8] Among the dancers were men of all sizes, figures, and heights. There was one, who might almost have been called a giant, on account of his great size, and one although a man in age, and had made no little progress in the perpetuity of his kind, might justly have been classed among the race of dwarfs. Our brothers of the Ho-de-no-son-nee, admiring and wondering at the huge size of the former and being surprised at the ease and grace with which he managed his wonderful proportions very justly proposed giving him a present of two plugs of tobacco, remarking that they fancied it would be enough for one chew (or cut). He received it with seeming pleasure, and at the conclusion of the next song he proposed to return his thanks to our brothers for their present, adding that his intellectual capacities corresponded very justly with his physical dimensions, and he hoped that our brothers would publish his fame from the rising to the setting sun.

After the conclusion of a few more songs, our brothers through Isaac Shanks again called the attention of the people to a few words which they wished to say in reply to the speech of the big man. They replied that before they had heard him speak, they had hoped and indulged the idea that he might possibly be an able man. But the attempted display of his puny powers had sadly disappointed them. In his strivings to rise, he was falling lower and lower, and they wanted fain [to] give him another present, but could not. They would therefore give a present to the man in shaggy clothes, and requested that he would come over close to them, to see if they could not recognize him.

Soon after, our brothers through Isaac Shanks, desired to make a present to the women who had assisted in preparing the feast, but as they could [not] give all presents, they requested to see the one who had that day eat[en] the most beef, and who was considered the most greedy, and wished her to come forward and receive the present. This was promptly complied with though we cannot say whether our brothers were aware of the import of the speech that had just been made in their name, and of course did not scrutinize the physiognomy of the women.

After a few more songs, Dennis Sky again spoke. In his remarks he deplored deeply the ill fate of the Iroquois people. He gloried in the day of its highest prosperity, but he beheld with sadness the present declining state of his noble race. He dwelt much upon the keen sightedness, cunning, and sagacity of the white race. The formation of an Iroquois Society, to assume its name and forms and ceremonies among the whites, argued strongly the inevitable extinction of the Indian race, but he sincerely hoped, and he craved one blessing only, that they might be allowed to live upon their own lands, to cultivate their own fields, and to drink from their own springs and creeks, and to mingle their bones with the ashes of their venerated ancestry.

He requested that the Iroquois Society might look into this and see if they could not lend effectual aid to them.

Isaac Shanks followed nearly in the same strain of remarks. He added that many winters ago, our wise ancestors predicted that a great monster with white eyes would come from the east, who would as he advanced eat up all the land, and our ancestors advised their children when their land began to grow weak by the continued gnawings of this white-eyed monster, to look around them for some great tree, whose great roots extended one toward the east, one to the south, another to the west, and another to the north, and around the roots of the tree to collect themselves, and live and die there. This tree he proposed should be the Tonawanda reservation, here they should gather, and here die. He requested all to regard our newly adopted brothers, and to have full faith in them, and their promises to assist the oppressed Indian.

A few more songs being concluded, I requested the audience to lend me their ears for a few moments, while I spoke in behalf of the newly adopted Senecas. I told the people that it was with much feeling they (the brothers) had listened to the mournful tale of the ill fate of the Iroquois people. As a new confederacy of Iroquois, they had come into existence too late to avert the sad calamity. They had come into life just at the moment their elder brothers were stepping into the grave. They very much regretted to see their elder brothers' grey hair bedewed with sorrow, and they would promise, as a society that has now taken the mantle the old Iroquois had thrown off, with all their forms and ceremonies, to make an effort to ease his declining years, and to soften his bed of affliction. They beheld with sorrow the grown attempts made without the least shadow of right to rob and despoil them of their lands, the only and last heritage left them by their fathers. They promised upon the sacred word of adopted Senecas to make an effort to avert this dreadful calamity, and to save if possible the old Iroquois remnants from an ignominious grave. They would also use all their endeavors to unprejudice the public mind against the Indian race. And to effectively accomplish this object, they urged the Indians to unity of counsel and action, for on this alone depended their safety. Without it, no effort of the young Iroquois could save them. They commended them to the kind care and protection of the Great Spirit.

After another song the dance closed and then followed the Grand Religious dance, sometimes called the Corn dance. The two singers sat on a long bench facing one another, the one having a turtle shell rattle and the other, a string of small bells, with which they beat time to their songs, while the dancers kept strict time with them, sometimes making a slow and again a quick step. The dancers seemed animated and pleased in this dance, and it was very exciting to the spectators. Following this dance came the Fish dance, which I have already described. Then came the Trotting dance, which is similar to the Fish dance, except the singers instead of sitting on a bench are the leaders. After this came the Squaw or Shuffling dance. This [was] composed wholly of women. They choose their own singers, who sit on a long bench facing one another, in a circle around the bench.

After this came the feast, which unluckily happened to fall far short of satisfying the great crowd, who all expected to get a taste at least of the meats, and they justly needed it for it was now nearly 2 o'clock Sunday morning. Our brothers had retired before Sunday, I believe, which left the Indians alone transgressors of this holy day. So ended the adventures of our brothers, of which I have attempted to give a faithful record, though very much condensed. But it gives a slight idea of what our pale faced brothers experienced while at our village at Tonawanda.

The first three of the "Letters on the Iroquois" appeared in the February 1847 issue of the *American Review*; five in the March issue; and three in the May issue. At the same time, Morgan was expanding his paper on Iroquois trails and geography, which he read before the New York Historical Society on May 4, 1847. Slightly condensed, this study was published as the last three "Letters on the Iroquois" in the November and December issues of the *American Review*.

Although the members of the Grand Order of the Iroquois envisioned that their society would replace the "old" Iroquois confederacy, which they believed was dying, that proved not to be the case. An anniversary meeting of the order was held in Palmyra, New York, in August 1847. It was largely attended, but it was the last such gathering. The new confederacy quickly died; the old continues to this day.

A further attempt was made in 1847 by Ely Parker and others to get the U.S. Senate to overturn the provisions of the Compromise Treaty of 1842, but the effort failed. The Tonawanda Senecas then took their case to the courts, and after the Supreme Court rejected their argument, the Senate reached the agreement signed in 1857.

In 1847, also at the urging of Governor John Young, the regents of the University of the State of New York decided to add a "historical and antiquarian collection" to the State Cabinet of Natural History. In the furtherance of this goal, the regents asked the citizens of the state for help. One of those replying was Morgan, who, having essentially completed his study of Iroquois sociopolitical organization with the publication of "Letters on the Iroquois," offered his collection of "Indian antiquities and relics" and plans of five archaeological sites he had mapped.

The interest of the regents in adding Indian materials to the state cabinet induced Morgan to take up further ethnographic work, suggesting to the regents that the state make a collection of ethnographic articles of Iroquois manufacture, a project he offered to supervise. The regents accepted the offer and gave Morgan $215 to make the collection. The following year, at Morgan's urging, the regents appropriated $250 for a further collection.

Many of the articles supplied to the state were made by various members of the Parker family; in fact, the making of these collections became a Parker family project. As Morgan saw it, it was not sufficient just to collect these items of Iroquois manufacture; information on their use should also be obtained. To procure it, Morgan went to Tonawanda in the fall of 1849. One year later, he made two more trips: one to the Grand River Reserve in Canada and other to Tonawanda. From these trips came two reports, written by Morgan and illustrated with engravings of the objects themselves: one published in 1850 in the *Third Annual Report of the Regents* and the other written in 1851 but not published until 1852 in the *Fifth Annual Report* (Morgan 1850, 1852).

About the time he was writing the last of these reports, Morgan was also assembling materials for his *League of the Ho-dé-no-sau-nee, or*

Iroquois. As published, *League of the Iroquois* is divided into three books. In book 1, on the structure of the League, Morgan reprinted the nine "Letters on the Iroquois" that described Iroquois social and political organization, which he prefaced by two chapters: one on Iroquois history and one that reprinted the first of the three "Letters" on Indian geography. For book 2, Morgan wrote three chapters on religion, the second being an account of the calendric rituals probably based on information gathered on a field trip in 1850 for which no record exists, and the third being Ely Parker's translation of Jemmy Johnson's speech at the 1848 fall council, which Parker sent to Morgan in 1850. Three more chapters, in part rewritten from the *Third Annual Report of the Regents*, completed book 2. Book 3 comprised four chapters: most of the first was rewritten from the *Third Annual Report of the Regents*; the second reprinted the "Letter" on language; the third, the final two "Letters" on Indian geography. A concluding chapter discussed the future of the Indian.

The volume was illustrated with plates and figures used in the *Third Annual Report of the Regents*, two plates later used in the *Fifth Annual Report*, and two engravings, one of Levi Parker and the other of Caroline Parker, wearing the clothing collected in 1849 and illustrated in the *Third Annual Report of the Regents*. Also included was a large map of the state with Iroquois names for villages, lakes, rivers, and ancient territories.

With the collections he made for the state in 1850 sent to Albany along with his report on them, and *League of the Iroquois* published, Morgan finally freed himself from what in the spring of 1849 he called "this Indian fanaticism" to devote more time to the law—"more profitable, and at times a great deal more interesting" (Morgan 1849). On August 13, 1851, he married his cousin, Mary Elizabeth Steele, daughter of his mother's brother. A half dozen years passed before he took up anthropological studies again. When he did, it was to answer through extensive comparative research questions posed by his Iroquois data. In 1871, the Smithsonian published his seminal study of kinship terminologies, *Systems of Consanguinity and Affinity of the Human Family*; in 1877, Henry Holt published his *Ancient Society*; and in 1881, John Wesley Powell, then director of the Bureau of (American) Ethnology, published his *Houses and House-Life of the American Aborigines* shortly before Morgan's death on December 17.

In 1865, the year Morgan finished writing the first draft of *Systems*, three seminal books were published in England: John F. McLennan's *Primitive Marriage*, John Lubbock's *Pre-historic Times*, and Edward B. Tylor's *Researches into the Early History of Mankind and the Development of Civilization*. A few years later, as *Systems* was being published, two more influential books appeared: Lubbock's *The Origin of Civilisation and the Primitive Condition of Man* in 1870 and Tylor's *Primitive Culture* in 1871. None of these men had done fieldwork. Their studies were syntheses of published data, in some sense, data shipped from the colonies back to England for processing. Only at the end of the century did anthropologists living permanently in England begin to go abroad to conduct fieldwork themselves. The experience was a transforming one, and coming as it did at the time of the professionalization of the discipline, it became a mark of the professional anthropologist. The method that came to be espoused was "participant-observation," the goal being to understand the Natives' culture as they themselves did. For some, adoption was a step in gaining this understanding.

It is difficult to know at this distance in time why Morgan wanted to be adopted by the Tonawanda Senecas. In the nineteenth century, fieldwork had not become the mark of an anthropologist. Rather, those interested in the subject and having access to members of other cultures simply did what Morgan did: interview and observe. Coming as it did after Morgan had done most of his Iroquois fieldwork, Morgan's primary desire to be adopted by the Tonawanda Senecas seems not to have been any expectation that it might be of aid in the collection of information. More likely, it was grounded in ideas that informed the Grand Order of the Iroquois. Chapter meetings of the order featured adoption along with the dancing of Indian dances in Indian costume. Members regarded the order, based on the same principles, as successor to the Iroquois League, and Morgan may have regarded adoption by the Tonawanda Senecas as confirming that belief. In its turn, this idea rested on the older Western notion that the peoples of each continent had their own distinctive characteristics and that those who came to live there acquired these characteristics. Then, too, after the American Revolution, white Americans needing a history separate from that of England turned to Indian culture and history for symbols of national identity, thus strengthening the idea that those living on the continent were, indeed, distinctive.

Perhaps, then, these ideas underlay Morgan's desire to be adopted, as perhaps similar ones also have for other ethnographers adopted by North American Indians.

NOTES

Ely S. Parker's "Report of the Adventures of Lewis H. Morgan" is published here by kind permission of the Department of Rare Books and Special Collections, University of Rochester Library.

1. Handsome Lake was Jemmy Johnson's mother's mother's mother's sister's son, "grandfather" in Seneca kinship terminology.

2. This error is repeated in *League of the Iroquois* (Morgan 1851:79).

3. The order adopted the title of Grand Tekarihogea for its Grand Sachem on the basis of a statement in Stone's *Life of Brant* (1838, 2:500): "The official title of the principal chief of the Six Nations, is Tekarihogea." The title is the first Mohawk name-title, and hence the first name-title on the Roll Call of the Chiefs. It has war associations.

4. Schoolcraft's address and Hosmer's poem were published by the order the following year (Schoolcraft and Hosmer 1846).

5. This address was published by Arthur C. Parker (1928).

6. Porter's reminiscence of this trip written in 1901 is published in the Lloyd edition of *League of the Iroquois* (Morgan 1901, 2:157–160). All I can discover about Thomas Darling is that he lived in Auburn. Circumstantial evidence in Parker's account of the adoption ceremony suggests that Darling was editor of the *Spirit of the Times*, which I also have been unable to identify.

7. Ely Parker (1847, 1891) elsewhere stated that this name belonged to Horatio Jones (1723–1836). Jones was captured by the Senecas in 1781 and adopted into the Hawk clan. He later became one of the two most prominent Seneca interpreters (Jasper Parrish was the other). If Parker is correct, this name would appear to be the one given to Jones later in life and perhaps referred to his role as interpreter. The name given to Jones by his adoptive Seneca family was

Ho-sa-gowwa (Handsome Boy), the name of one of his adoptive family's sons killed not long before Jones's capture.

By Iroquois custom, personal names are "owned" by the matrilineal clans. A child receives a "baby" name belonging to his clan then "not in use," a name that had once belonged to an individual who had died or who had given it up in favor of an "adult" name. Some of these names have associated duties, such as those belonging to the fifty chiefs of the League of the Iroquois, formerly some war chiefs, and at least more recently Faithkeepers (positions resembling those of deacons and deaconesses in some Christian churches).

The Iroquois extended this principle to the naming of colonial officials. For example, governors of New France were called Onontio (Big Mountain), a translation into Iroquois of the name of the first governor of New France, Charles Huault de Montmagny. Governors of Pennsylvania were called Onas (quill, pen) because the first governor of the colony was William Penn. English governors of New York beginning with Edmond Andros (first governor after the English had retaken New Netherlands from the Dutch) were named Corlear after Arent van Curler (or Corlear), chief Dutch negotiator with the Indians. Just as van Curler had gone to Mohawk country in 1643 to negotiate the first treaty between the Dutch and the Mohawks, so also had Andros visited the Mohawks in 1675, not long after his appointment.

8. Morgan published Parker's examples in *League of the Iroquois*, to which he added at the beginning of this passage a series of three speeches in a war dance he had witnessed on the evening of December 3, 1849, while at Tonawanda collecting articles for the state. He also combined the speeches of Dennis Sky and Isaac Shanks that follow in Parker's manuscript, attributing the whole to Shanks. This passage in *League of the Iroquois* concludes with another speech from the December 3, 1849, performance of the war dance (Morgan 1851:274–278).

Nicholson H. Parker, brother of Ely Parker, later used the chapter in *League of the Iroquois* in which this passage appears (Morgan 1851:260–290) with some deletions, rearrangement, and minor changes in wording in one of his lectures, a portion of which his son, Arthur C. Parker, published in his *Life of General Ely S. Parker* (1919:279–286).

BIBLIOGRAPHIC NOTE

The standard biography of Morgan is Carl Resek's *Lewis Henry Morgan: American Scholar* (1960). Bernhard J. Stern's earlier *Lewis Henry Morgan: Social Evolutionist* (1931) contains a number of quotations from the Morgan Papers in the University of Rochester Library, but is marred by error. Additional information on Morgan's life may be found in two more specialized studies: my *Lewis H. Morgan on Iroquois Material Culture* (1994) and Thomas R. Trautmann's superb *Lewis H. Morgan and the Invention of Kinship* (1987).

William H. Armstrong's excellent *Warrior in Two Camps: Ely S. Parker, Union General and Seneca Chief* (1978) supersedes Arthur C. Parker's earlier biography of his great-uncle, *The Life of General Ely S. Parker* (1919).

Perhaps the best recent scholarly survey of Iroquois culture and history is to be found in various articles in volume 15 of *Handbook of North American Indians* edited by William C. Sturtevant and Bruce G. Trigger (1978).

REFERENCES

Armstrong, William H. 1978. *Warrior in Two Camps: Ely S. Parker, Union General and Seneca Chief*. Syracuse: Syracuse University Press.

Brinton, Daniel G. 1886a. Anthropology. *Iconographic Encyclopaedia* (Philadelphia: Iconographic Publishing), 1:17–56.

———. 1886b. Ethnology. *Iconographic Encyclopaedia* (Philadelphia: Iconographic Publishing), 1:57–184.

Hill, David J. 1885. *Lecture Notes on Anthropology*. Lewisburg: Lewisburg University.

Lubbock, John. 1865. *Pre-historic Times*. London and Edinburgh: Williams and Norgate.

———. 1870. *The Origin of Civilisation and the Primitive Condition of Man*. London: Longmans.

McLennan, John F. 1970 [1865]. *Primitive Marriage: An Inquiry into the Origin of the Form of Capture in Marriage Ceremonies*. Chicago: University of Chicago Press.

Morgan, Lewis H. 1843a. Aristomenes the Messenian. *Knickerbocker* 21:25–30.

———. 1843b. Thoughts at Niagara. *Knickerbocker* 22:193–196.

———. 1843c. Mind or Instinct: An Inquiry Concerning the Manifestation of Mind in the Lower Orders of Animals. *Knickerbocker* 22:414–420, 507–515.

———. 1844. Vision of Kar-is-ta-gi-a, a Sachem of Cayuga. *Knickerbocker* 24:238–245.

———. 1845. Letter of Lewis H. Morgan to Henry R. Schoolcraft, October 7, 1845. Schoolcraft Papers, Library of Congress, Washington DC.

———. 1847. Letters on the Iroquois, by Schenandoah: Addressed to Albert Gallatin, LL.D., President New York Historical Society. *American Review* 5:177–190, 242–257, 447–461, 6:477–490, 626–633.

———. 1849. Letter of Lewis H. Morgan to Ephraim George Squier, April 19, 1849. Squier Papers, Library of Congress, Washington DC.

———. 1850. Report to the Regents of the University, upon the Articles Furnished the Indian Collection. In *Third Annual Report of the Regents of the University, on the Condition of the State Cabinet of Natural History, and the Historical and Antiquarian Collection, Annexed Thereto* (New York State Senate Document, no. 75), 65–97. Reprint, Albany: Weed, Parsons, 1850, 63–95; reprinted in Tooker, *Lewis H. Morgan on Iroquois Material Culture* (Tucson: University of Arizona Press, 1994), 163–171.

———. 1851. *League of the Ho-dé-no-sau-nee, or Iroquois*. Rochester: Sage and Brother.

———. 1852. Report on the Fabrics, Inventions, Implements, and Utensils of the Iroquois. In *Fifth Annual Report of the Regents of the University, on the Condition of the State Cabinet of Natural History, and the Historical and Antiquarian Collection Annexed Thereto* (New

York State Senate Document, no. 30), 67–117. Albany: Charles van Benthuysen.

———. 1868. *The American Beaver and His Works*. Philadelphia: J. B. Lippincott.

———. 1871. *Systems of Consanguinity and Affinity of the Human Family*. Smithsonian Contributions to Knowledge 7. Washington DC: Smithsonian Institution.

———. 1877. *Ancient Society*. New York: Henry Holt.

———. 1881. *Houses and House-life of the American Aborigines*. Contributions to North American Ethnology 4. Washington DC: U.S. Geographical and Geological Survey of the Rocky Mountain Region.

———. 1901. *League of the Ho-dé-no-sau-nee, or Iroquois*. Edited by Herbert M. Lloyd. 2 vols. New York: Dodd, Mead.

Parker, Arthur C. 1919. *The Life of General Ely S. Parker: Last Grand Sachem of the Iroquois and General Grant's Military Secretary*. Buffalo NY: Buffalo Historical Society.

———. 1928. *Government and Institutions of the Iroquois by Lewis Henry Morgan*. Researches and Transactions of the New York State Archaeological Association, Lewis Henry Morgan Chapter 7(1). Rochester: Lewis Henry Morgan Chapter.

Parker, Ely S. 1847. Undated newspaper clipping, c. 1847. Parker Papers, American Philosophical Society Library, Philadelphia.

———. 1891. Letter of Ely S. Parker to George H. Harris, August 19, 1891. Parker Papers, Huntington Library, San Marino CA.

Powell, John Wesley 1880. Sketch of Lewis Henry Morgan. *Popular Science Monthly* 17:114–121.

Resek, Carl. 1960. *Lewis Henry Morgan: American Scholar*. Chicago: University of Chicago Press.

Schoolcraft, Henry R., and William H. C. Hosmer. 1846. *An Address, Delivered Before the Was-ah Ho-de-no-son-ne or New Confederacy of the Iroquois, by Henry R. Schoolcraft, a Member: at Its Third Annual Council, August 14, 1845. Also, Genundewah, a Poem, by W. H. C. Hos-*

mer, a Member: Pronounced on the Same Occasion. Rochester: Jerome and Brother.

Stern, Bernhard J. 1931. *Lewis Henry Morgan: Social Evolutionist*. Chicago: University of Chicago Press.

Stone, William L. 1838. *Life of Joseph Brant-Thayendanegea*. 2 vols. New York: Alexander V. Blake.

————. 1841. *The Life and Times of Red Jacket, or Sa-go-ye-wat-ha*. New York and London: Wiley and Putnam.

Sturtevant, William C., and Bruce G. Trigger, eds. 1978. *Handbook of North American Indians*. Vol. 15, Northeast. Washington DC: Smithsonian Institution.

Thatcher, B. B. 1832. *Indian Biography*. 2 vols. New York: J. and J. Harper.

Tooker, Elisabeth. 1990. A Note on Undergraduate Courses in Anthropology in the Latter Part of the Nineteenth Century. *Man in the Northeast* 39:45–61.

————. 1994. *Lewis H. Morgan on Iroquois Material Culture*. Tucson: University of Arizona Press.

Trautmann, Thomas R. 1987. *Lewis Henry Morgan and the Invention of Kinship*. Berkeley: University of California Press.

Tylor, Edward B. 1865. *Researches into the Early History of Mankind and the Development of Civilization*. London: J. Murray.

————. 1871. *Primitive Culture*. 2 vols. London: J. Murray.

————. 1881. *Anthropology: An Introduction to the Study of Man and Civilization*. New York: D. Appleton.

2

Ethnographic Deep Play

Boas, McIlwraith, and Fictive Adoption on the Northwest Coast

Michael E. Harkin

THE ADOPTION GAMBIT

Adoption of anthropologists by aboriginal groups is a phenomenon as old as North American anthropology itself, dating back to our apical ancestor, Lewis Henry Morgan (see chapter 1). It has been seen as a valuable token of important things: rapport, solidarity, familiarity, good works, but above all privileged access to valuable information. Indeed, it is often a mark of one or more of these things, and the anthropologists who benefit from it are often privileged to obtain data with which to produce superior ethnographies. However, a truly ethnographic account of such adoptions would show it to be a phenomenon of great interest, but one not always meaning exactly what anthropologists have claimed or assumed it to mean. With adoption there is both more and less than meets the eye.

Morgan's case, although outside the focal area, provides an interesting starting point for an examination of anthropologist adoption. Morgan's adoption into the Seneca tribe in 1846 was facilitated by his friendly relationship with Ely S. Parker, a man whom he had met in Albany. However, Morgan's relationship to Indian identity was much more complex than this friendship would suggest. Less significant than his adoption into the Senecas was his self-designation as an Iroquois, taking the name Schenandoah. His involvement with the "New Confederacy," a secret fraternal organization in upstate New York that he founded, was in fact the impetus for his ethnographic study of the Iroquois. This hints at the ludic quality inherent in any impersonation.

Taking on a temporary identity is similar to the wearing of a mask in ritual. (Indeed, on the Northwest Coast, the connection is made explicitly.) Thus, the assumption of an alternate identity is always a form of what Philip Deloria (1998) calls "playing Indian." This does not imply that such play lacks value, scientific or otherwise. As Deloria carefully points out, Morgan's sympathetic and accurate portrayals of the Iroquois, as well as his legal pro bono work for them, resulted from this play. As we will see with Boas and McIlwraith, an element of play is mixed in with the professional aspects of anthropological adoption. Indeed, we could call this a form of "deep play," in the Geertzian sense in which fundamental values of an ideological system (in this case, anthropology itself) are "in play" (Geertz 1973:412–454).

The psychological dimensions of deep play are clear. In such a dynamic situation, in which questions of identity, both professional and personal, are at stake, feelings of deep fulfillment and anxious frustration, as well as identity conflicts, are likely to arise. The genre of reflexive ethnography, although not usually foregrounding adoption, tends to bear this out (Geertz 1988:91–101). In such a stressful situation, instrumental action gives way to play. Morgan gives us a broad hint about the psychological status of such game-playing in his mention of the "boyish" aspects of his role-playing (Deloria 1998:88). Indeed, his quest was for innocence, both personal and world-historical, which found fulfillment in the adoption of an Iroquois identity. Deloria's provocative title, "playing Indian," connects such cultural practices with juvenile play, and the dream of return to a prelapsarian (and pre-pubescent) golden age. Deloria convincingly places this within the context of historical tendencies in American culture. However, one can easily find such beliefs in Europe as well (see Feest 1987).

The ludic quality of adoption, evident in Morgan's case as well as the cases of Thomas McIlwraith and Franz Boas, by no means contradicts the serious nature of adoption. Indeed, the concept of deep play, which Geertz borrows from the Utilitarian philosopher Jeremy Bentham, includes both aspects, the ludic and the deeply serious (see Huizinga 1955:5–6). Bentham describes deep play as a bet in which the stakes are irrationally high, so high that neither party can afford to lose. What for Bentham was rationally unfathomable is, using a less reductive psychology, eminently comprehensible. The enactment of deep play deflects attention away from the high stakes and the threat of loss, and yet allows the player to operate upon the contested elements, within the self-limiting context of the game.

NAMING

When Northwest Coast Indians adopted anthropologists or others, this act of adoption was always a name-giving. In Northwest Coast cultures, as elsewhere, the personal name is a marker of social identity and group membership. Traditional feast names are explicitly conceived of as titles, as claims to social, ritual, and political status and even property rights. Such title names have lives of their own and are detachable from individual holders. The act of attaching a title to an individual is always a public one, requiring a distribution of goods by the person assuming the title or someone acting on his or her behalf. At an early age (ten months), Heiltsuk children were given their first names. This coincided with their being considered fully human; young children who died before naming were not formally mourned (Harkin 1990). Naming at this precise point in the life cycle is associated with the period of human gestation, believed to be ten months. Naming was thus a second birth, a rebirth into society. Naming is always an assignment of social and political status. Thus, the process of naming and renaming, which continued until a person reached old age, involved at each stage a social transformation. Generally, this marked transitions in the life cycle, such as adolescence, marriage, and middle age, and a movement up and down the hierarchical scale of statuses.

In certain extraordinary cases, the transition might be glossed as "adoption," such as when a nineteenth-century Heiltsuk chief took a name in the Raven clan of his own village, because the Raven clan was ranked highest (Olson 1935, 5:38). Interethnic adoption was not uncommon, such as between Heiltsuks and Nuxalks (Bella Coolas) who intermarried frequently and shared a village (McIlwraith 1948, 1:19–20). This extensive contact required a merging system of title names, which was, however, never fully unified.

Traditional "Indian names" are not proper names in the classic sense developed by western philosophers, who for the most part have viewed proper names as meaningless tags whose only function is to ensure correct reference (see Gardner 1954; Searle 1969:162–174). Personal names may develop connotations through connection with their holders, but they are only associated with characteristic qualities "in a loose sort of way" (Searle 1969:170). By contrast, "Indian names" have semantic content, and thus intrinsic denotation as well as connotation (see Mill 1895:34–41). In particular, these names refer to social characteristics of persons, such as wealth or generosity, and to family and clan connections. Naming is more than a means of achieving successful reference, but it brings the named within a common social and moral universe.[1]

Based on my reading of Mauss, I have argued that such titles are personae, or public identities (Harkin 1990; Mauss 1985). The original Latin meaning of *persona* as mask (literally "speaking, or sounding through"), of which Mauss was highly conscious, is particularly relevant here. The name (often associated with the right to perform certain masked dances) provides a medium through which the individual is able to communicate to social others, with the ability to make believable, authoritative statements. The individual is thereby transformed into a social actor. Although Mauss presents an overly mechanistic view of Heiltsuk society, his basic point, that social roles derived from a permanent structure of statuses, is essentially correct. Rather than a mere instantiation of an ancestral spirit, the situation is more of a dialectic, in which individual qualities are expressed through a status. Masks, as physical objects, were constructed anew for individual holders of statuses, with the best examples expressing something of the character of the individual holder. Masks were usually destroyed upon the death of the holder. However, once the dialectical relationship between status and individual identity was successfully consummated, the former overwhelmed the latter, as is evident in the fact that the use of vocative kin terms was determined by the relation between the previous holder of the speaker's name and the addressee (Hilton 1990:317; Olson 1954:253, 1955:335).

The "public face" represented by the title name is a requisite for meaningful social action. To speak in public, one needs a position from which to speak, what Boas called a "standing place" (Boas 1966:50–52). In a general sense, this is why Native people have been inclined to give outsiders—missionaries, merchants, Indian agents, as well as anthropologists—titles or "Indian names." It is a means of socializing these persons, of resolving the ambiguity of their status of stranger, "a person afflicted with the incurable sickness of multiple incongruity"

(Bauman 1990:150; Simmel 1950). To do so is to resolve the contradiction of a person who is a local actor—often a very important one—but who lacks any position within the social grid. As I will argue below, this represents an attempt to exercise some control, at least on the level of interpretation, over the actions of this interested, powerful stranger.

Beginning in the late nineteenth century, an increasingly large number of titles lay dormant, without real persons to maintain them. At first due to demographic decline, this trend continued because of the suppression of the potlatch by missionaries and civil authorities and, later, the lack of interest among many Native people in reviving the traditional status system. This trend reached its peak in the 1960s, when relatively few Native people held titles. Only recently has it been reversed. However, during the period I am considering—the 1800s through the 1920s—the system of title names had not yet been destroyed, as social actors generally still had titles, even if many titles went unused. The system of names still constituted a primary social framework.

THE APPEARANCE OF THE WHITE MAN ON THE NORTHWEST COAST

For Native groups on the Northwest Coast, the nineteenth century was a period of radical dislocation. At the beginning of the century, all the groups were autonomous. By the 1880s, most groups were, at the very least, beginning to be encapsulated by colonial society. The Heiltsuks, long considered the most resistant of the British Columbia tribes, had by 1880 accepted Methodist missionaries and begun the rapid process of acculturation (Harkin 1997). At the outset, contact with Europeans was rare: individual explorers such as Vancouver, Mackenzie, and Mozino and, soon thereafter, maritime fur traders were infrequent visitors to Native shores. Many local groups went years between such visits. However, within a few decades, the European presence was permanent and pervasive, with Russians, British, and Americans establishing trading posts and settlements.

This increased face-to-face contact with Europeans resulted in the development of mental schemas for conceptualizing these interested others. In the early stages of contact, individuals were considered *sui generis*, possibly human but extraordinary bearers of wealth and power. Thus, in 1834 the Heiltsuks possessed relics of Vancouver's 1793 visit sewn into a dance apron, treated as objects of power (Tolmie 1963:295). Over time this schema, in which the appearance of whites was assimilated to indigenous narratives of contact with nonhuman beings, proved inadequate (Harkin 1997). Not only were whites more obviously driven by pragmatic concerns in the fur trade, similar to those motivating the Natives themselves, but the appearance of many such people was evidence for the existence of a class of humans previously unknown.

This class of persons required effective reference, of course. It also exhibited certain characteristics that, in aggregate, suggested intentional features. That is, whites were not merely an accidental assortment of individuals who happened to appear within a certain time frame; they constituted a definite category of being. Just as bears were thought to have certain common essential qualities, so too the case with whites. A new mental schema was forming.

THE UNSOCIALIZED OTHER

At some point in the mid–nineteenth century this perception that Europeans and Euroamericans represented a separate and distinct class of humanity was crystallized by the designation of a generic name to describe the "white man." George Hunt describes his interview with a Haisla man who described the "baptismal event":

> I was talking with a Xae'sEla [Haisla] and I asked him Why the Hełdzaqᵘ [Heiltsuks] called the White people Q!wEmx·siwa [q'ʷémxsiwa].
>
> He said, when the White people came first to our place there were many Xae'sEla who went and sat on the deck of the ship
>
> And it is said the bell was ringing. And as soon as the bell stopped ringing then all the White men went down below.
>
> It is said that the chief of the Xae'sEla said that all q!wEmx·siwam (have gone down below).
>
> This is what is called by the Kwakiutl q!wEmx·bEta.
>
> That is the beginning when the Hełdzaqᵘ and Xae'sEla called the White people Q!omx·siwa.[2] (Hunt n.d.)

This curious fragment ascribes the naming of the white man to an encounter on board ship in the early postcontact period. This name, although Heiltsuk or Haisla in origin, is known widely along the central British Columbia coast. This narrative is to be read as an "epitomizing event" in which a complex or drawn-out process is condensed into a symbolic and easily remembered form (Fogelson 1984:260; Harkin 1997:48–65). Thus, the process of establishing relations with whites is represented in the bestowal of a name.

Like other Indian names, q'^{w}émxsiwa has semantic content. An actual translation of the word q'^{w}émxsiwa, in use today, is difficult, but a semantic analysis is possible. The word is composed of the root /q'^{w}m/, meaning "to stick out" and the suffix /siwa/, meaning "through, emerging, expanding" (Lincoln and Rath 1980; Hilton and Rath 1982:102; Rath pers. com. 1987). The phallic symbolism of this is apparent, as the white man is characterized by penetration and expansion. This may refer both to his reputed enormous sexual appetite, a feature that is today one of the connotations of this term among Heiltsuk speakers. It may as well refer to the quality of whites in the colonial period and after to penetrate Native lands and expand into them.

This suffix /siwa/ occurs as well in the name of the cannibal monster Báx^{w}bak^{w}álánusiwa, who is the spirit of the Cannibal Dance, the most powerful performance in the Winter Ceremonial. On one level this suggests the idea of extrahuman power. There is good evidence to support this view. In a complementary narrative, in which Europeans give a name to the Heiltsuks, the white man is seen as a possessor of great power (Harkin 1988). More direct evidence that q'^{w}émxsiwa is considered a powerful name is the fact that it was taken as a title by a Heiltsuk chief in the early part of this century (Drucker 1936–37:7).

If we consider the characteristics of Báx^{w}bak^{w}álánusiwa, certain clues to the perceived character of the white man emerge. The cannibal is associated, especially in Kwakiutl culture, with wealth. Indeed, Hunt suggests as much. But rather than simply wealthy, Báx^{w}bak^{w}álánusiwa is in fact voracious for wealth and human flesh; the two are viewed as equivalent at certain ritual moments. In this sense Báx^{w}bak^{w}álánusiwa may be classified with other ogres and monsters characterized by exaggerated appetites (see Lévi-Strauss 1982). At the heart of the matter is a lack of sociability. The cannibal monster and ogres such as Dzonokwa—a cannibalistic woman who steals children and places them in her basket—approach human society as predators;

only when fully "tamed" can the dancers who impersonate them return to social life.

Consider again the brief Hunt narrative. In the section where the name is actually bestowed, it appears as a description of the white men's actions.

> And as soon as the bell stopped ringing then all the White men
> went down below.
> > It is said that the chief of the Xae'sEla said that all
> q!wEmx·siwa (have gone down below).

Here, *q!wEmx·siwa* is presented as the equivalent of the action of going below. This is evident not only in the English text, where the phrase appears in parentheses, but in the facing Kwakw'ala text, where it is absent altogether. Clearly, *q!wEmx·siwa* is meant as a definite description of the whites, of their going belowdecks. What does this signify? In essence, a refusal to engage in reciprocal exchange. The reason for Indians being on the deck of a ship in the first place could only be to trade. The white failure to engage in trade bespeaks a drastic lack of sociability. The curious business of the bell may be read as an interpretation of the highly regimented nature of life aboard ship and the fact that the behavior of whites was both unpredictable and regulated, even ritualized, by mysterious forces. Similarly, the Winter Ceremonial initiate was slave to an esoteric regimen involving seemingly arbitrary symbols and cues.[3]

Interestingly, this narrative bears some similarity to a narrative I collected describing the bestowal of the name "Bella Bella" upon the Heiltsuks (Harkin 1988). Both narratives involve ships and the idea of proceeding belowdecks. In the Heiltsuk narrative, an old man and a woman are taken below and given presents. In the Haisla narrative, the sailors go below, forestalling the possibility of trade. The space below decks—which was novel to people who had canoes—is a womb-like space, reminiscent of the magical spaces of caves in narratives of supernatural encounter (see Berman 1991). Powerful objects reside in such spaces. In the Heiltsuk narrative, they are parceled out; in the Haisla narrative they are hoarded. In the former, a name with positive connotations is given; in the latter, one with negative connotations is produced by the actions of whites.[4]

Whites were not, as such, amenable to the normal rules of social intercourse. As *q'ʷémxsiwa*, whites were not available as trading or marriage partners. However, *individual* whites might be approached, so long as they were part of a common social and ethical universe. Naming was alternatively a means of recognizing this fact (as in the case of a long-serving missionary) or attempting to achieve this state of commensalism (as in the case of government agents and other powerful, distant figures). If the *q'ʷémxsiwa* was an unsocial character, resistant to the ethical demands of reciprocity, like Báxʷbakʷálánusiwa, giving the individual *q'ʷémxsiwa* an "Indian name" was akin to taming the Cannibal Dancer in the Winter Ceremonial. This logic of bringing otherness within the body of society, domesticating and controlling it, was a characteristic means for the Heiltsuk and other groups to deal with Europeans.

NAMING AND ASYMMETRICAL SYMBOLIC EXCHANGE

The hopes of First Nation peoples to establish balanced reciprocity with whites were not to be fulfilled. By the late nineteenth century, these groups were relatively powerless in the face of colonial agents, including, in certain cases, anthropologists. Indeed, such exchanges turned out to be highly asymmetrical.

Consider the primary task of the ethnographer. It is to define a community for study, to frame it, and above all to name it. This naming may take the form of a baptismal event as it did for Boas and the "Kwakiutl," who had not been so called before (Codere 1990:376). Or it may take the form of a definition, that is setting up terms for correct reference. Boas attempted this, although with less success, as he never established context-free criteria for determining the referential extension of his ethnonym, which could extend minimally to the Kwakw'ala-speaking peoples living around Fort Rupert and maximally to all speakers of North Wakashan languages (see Lincoln and Rath 1980). While the field was considerably more settled when Thomas McIlwraith began his research in 1921 at the behest of Edward Sapir, he chose to employ the ethnonym *Bella Coola*, used by the local whites, rather than the native ethnonym *Nuxalk*. In so doing he enshrined the former term in the ethnographic record.

The Heiltsuks are the only Northwest Coast group explicitly to consider the renaming of their group, as "Bella Bella," a type of ritual exchange (Harkin 1988; 1997: 48–65). However, given the importance of names as social markers and representations of power and spiritual status, it is unlikely that such associations went unnoticed by other First Nations. Naming of anthropologists through adoption is thus an attempt to assert reciprocity, even when that reciprocity is asymmetrical.

If this all seems trivial, consider the uses to which names are put. Ethnonyms, as well as personal names, were imposed upon Native peoples in British Columbia in the late nineteenth century as a means of exercising legal and political control over persons and groups. Anglicized and christianized names marked individuals more clearly and permanently than did Native titles. Anglicized names could be filed and sorted alphabetically, opening up new possibilities of bureaucratic and carceral supervision. Similarly, ethnonyms with agreed-upon definitions allowed for what Scott calls "cadastral mapping" and state control, especially over the crucial question of land and resources (see Scott 1998). After the 1871 Act of Union, First Nations were stripped of any titular rights to land; these would be returned in a very limited fashion through the reserve system, which parceled out lands to named groups (MacDonald 1994). That is, the existence of a legally named entity, such as the Kwakiutls, was a necessary stage in the process of expropriation, a mediation between the aboriginal social world of the early postcontact period and the reserve period of political, legal, and economic domination.

Faced with this intolerable and in many ways inconceivable situation, in which Eurocanadian strangers were redefining their very terms of existence, First Nation peoples used the renaming of key white players to attempt to make sense of and exercise control over events. By bringing them within their social sphere, it was hoped they would conform to common values of First Nation cultures.

FRANZ BOAS AND THE "KWAKIUTL"

As anthropologists we often flatter ourselves in thinking that our professional relations with our native consultants separate us distinctly from other outsiders, especially missionaries and government agents. That Boas was, at least in the early days, considered just another interested stranger by the Kwakwaka'wakw people of Nawiti is evident in their confrontation with him in October 1886. As Boas recorded in his diary: "I must add that the natives were not too clear about why I was there and what I wanted and that they were making all kinds of conjectures. At first they thought I was a priest, and now, because I had bought nothing, they thought I might be a government agent come to put a stop to the festival" (Rohner 1969:33). Boas, in response, rises to his feet and gives an oration in English about the mission of the anthropologist: "My people live far away and would like to know what people in distant lands do, and so I set out. I was in warm lands and cold lands. I saw many different people and told them at home how they live" (Rohner 1969:34). It is significant that he makes the further claim that, as a German, he cares neither what the queen nor the Indian agent may think of the potlatch. Such distancing is a technique familiar to modern anthropologists, who are likewise taken for spies or representatives of faraway powerful interests.[5]

The Kwakwaka'wakw concern over the potlatch was real and deeply felt. However, it is possible to see it as well as a symbol of the larger conflict between Kwakwaka'wakw and Eurocanadian legal systems and worldviews (see Bracken 1997). The potlatch was, as Loo (1992) calls it, a "site of struggle," an arena in which opposing ideas about power, personhood, and property were rhetorically contested.

In November 1894, Boas was familiar enough to the Kwakwaka' wakw of Fort Rupert to be given a name. Judging by the very small distribution made, it was not a high-ranking title, but it gave him membership in the community. As Boas phrased the matter in a letter to his wife, "I gained the good will of these people and received invitations to all the feasts which are taking place here" (Rohner 1969: 178). Boas does not specify from what family the name came, although we know it was given to him by George Hunt. Indeed, his attitude toward the whole process was rather casual. He mistakenly glosses his title Heiltsakuls as "the silent one" in his letter; later in a publication it is glossed "the one who says the right thing" (Boas 1896:232, quoted in Rohner 1969). The latter translation is correct. The root /heil/, which also occurs in the ethnonym *Heiltsuk*, means to do something correctly. However, there is some question as to whether that is the name actually given to Boas, or whether, as George Hunt's daughter stated, it was really HeiLakwalets (Rohner 1969:177).[6]

If, for Boas, naming was a means of gaining access, for the Fort Rupert Kwakwaka'wakw it was a means of "domesticating" the anthropologist who had already spent considerable time in the community. The specific reasons for the "adoption" at this time are not clear, but I would suggest that they are related to the research agenda Boas was pursuing. He was undertaking the work on the Winter Ceremonial that would culminate in his masterpiece, *The Social Organization and Secret Societies of the Kwakiutl* (1897). By definition, the Winter Ceremonial was a web of secrecy in which information was not allowed to circulate beyond certain sociological boundaries. Although George Hunt collected most of the secret information, Boas himself participated in the more public performances. In order to participate even on that level, it was necessary to possess an official standing in the community, represented by the title name. Perhaps, secondarily, the Kwakwaka'wakw experienced discomfort at the idea of this information circulating beyond the closed community of the "ritual congregation," as Goldman (1975) called the translocal community of initiated Kwakwaka'wakw adults. Naming Boas a member of that congregation was a means of avoiding the primary leakage of information to the anthropologist himself, although, of course, it did nothing to prevent its dissemination to readers in Boas's land "far away."

THOMAS MCILWRAITH AND THE POLITICS OF SECRECY

Thomas McIlwraith was among the first generation of home-grown Canadian anthropologists. He studied anthropology at Cambridge under Rivers and Haddon, and was a star student who was asked to stay on as a lecturer for one year (Sapir 9 Aug 1921). Although he had only an undergraduate degree, he returned to Canada to carry out field research under the direction of Edward Sapir at the Victoria Memorial Museum (later National Museum of Man). Sapir sent him to Bella Coola to complete a monograph on the Nuxalk or Bella Coola Indians, which resulted in the classic two-volume tome *The Bella Coola Indians* (1948). This work was actually completed in the 1920s, but it was held back from publication for twenty years over questions of "obscene" material (Jones 1983). McIlwraith refused to translate certain sexual passages into Latin, as was the custom. McIlwraith held a temporary academic post at Yale before being hired at the University of

Toronto, the first anthropologist at a Canadian university (McIlwraith Papers B79–0011).

Sapir sent McIlwraith to Bella Coola as a "field assistant" in December 1921 (Sapir 30 Nov 1921). McIlwraith began to work immediately upon his arrival in March 1922 with Joshua Moody, a Christian who was knowledgeable about traditional culture (Barker 1992; Tepper 1991). McIlwraith's comments about Moody are worth quoting at length: "I think I have flattered my way into his good graces, and at any rate he has shown me his secret dance whistles and so on. Joshua realizes that the old order is changing rapidly, and is willing, therefore, to describe customs which were secret in olden times, and which he does not want to have other Indians know about his communicating to me. Unluckily, he is very jealous and any attempt on my part to go to other people, even to purchase specimens, would check the flow of information from him" (Sapir 2 Mar 1922). Several points are interesting. Moody's perceived "jealousy" and tetchiness are at best only partly due to his personality. It is clear that he is in a precarious position, having let McIlwraith into secrets of the Winter Ceremonial. In the postcontact period, such violations could have resulted in death to either party (McIlwraith 1948, 2:11–12). He is especially concerned that others would find out about his divulgences, which indeed happens later. Although Moody is a Christian, and thus theoretically protected from both supernatural and social retribution, he still has reason to worry.

To a man attempting to live in both worlds, the appearance of the anthropologist presents both opportunities and dangers. Moody had worked with Harlan Smith two years prior to McIlwraith's arrival in Bella Coola (Barker 1992). Clearly, his willingness to work with anthropologists was a function of his position in society. Such persons as Moody and Boas's assistant George Hunt were best able to interpret Native culture to anthropologists, as they were themselves in a position somewhat external to it; however, they were equally responsible at least indirectly for any interpretive violence done by the anthropologist to the cultural fabric (Crapanzano 1992:6).[7] From the Native perspective, allowing the anthropologist to record cultural data involved both benefits and costs. The obvious benefit of having cultural practices and beliefs recorded are partly offset by the fact that the an-

thropologist and his or her Native consultant(s) selected and organized the data.

McIlwraith's and his consultants' ambiguous and dangerous positions with respect to esoteric knowledge was resolved when McIlwraith was "adopted" into the community. This occurred when one of
his consultants, a monolingual traditionalist named Captain Schooner, named McIlwraith his "son" in 1923 (Sapir 29 Sept 1923). Schooner died shortly thereafter. This was a serious blow to the small
community of traditionalists; a gap was left in the knowledge and personnel required to perform the Winter Ceremonial (Barker 1992).
Into this breach stepped McIlwraith, whose knowledge, competence,
and friendship with several of the elders made him a logical candidate to succeed Schooner (Sapir 4 Mar 1924). This involved taking
Schooner's name, Xwots Konis (Barker 1992). Not only was a name
given to McIlwraith, but one was given to Sapir as well. In a postscript
to a letter to Sapir, McIlwraith writes: "I have always forgotten to tell
you that the Bella Coola name Ałqunłam has been legally conferred
on you—as my chief. I protested, not having been given as exalted a
name myself but the community wished to honour you for sending
me to Bella Coola" (Sapir 4 Mar 1924). That naming has a political dimension is undeniably evident in this case. While McIlwraith was
known and well liked in Bella Coola, Sapir was not known personally,
and he resided in distant Ottawa, the seat of federal power (and, as
such, second in importance to the provincial capital Victoria, but important nonetheless). Providing Sapir with a chiefly name can only be
understood within the framework of an attempt to exercise control
over the terms of their own representation in the Eurocanadian world.
McIlwraith's forgetting to inform Sapir of this honor demonstrates
the rather frivolous manner in which he understands and speaks about
"adoption." For McIlwraith, naming was simply a mark of rapport
with his consultants, a value stressed by the Cambridge anthropologists who trained him (Barker 1992). The existence of such rapport,
and its ethnographic benefits, are undeniable in McIlwraith's case.
However, other aspects are primary, since they provided the motiva-
tion for these namings.

The benefits of naming to McIlwraith and his generations of readers, including Nuxalk ones, are quite substantial. In the 1923–24 season, McIlwraith was allowed to participate in the Winter Ceremonial

performances, rather than merely record consultants' secondhand accounts. There is evidence that this turn of affairs was beneficial to the Nuxalks as well, for McIlwraith threw himself, albeit somewhat reluctantly, into the practical management of the performances: "The greatest time-killer has been the dances, which have taken place nightly for the last six weeks. Luckily (or unluckily) I have an official place in the choir; the words of the songs are given to me when composed, then when they are to be sung I am established by Jim Pollard and whisper them to him to call out when necessary. . . . The dances are really going off better than they would were I not present and several speeches of gratitude have been made to me, while I take my just share of whatever is being distributed" (Smith 7 Jan 1924). McIlwraith says much the same in a letter to Sapir, but is more expansive on his own role in the dances: "Speeches have been made thanking me for my help, and I have certainly become popular. I have danced myself four or five times, and have stepped into the shoes of an old man who last year adopted me and has since died. As a result I have made ritual speeches in Bella Coola and have the theoretical right to kill anyone who errs in the ritual" (Sapir 26 Dec 1923). The playful, even flippant tone of these passages reflects in part youthful enthusiasm, but more the inherently ludic quality of a Cambridge man dressing up and acting as though Nuxalk. He was certainly aware of the seriousness of the religious themes expressed in the ceremony, as well as the seeming precariousness of the ceremony's continued existence, with the loss of a key actor for whom McIlwraith fills in during that 1923–24 season.

Thomas McIlwraith became an important figure in the Winter Ceremonial of that year, which was the culmination of his two years in the field. He clearly achieved the role of significant social actor within the Nuxalk social universe. This adoption was a culturally characteristic response to the ambiguous state of affairs that saw a person with no formal standing in the community becoming privy to powerful secrets. Such adoptions were not without precedence in historical Nuxalk culture. On one occasion a mask slipped off during a public performance of the *kusiut* ceremony. As the uninitiated beheld in shocked silence the secrets behind the workings of this ceremony, a senior member of the society barred the doors of the dance house and proceeded to initiate the uninitiated (McIlwraith 1948, 2:12). Something similar happens when the anthropologist arrives in a commu-

nity and rather suddenly gains access to previously secret information. The contradictory nature of the situation gives rise to alternative
extraordinary measures to resolve the ambiguity, either expulsion or
adoption. For successful anthropologists, through luck, persistence,
or strength of personality, the latter is the outcome. Indeed, the ethnographic outcome of fieldwork and the trajectory of anthropological careers depend upon such hazards.

THE CULTURAL POLITICS OF ADOPTION

The concept of adoption is, along with the related idea of the anthropologist as child in the community he or she studies, part of a natu-
ralizing discourse that masks the complex, ambiguous, and power-
saturated conditions of fieldwork (see Rosaldo 1989:168–195).[8] Despite
attempts on the part of both anthropologist and aboriginal to resolve
or at least displace these contradictions by hiding them, the fact remains that the anthropologist is not socially identical to the locals,
that he or she controls the information presented to him or her in a
way not available to the Native, and that he or she is bound to leave
the community sooner or later. The primary locus of anthropological
praxis is not "in the field" but elsewhere, in the academy and governmental institutions.

This fiction, mutually constructed by anthropologist and Native
consultant as well as by the host community at large, is a powerful
means of addressing the contradictions entailed by the presence of
the intimate stranger. Other sorts of contradictions involving non-
anthropological actors may also be dealt with in this way. Thus George
Darby, a longtime missionary among the Heiltsuks, was given a high-
ranking title, ironically, despite Darby's work to destroy the traditional
feasting system (Harkin 1993; McKervill 1964:144). Likewise, Indian
agents whose power is based upon principles contradictory to the aboriginal system may be similarly honored. Such honorings are not
pure Machiavellian attempts at realpolitik, nor are they necessarily or
exactly statements of affinity.

Rather, adoption by naming is precisely the creation of a fictive
kinship, a relationship that gives the namer a certain kind of tenuous
and provisional claim upon the named. Although the practical advantages of naming are very limited (except to the anthropologist), it al-

lows for symbolic control over uncontrollable events and actors, in a sense not too different from Malinowski's theory of magic as a means of controlling nature (Malinowski 1954:28–30). Like nature, the anthropologist is generally resistant, because he or she has no choice, to the claims implied in the relationship of adopter and adoptee.

For the anthropologist, the overtly ludic dimensions of "playing Indian" may be foregrounded, as with Morgan, or suppressed, as with Boas. Nevertheless, deep play, in which identities, professional and personal, are at stake, characterizes the ethnographic encounter in general and the practice of adoption in particular. The fact that first fieldwork occurs for most anthropologists during early adulthood or even late adolescence is part of the paradigm of professionalization. Identity transformation is bound to occur; fictive adoption by the host people (or, more commonly, a family) is a particularly overt and material form of this transformation, and thus it is seen as desirable or even necessary. Moreover, as Michael Jackson has said, adoption fulfills the anthropologist's need to repay the psychological debt owed to those who have "recognized one's humanity, rescued one's ego, saved one's face" (Jackson 1998:104).[9]

Deep play arises in part from the contradictory nature of the ethnographic role: intimate stranger, alien kinsman. As Philip Deloria has observed of "playing Indian" in American history, such play arises at moments when contradictions within American identity become foregrounded. Playing Indian "is both precarious and creative, and it can play a critical role in the way people construct new identities" (Deloria 1998:7). Similarly, ethnographic deep play strives not to deny contradictions in an emerging professional identity but rather to represent and deploy those contradictions creatively.

Indeed, both anthropologist and Native participate in ethnographic deep play, in which much more than the credentialing of the anthropologist is at stake. The entire repertoire of expressive culture, for example, may hang in the balance as insiders decide whether or not to allow access to outsiders who may not always be easily identifiable as friend or foe. (Some of the staunchest opponents of traditional culture, such as the aforementioned George Darby of Bella Bella, were also the most devoted friends of the Indians as individuals). The famous interrogation of Franz Boas raises the issue with an unusual degree of explicitness, but such questions have always been, and remain, at the very heart of the relation between anthropologist and Native.

From the aboriginal side, ethnographic deep play is both deadly serious and overtly playful. Although not recorded, we can imagine the amusement on the faces of older Nuxalks upon seeing a young white man from Ottawa acting out his role in the chorus of aged Indians.[10] It is inconceivable that the humor and novelty of the situation were lost on them.

NOTES

1. Names have something of this function of social identification in western cultures, especially in societies that maintain fraught social or "ethnic" boundaries. Consider the powerful connotations in American society of a "Jewish name," which have survived in some segments of society until the present day. Additionally, social class connotations of personal names are very strongly pronounced and very likely have an impact on a child's life opportunities (e.g., "Crystal" as opposed to "Emma").

2. It is difficult to understand why Hunt recorded three separate orthographies of this word: q!wEmx·siwa, Q!wEmx·siwa, and Q!omx·siwa in this short passage. It will be noted that the latter are capitalized, and thus can be taken to be the "name" the white people are called, while the former is a description. The difference in the initial vowel may be attributed to the Boasian method of phonetic, not phonemic, transcription.

3. The best example of this supposed arbitrariness of behavior in the Winter Ceremonial was the "taboo word" of the Cannibal Dancer. It was a word, seemingly unconnected to the themes of the dance, that, when spoken, sent the initiate into a frenzy of biting.

4. The contrast between the two narratives may refer to the difference between two historical periods, as the Heiltsuk narrative is of the "first contact" genre. The Haisla narrative suggests a greater degree of familiarity with whites. What is certain is that the structural opposition between the two narratives contrasts generous with antisocial behavior.

5. When undertaking fieldwork among Nuu-chah-nulths in Clayo-quot Sound, British Columbia, in the early 1990s, I was accused of spying for MacMillan-Bloedel, the logging corporation that was seeking to clear-cut much of the area. These accusations did not derive from important figures in the community (who were very familiar with the players in that ecopolitical drama) and so did not impede research, but they were nonetheless unsettling.

6. Much later, in 1930, Boas was honored with the name Mullmum-laeetlatre, which, he said, meant "If you put water on him the southeast wind will blow" (Rohner 1969:292).

7. George Hunt was, as is well known, of mixed Tlingit and Scots de-scent and was himself "adopted" into Kwakwaka'wakw society.

8. It is important to note that not all the power resides with the an-thropologist. Local people have almost always had the power not to respond to ethnographic inquiries and to throw out such un-wanted unofficial visitors. Anthropologists, especially novices, of-ten cut a rather pathetic figure: a pathos that often facilitates their entry into the community. However, the interaction is nonethe-less power saturated. Following Foucault, we can view the ethno-graphic encounter as a crucial nexus of power flowing through, but not effectively wielded by, local actors. That is to say, the conditions of the larger world, including the hegemony of the ethnographer's culture, impinge upon the encounter in multiple ways.

9. Jackson's observations, based on long field experience, are worth quoting entire: "The intimate and incorporative bonds of fictive kinship and friendship that belong to the fieldwork situation are frequently opportunistic and transitory; what they often connote is a deep sense of gratitude that the ethnographer feels toward his host community for having saved his or her sense of dignity in a cultur-ally disorientating and debilitating environment. It is an overcom-pensatory gesture to the other for having recognized one's human-ity, rescued one's ego, and saved one's face" (Jackson 1998:104).

10. The members of the chorus would have been fairly old. The younger men (and some women) constituted the initiates.

Barker, John. 1992. Introduction to *The Bella Coola Indians*. Toronto: University of Toronto Press.

Bauman, Zygmunt. 1990. Modernity and Ambivalence. In *Global Culture: Nationalism, Globalization, and Modernity*, ed. Mike Featherstone, 143–169. Theory, Culture, and Society, vol. 7. London: Sage.

Berman, Judith. 1991. The Seals' Sleeping Cave: The Interpretation of Boas's Kwakw'ala Texts. Ph.D. thesis, University of Pennsylvania.

Boas, Franz. 1896. The Indians of British Columbia. *Bulletin of the American Geographical Society* 28:229–43.

———. 1897. The Social Organization and the Secret Societies of the Kwakiutl Indians. United States National Museum, report for 1895:311–738.

———. 1966. *Kwakiutl Ethnography*. Edited by Helen Codere. Chicago: University of Chicago Press.

Bracken, Christopher. 1997. *The Potlatch Papers: A Colonial Case History*. Chicago: University of Chicago Press.

Codere, Helen. 1990. Kwakiutl: Traditional Culture. In *Handbook of North American Indians*, vol. 7: *The Northwest Coast*, ed. Wayne Suttles, 359–377. Washington DC: Smithsonian Institution Press.

Crapanzano, Vincent. 1992. *Hermes' Dilemma and Hamlet's Desire: On the Epistemology of Interpretation*. Cambridge: Harvard University Press.

Deloria, Philip. 1998. *Playing Indian*. New Haven: Yale University Press.

Drucker, Philip. 1936–37. Field notes taken at Bella Bella. File no. 4516(46). Washington DC: Smithsonian Institution, Bureau of American Ethnology Archives.

Feest, Christian. 1987. *Indians and Europe*. Aachen: Edition Herodot.

Fogelson, Raymond. 1984. Who Were the Aní-Kutáni? An Excursion into Cherokee Historical Thought. *Ethnohistory* 31:255–63.

Gardner, Alan H. 1954. *The Theory of Proper Names: A Controversial Essay*. 2d ed. Oxford: Oxford University Press.

Geertz, Clifford. 1973. *The Interpretation of Cultures*. New York: Basic Books.

———. 1988. *Works and Lives: The Anthropologist as Author*. Stanford CA: Stanford University Press.

Goldman, Irving. 1975. *The Mouth of Heaven: An Introduction to Kwakiutl Religious Thought*. New York: John Wiley and Sons.

Harkin, Michael. 1988. History, Narrative, and Temporality: Examples from the Northwest Coast. *Ethnohistory* 35:99–130.

———. 1990. Mortuary Practices and the Category of Person among the Heiltsuk. *Arctic Anthropology* 27:87–108.

———. 1993. Power and Progress: The Evangelic Dialogue among the Heiltsuk. *Ethnohistory* 40:1–33.

———. 1997. *The Heiltsuks: Dialogues of History and Culture on the Northwest Coast*. Lincoln: University of Nebraska Press.

Hilton, Suzanne F. 1990. Haihais, Bella Bella, and Oowekeeno. In *The Handbook of North American Indians*, vol. 7: *The Northwest Coast*, ed. Wayne Suttles, 312–322. Washington DC: Smithsonian Institution Press.

Hilton, Suzanne F., and John Rath. 1982. Objections to Franz Boas's Referring to Eating People in the Translation of the Kwakw'ala Terms of Baxubakwalanuxusiwe and Hamats!a. Working paper, 17th International Conference on Salish and Neighboring Languages. Portland State University.

Huizinga, Johan. 1955. *Homo Ludens*. Boston: Beacon Press.

Hunt, George. n.d. The Name for White People. Kwakiutl Ethnographic Texts with Translation. Boas Papers W1a.19 F1938, p. 81a. American Philosophical Society, Philadelphia PA.

Jackson, Michael. 1998. *Minima Ethnographica: Intersubjectivity and the Anthropological Project*. Chicago: University of Chicago Press.

Jones, Donald. 1983. Anthropologist Fought Twenty Years of Censorship. *Toronto Star*, May 14, 1983, G22.

Lévi-Strauss, Claude. 1982. *The Way of the Masks*. Seattle: University of Washington Press.

Lincoln, Neville, and John Rath. 1980. *North Wakashan Comparative Root List*. National Museum of Man, Mercury Series, Canadian Ethnology Service, paper no. 68. Ottawa: National Museums of Canada.

Loo, Tina. 1992. Dan Cranmer's Potlatch: Law as Coercion, Symbol, and Rhetoric in British Columbia, 1884–1951. *Canadian Historical Review* 73:125–165.

MacDonald, James. 1994. Social Change and the Creation of Underdevelopment: A Northwest Coast Case. *American Ethnologist* 21:152–175.

McIlwraith, Thomas F. 1921–64. McIlwraith Papers, University of Toronto Archives, Fisher Rare Book Library, Toronto.

————. 1948. *The Bella Coola Indians*. 2 vols. Toronto: University of Toronto Press.

McKervill, Hugh. 1964. *Darby of Bella Bella*. Toronto: Ryerson.

Malinowski, Bronislaw. 1954. *Magic, Science, and Religion and Other Essays*. Garden City NY: Doubleday Anchor.

Mauss, Marcel. 1985. A Category of the Human Mind: The Notion of the Person, the Notion of the Self. Translated by W. D. Halls. In *The Category of the Person: Anthropology, Philosophy, History*, ed. Michael Carrithers, Steven Collins, and Steven Lukes. Cambridge: Cambridge University Press.

Mill, John Stuart. 1895. *A System of Logic: Ratiocinative and Inductive*. New York: Harper and Brothers.

Olson, Ronald. 1935. Field notes from Bella Bella and Rivers Inlet. 6 vols. University of California Bancroft Library, Berkeley CA.

————. 1954. Social Life of the Owikeno Kwakiutl. *Anthropological Records of the University of California* 14:213–259.

———. 1955. Notes on the Bella Bella Kwakiutl. *Anthropological Records of the University of California* 14:319–347.

Rath, John C. 1980. *A Practical Heiltsuk-English Dictionary with a Grammatical Introduction*. 2 vols. National Museum of Man, Mercury Series, Canadian Ethnology Service, paper no. 75. Ottawa: National Museums of Canada.

Rohner, Ronald. 1969. *The Ethnography of Franz Boas: Letters and Diaries of Franz Boas Written on the Northwest Coast from 1886 to 1931.* Chicago: University of Chicago Press.

Rosaldo, Renato. 1989. *Culture and Truth: The Remaking of Social Analysis*. Boston: Beacon.

Sapir, Edward. 1921–23. Edward Sapir Correspondence. I-A-236M, box 427, file 82. National Museum of Civilization, Hull, Quebec.

Scott, James. 1998. *Seeing like a State: How Certain Schemes to Improve the Human Condition Have Failed*. New Haven: Yale University Press.

Searle, John R. 1969. *Speech Acts: An Essay in the Philosophy of Language*. Cambridge: Cambridge University Press.

Simmel, George. 1950. The Stranger. In *The Sociology of George Simmel*, ed. and trans. Kurt H. Wolff, 402–408. New York: Free Press.

Smith, Harlan I. 1923–24. Smith Correspondence. I-A-242M, box 216, file R. National Museum of Civilization, Hull, Quebec.

Tepper, Leslie H. 1991. *The Bella Coola Valley: Harlan Smith's Fieldwork Photographs, 1920–1924*. Canadian Ethnological Service, paper no. 123. Ottawa: National Museum of Civilization.

Tolmie, William Fraser. 1963. *The Journals of W. F. Tolmie, Physician and Fur Trader*. Vancouver: Mitchell Press.

3

He-Lost-a-Bet (Howan?neyao)
of the Seneca Hawk Clan

William N. Fenton

The Iroquois have a long history of adoption. Indeed, adoption was public policy of the Iroquois Confederacy from earliest times. During the seventeenth and eighteenth centuries, the Confederacy took in whole populations to replace losses from epidemics and warfare. Invariably colonial officials with whom they dealt acquired Indian personal names, often puns on their English or French surnames, for everyone in Iroquois society must have a name and occupy a niche in the social system so as to move socially and deal politically. Clan affiliation of those early names remains obscure; but in later times we know that the Seneca Hawk clan awarded a name to L. H. Morgan at mid–nineteenth century, and they honored New York governor Nelson Rockefeller a century later. After me, they gave a name to anthropologist George S. Snyderman, and not to be outdone, the Seneca Turtle clan conferred Gahe?dago:wa: (Great Porcupine) on Frank G. Speck, whom we all greatly admired. So I was not alone, although the account of my adoption may be unique.

The Fentons of Conewango valley in western New York and the family of Amos Snow of the Seneca Nation kept up an association going back to the 1860s. The Fenton farm on Flat Iron Road lay halfway between the Cattaraugus and Allegany Reservations of the Seneca Nation, and Seneca families "going to the other side," as they said, camped on the hemlock ridge at the back of the farm. One bitter winter morning, my father's father at chore time reported to his widowed mother that smoke was rising from the hemlock ridge beyond the swamp. His mother suggested that he go see how the Indians were faring. He took an ax and went afoot, intending to split up some firewood that he had felled. He found an Indian family encamped in a lean-to that they had constructed of hemlock bows: a man, an old woman, and a young girl with a newborn baby. They were shivering. When he returned to the house for dinner, he reported what he had seen to his mother. She insisted that he hitch the team to the pung, fill the bed with straw, throw in a buffalo robe, and go fetch the family to the warm farmhouse. By suppertime she had installed the Indian family in the hired girl's room off the kitchen.

The Seneca family stayed for a week until the weather moderated and permitted travel. When they departed, the old lady thanked my great-grandmother for shelter, sustenance, and hospitality, saying it was the first time they were invited to sleep and eat in a white home. It was an Indian custom, she added, to bind a friendship with a present, whereupon she unfolded an old burden strap, an obvious heirloom, that was decorated with dyed deer hair and porcupine quill embroidery worked in a geometric pattern, and edged with seed beads, which she handed to my great-grandmother, Fanny Carr, widow of Captain William Fenton, the seafarer.

The Seneca hunter was Amos Snow, a stout, jovial fellow who became a lifelong friend of my grandfather: companions on squirrel and pigeon-shooting expeditions, trotting horse fanciers, good for shared labor on the farm. On occasion Amos would show up with his young family and stay for a meal. At some point he entrusted to my grandfather two old wooden False Faces that he produced from under the wagon seat. My grandfather kept them in a round wooden cheese box (Fenton 1987:248). Later, Amos left a string of purple wampum that commemorated some event long since forgotten. These items, however they came to us, formed the nucleus of an ethnological collection that was kept in a special attic room known as the "Indian collection," where I was privileged to climb steep stairs on a rainy summer afternoon. When visitors, sometimes Indians, came to the farm, I was allowed to tag along and listen. I recall Warren King Moorehead from Andover Academy, on the way to or from the Ohio mounds; Arthur C. Parker, the New York State archaeologist, himself of Seneca descent; and M. R. Harrington of the American Museum of Natural History. Their comments aroused my curiosity.

Amos Snow's son Jonas lived at Allegany Reservation and worked on the Erie Railroad with the "regular gang." Jonas and my father shared an interest in the arts, one carved masks and made snapping turtle rattles; the other was a painter. After my family acquired a Buick in 1916, going to the reservation to visit the Snows and their neighbors became favorite summer outings. We could depend on Jonas's wife to have huckleberries, which she picked along the Erie tracks and shared with us. Sometimes I played with the Johnny John boys—Arthur and Richard, by their English names, while Father sketched along the Allegheny River. Chauncey Johnny John, their grandfather, amused my father with tales of other collectors, including George Heye of the "Indian Museum" in New York City. I witnessed my first green corn dance in 1924 when the then unintelligible speeches in Seneca and the singing puzzled me. I still remember watching Johnny Armstrong perform in the drum dance.

Years later, as a graduate student at Yale, when approaching my first fieldwork in ethnology, and deciding where to go, I recalled the Snow connection and the Coldspring longhouse community, and I mentioned this to Edward Sapir, who said he had money to support my research. (Sapir had directed a program of Iroquois research on the Six Nations Reserve while chief of the Anthropological Survey of Canada, 1910–25.) He encouraged me to take up the Allegany connection while advising me to find a field of concentration early so that I should have a subject for a dissertation, and not just to collect field notes. He suggested ceremonialism, with asides in material culture. He urged me to make a census so as to get acquainted and to afford data on social organization.

I had attended Sapir's seminar on phonetics where we practiced on various languages, but the Seneca language would be new to me. To get me started, he loaned me a copy of *Phonetic Transcription of American Indian Languages*, of which he was joint author. These hints would prove a boon to a novice fieldworker, but I soon sensed that the Seneca themselves would control my learning and that their interest would govern its progress.

Snow Street was a short cut connecting Highway 17 from Steamburg east to the road coming north from Quaker Bridge that passes the Coldspring longhouse, forming a triangle within which most of the community activity took place. That first summer I set up a tent in Jonas Snow's dooryard where I became an adjunct to his house-hold. From this vantage point I kept a journal, which is a miscellany of family life, medicines, rattlesnakes, turtles, drunks, feuds, friends, ball games, singing society sessions, mutual aid activities, and social dances at the longhouse. It was all quite confusing at first.

My progress was affected more by accident than by the good advice of my professors or the strategy I had worked out for my fieldwork. Members of the Snow family helped me sort out the bits and pieces that came to me all at once, but they had concerns of their own that left little time for my queries. Whenever they could, they included me in their activities.

Formal work with an informant on herbal medicines yielded sys-tematic data, and by way of getting acquainted I recorded family ge-nealogies, noting personal names belonging to the several clans that later enabled me to identify participation in ceremonies.[1] But it was not these structured efforts at ethnology that were most rewarding. It was the after-hours informal activities that I shared with members of my "family" that brought me in touch with the culture and enabled me to experience Seneca society as a going concern.

Evenings, the Snow boys—Windsor and Linus (Kala) (afterward a casualty at Saint-Lô during World War II)—led me on the paths that cut through the brush to the ball ground where we fielded grounders or practiced lacrosse. Or perhaps we poled over the river in a john boat (a flat-bottomed skiff with square ends) to Crick's Run, or at night we went "torching" (spearing fish with a light), or we swam in the gravel pit where I taught Seneca lads to swim the six-beat crawl. Coming home we stopped at a house where we heard singing.

The singers sat facing each other on two rows of chairs or benches. The lead singer held a water drum and beater, with which he lined out the song, while the others kept time beating horn rattles in the palm of one hand while bumping their heels with the drum beat. Then they repeated the song together, drum and rattle vibrato, while maintain-ing the slower tempo with their heels. The song belongs to the reper-toire of *en:ska:nye:ʔ*, "Women's shuffle dance," I was told. The singers formed a mutual aid society that performed charitable work in the Coldspring community. The hostess passed me a brimming bowl of hulled corn soup, saying, "His face is white, but maybe he likes soup. Perhaps later he may learn to sing."

Presently, Albert Jones of the Snipe clan, then married to Jonas Snow's sister of the Hawk clan, having gathered the horn rattles from the singers and put them with the drum in a hand basket, paused at the door to say to me, "We are glad that you came. You are welcome to sit with us. We will let you know where we next meet." I had found the Senecas a charitable people.

At midnight Jonas Snow, Linus, and I walked home along Snow Street. I remarked on the brilliant night sky, which prompted Jonas to designate several constellations by their Seneca names—the "Dancing Boys" (Pleiades), which I would later learn regulated the Seneca calendar; the Loon; and the North Star in Ursa Major.

Singing societies are found in other longhouse communities, and learning to sing that summer at Coldspring would afford a passport later at Tonawanda and at Six Nations, for the water drum and horn rattle are to the Iroquois what the violin and tambourine are to the gypsies.

Sessions for rehearsing songs are social occasions that afford the setting for conversations. People soon asked me what clan I was going to join. They assumed it would be the Hawk clan, that of Jonas Snow, his sisters Alice Jones and clan matron Emma Turkey, and their children, particularly my interpreter, Emma's daughter Clara Redeye. The question came from two members of the Snipe clan who were married to Hawk women. Hawk clan was the logical choice, although I sensed that the Snipes would accept me. Only later would I learn that a clan functionally includes a fringe of spouses—men who had married in.

The Hawk clan regarded my beat-up station wagon as a means of transportation. Of a Sunday my family decided to visit their relatives at Cattaraugus and attend the lacrosse match at Pine Woods. Our company included Jonas's then current drinking companion, otherwise the village villain, which called for stops at the back of taverns to visit bootleggers in East Randolph and at Lawtons by Cattaraugus, after which our progress included calls on Jonas's maternal kin. Between pauses, my vehicle served as a taxi between drinks and the ball ground, as Jonas picked up friends and relatives, while introducing me to the elite of Seneca informants.

On a visit one touches base with one's clansmen. We stopped at a log house, the home of Jonas's mother's sister. The old log house was spotless and surrounded by well-kept grounds and a weedless garden.

The old lady, victim of several strokes and bedridden, nevertheless appeared glad to see me. When Jonas explained my family connection, her face brightened. I thought she said she was the one born in the shanty on the hemlock ridge, but I later learned that I was mistaken. But she surely knew of the incident. Before we sat down to dinner, our hostess insisted that I read to her from the Bible, which made me think that she was a Christian. But the gesture was a courtesy to me, for she was later to be buried from the longhouse. Whatever this reunion of the Hawk clan lineage of Jonas's mother's mother might mean to Jonas's immediate family, to me it represented a symbolic reinforcement of the link between the Fenton family and the Senecas. I was beginning to find it difficult to separate my role as anthropologist from my role in my adoptive family. The Sunday visit to Newtown on Cattaraugus served as prelude to a summer's fieldwork.

My involvement in the affairs and concerns of the Hawk clan intensified during the next two months. As the Green Corn Festival approached in late August, the sisters of Jonas Snow discussed giving me an Indian name. Formal adoption in the Hawk clan would establish my place in the community. But for some reason they did not get around to naming me at Green Corn, which postponed my formal adoption until I returned for the Midwinter Festival. The third day of Green Corn and the eighth day of the Midwinter Festival, or Indian New Year, are the two times when names are announced or changed for adults.

The death in September of Jonas's mother's sister, the old lady whom we had visited in early summer, put everything else aside. The bereaved relatives naturally turned to me for transportation to the funeral. This was my first opportunity as an anthropologist to observe a longhouse funeral, and it was surely under unique circumstances. As we drove the forty miles from Coldspring to Newtown that evening, I became aware that the people riding with me regarded me as next of kin. And that is how I was treated when we arrived. I sat with the mourners half of the night, and after midnight I went aloft to sleep. They assigned me a mattress near the wall. I can still visualize "my family" bedding down around me. Once I awakened to hear women dismissing drunks. Toward dawn I awoke to see not three feet away the beautiful face of the young woman who, throughout the long illness, had cared for her grandmother and conducted the wake, and who was now snatching a few moments of sleep before the funeral, secure in the taboos of exogamy, in the common bed of the Hawk clan (Fenton 1972:108–112).

An earlier extension of Hawk clan outreach occurred in July of that summer. One evening while writing up my journal on Snow Street, I could hear someone singing Seneca songs north of the Erie tracks. I asked the Snow family, "Who is that singing?" I was told, "That's Johnson Jimerson practicing his songs. He wants to learn." Johnson was then a lad of 15, some ten years my junior, and it was soon apparent that his eagerness to master and perform the ceremonial songs of the longhouse amused older, accomplished singers almost as much as my stumbling effort to acquire the Seneca language.

At the suggestion of George Herzog, then at Yale, I had brought an Edison wax cylinder (the then available recording devices) and found Coldspring singers willing to sing their repertoire of social dance songs into the metal horn. Johnson frequently attended these sessions. In a sense he and I were both beginners, although he spoke Seneca as a first language. But the old people did not accept Johnson as a singer; instead of encouraging him, they ridiculed his efforts, and ridicule is a powerful sanction in Seneca society. Somehow Johnson and I became friends. Perhaps it was evenings at the ball ground, going to the river, or swimming at the gravel pit—activities that required little verbal communication.

My journal entry for July 3, 1933, reads:

> Johnson Jimerson has been singing his songs after supper on the hill at Fatty's. [Sam Fatty, his material grandfather, specialized in making bent willow wood chairs, and his daughter Esther Fatty, Johnson's maternal grandmother of the Hawk clan, was one of four "head ones" in the longhouse, representing her moiety of clans. With this household Johnson should have been well connected.] Presently Johnson came down to Snow's. He seemed anxious to know whether I had heard him. He said that he wanted to record great feather dance [one of four sacred rites of the longhouse cycle]. He told me, and Jonas Snow agreed, that great feather dance has 36 songs, of which 16 are regularly sung as the first part; then comes old-time women's dance, after which 20 more songs follow. It would take 18 cylinders to record the cycle.

Unfortunately, we never got around to it, for I was hoping to persuade one of the reigning singers to record the cycle before I ran out of cylinders.

On a return visit to Sam Fatty's place, I found the old man working at his drawshave bench. He told me that Johnson was the son of a deceased daughter, but no one knew who his father was. Here was the fulfillment of the classic theme of "Thrownaway" in Seneca folklore: the fatherless boy, living on the margins, ridiculed by his elders but avid to learn, the outcast who would grow up to become a leading ritualist among his people.

And this is what happened. Years later, Johnson found a girl at Cattaraugus, but World War II intervened before he returned and raised a family. Having mastered everything of consequence in the Coldspring round of ceremonies, including the formal speeches and announcements, Johnson rose to become speaker of the Newtown longhouse. We had not seen each other in years.

At the moon of midwinter 1968, I returned to witness the ceremonies at the new Coldspring longhouse where it had been relocated during the Kinzua Dam flooding. The sixth night of the festival, or "Husk Face night," always brings visitors from Cattaraugus, Tonawanda, and sometimes Six Nations. I spotted Johnson in the crowd. The winner that night by acclaim of the impromptu dancing contest among the False Face beggars proved to be Johnson's son, whom the proud father brought over to meet me. I was fascinated to witness the learning that a father had transmitted to his son. Johnson had indeed, to use his words, "raised him right." Thrownaway of our youth at Coldspring had become a *hodi:ont*, or "Faith-keeper," in the Newtown longhouse and leader of the singing society where he now lived. We did not meet again, and it really sent me back to Snow Street to read of Johnson's passing in 1984.

It would be amiss to expect that other lineages of the Hawk clan would accept me that first summer at Coldspring. Esther Fatty, a powerful voice in longhouse matters, expressed her doubts to Jonas Snow and to his sisters about my presence, and old John Jimerson opposed my activities as an ethnologist on the floor of the longhouse. His remarks, however, prompted John "Twenty Canoes" Jacobs of the Bear clan, a respected elder with whom I had been working, to remind his age-mates that at least I listened while other young people ignored them, and it was clear that "this young man thinks what we do is worthwhile."

It was late in August before John Jimerson began to take me seriously and allowed me to climb High Bank for tutorials from his rocking chair. At best he was a difficult but learned informant. His youngest son, Avery, then a lad approaching 20, lived with his father. Avery liked to draw, and during one of my High Bank visits, he presented me with a pencil sketch of a Seneca masked dancer, which showed a considerable talent that he later converted to carving. Within a few years Avery would become the master carver of his generation (Fenton 1987:160, 257).

From opposition John had moved to a guarded rapport. When after Green Corn he decided to attend the renewal at Newtown of the "Little Water Medicine," the quintessential sacred rite in the Seneca cycle, he suspended doubts about me because I had a car. It was the first time for me of many such all-night sessions when I would hear the complete repertoire of songs, again at Coldspring and later at Tonawanda.

It was far easier to work within the lineage of Jonas Snow's elder sister, Emma Turkey. With her daughter, Clara Redeye, serving as interpreter, Clara's spouse, Sherman Redeye (Snipe clan), acting as intermediator, and his father, Henry Redeye (Bear clan), as primary source, we undertook systematic work on the ceremonies that first year. Henry, then speaker of the Coldspring longhouse, also preached the "Good Message" of Handsome Lake, and he had long since mastered the old forms. Sherman could fill in for his father any time. This would be my team the following year when they invited me to live with them.

Before returning home that fall, Henry clued me in on how to fix the date of the Indian new year. Watch for the "Dancing Boys" (Pleiades) during the fall until they are on the zenith at dusk during the full moon of "Short Days" (at the winter solstice), count twenty days, and the "Great ceremonial mark" (*gaiwanonskwaʔgo:wa:h*) should fall on the fifth day of the following new moon. This would be the second day of the Midwinter Festival, because the first, or preliminary, day is for naming children born since the Green Corn Festival. (Actually Henry depended on "Dr. Miles's calendar" to ascertain the phases of the moon.)

Following similar devices, in mid-January I took the Erie sleeper to

Salamanca, New York, where Albert Jones met me and drove me in his vintage Model-T Ford sedan over icy roads to Henry Redeye's place near Quaker Bridge. My kindred were there to greet me and install me overhead above the kitchen. (The family slept downstairs.)

Mornings Henry and I walked upriver to Coldspring, where he conducted the ceremonies, while Sherman and Clara stayed behind. Returning at noon, I shared my observations with Sherman, who explained what I should have seen and heard, for he knew what was significant and distinguished it from incidental behavior. Soon I began to sense the pattern of events, and within a week I knew what to expect.

My formal adoption into the Hawk clan took place on January 26, 1934, at Coldspring longhouse of the Seneca Nation. Naming of adults occurs on the eighth day of the Midwinter Festival during the celebration of Adon:weh (personal chant), which is the third of the Four Sacred Ceremonies prescribed by the prophet Handsome Lake. The other three were the great feather dance, the drum dance, and the great bowl games, each of which also has its day as at Green Corn (Fenton: typed field notes 1934).

Before a person is adopted, he must first be accepted by a clan, which is the basic unit of Seneca society. After being advanced by a particular maternal family within the clan and accepted by their clan relatives, one is taken into the larger group or community, which comprises the segments of eight clans. A public ceremony at the longhouse sanctions adoption. Ultimately, other Seneca communities recognize such actions.

The adoptee has a certain amount of choice. I recall that during the previous summer Albert Jones (Snipe clan), then spouse of my Hawk clan sponsor's sister advised me: "You must decide what clan you want to join." He was prepared to put me up in the Snipe clan, and Sherman Redeye was ready to second it. Although I was never told, I surmise that Clara Redeye advanced my candidacy with her mother, the Hawk clan matron, who in turn spoke to her younger brother, Jonas Snow, my host of the first summer, and persuaded him to sponsor me as a Hawk. The matter had been agreed upon at a family feast in my honor that was held the previous summer when my name was supposed to be awarded at the Green Corn Festival.

A Seneca man is privileged to grant a personal name that belongs to his clan set, a name that he himself has abandoned and is therefore free to offer an outsider whom the clan wishes to adopt and whom he agrees to sponsor. Jonas Snow (Hononwiya'gon, "He parts the riffles") of the Hawk clan, my host in 1933, formerly held the name Howan'neyao, "He loses a game, or a wager." This name was now free, and he wished to give it to me. Jonas was at the longhouse on the eighth morning prepared to release it.

An adoptee may have additional sponsors, known as "friends," who need not be of the clan of the primary sponsor and adoptee. Albert Jones (Snipe clan), husband of Jonas Snow's sister Alice, would be my friend. He had helped me get started in my research that first summer.

Having secured permission of the two male longhouse officers— Levi Snow (Heron) and Reuben White (Bear)—who represent opposite moieties, Jonas and Albert approached the speaker, Henry Redeye (Bear), to announce that Hononwiya'gon (Jonas Snow) was giving me his boyhood name. Albert (Hanoje:nen's) as conductor directed Jonas and me to sit together on the north end of the singers' bench, facing west toward the headmen. (The same setting is observed when raising *honondiont*, officers in the longhouse.)

The formal speech of adoption is called simply "Giving a name" (*howonseno:a'*). Phrasing depends on the speaker. Later Sherman and Clara Redeye recaptured the text for me, which follows in English:

> As it has happened in the past, names have been given to white
> men. That is the reason that the Hawk clan decided to award a
> name belonging to that clan, namely, the Hawk clan, whom we
> call *Hodiswen'ga:yo'*, "the striped kind." The name that they
> have given, which shall be his name, is *howan'neyao*. That is
> what you shall call him, the person whom you see here present,
> for he has come from the other side of New York. Here you see
> him where we are gathered [in this meeting]. He also thinks
> that it [what we do] amounts to something, for so he says.
> That is all.

Following the nominations speech, my two sponsors, the former holder of the name and my friend, stood me up and alternately performed Adon:wen' in my honor, marching me in measured cadence the length of the longhouse toward the women's side and back, while chanting their personal songs, Jonas first and then Albert, in a powerful voice. One or two other men repeated the gesture. Shortly thereafter, Sherman Redeye taught me to sing a personal song of my own taken from the Snipe clan repertoire: "Snipe woke me / Yeah, the Great Snipe woke me." There followed a public greeting, which amounted to a sanction by the community.

After the nomination is confirmed, a longhouse officer, usually a friend of the candidate, asks the adoptee and his sponsor to rise and accept pledges of friendship from the people. First, the women of the clan file by and shake hands with their new clansman. The men of the clan follow. The women say anything they wish, such as, "Nia:wenh ske:non" [Thanks, are you well?] The initiate may reply, "Do:gens" [Indeed]. [This is the ordinary greeting between friends.] Another person may inquire whether the initiate knows his name and ask him to repeat it, then tell him, "That shall be your name until the old people change it, or you assume office, or you die." All of this, and perhaps more, was said to me, as Clara Redeye afterward told me.

Next it is up to the "Head Ones" of the longhouse (two women and two men of opposite moieties), followed by lesser officers, to congratulate their new tribesman. In each rank the women take precedence over the men.

After these persons of exalted names, anyone may greet the adoptee. Sometimes a friend may approach him and in a joking way say: "You are a bad Indian, but if you are as bad as I am, everyone knows that you will be a pretty bad Indian." Then in a serious vein the joker may ask the recipient to address his new relatives, pledging his loyalty to them and his devotion in times of hardship. He must remember that whenever there are ceremonies at the longhouse that he should contribute. But it is not required that the recipient acknowledge the honor with a speech.

The above remarks are couched in the words of my hosts, Clara and Sherman Redeye. Indeed Clara was daughter of my clan mother, Jonas Snow's elder sister, formally Ganegojentha' but fondly known as Gojin. My notes say nothing further.

In following years I would learn more of the obligations of clanship, its benefits, and demands. The name given me followed or preceded me wherever I went among the Iroquois people. My name remained years later even when I stayed away. In the words of a recent correspondent, "My mom gave you that name in a ceremony many years ago. You can never be un-adopted!"

Tonawanda is the central hearth of the Handsome Lake religion. In going there the first time with the Coldspring Guardians of the Good Message, for whom I provided transportation, I met their peers from other longhouses during their annual September convention. I did not then have a name. Nor did I anticipate that I would serve for two and a half years there as community worker for the U.S. Indian Service. When I returned two winters later, my Indian name had preceded me. Tonawanda Hawk clan residents regarded me in a special way as one of theirs, and they were quick to imply my obligations. Older people daily addressed me in Seneca and expected me to reply, and as with children they coached me on what to say. Certainly I afforded them endless amusement. I sat with the Salt Creek Singers, a mutual aid society, who met at Jesse Cornplanter's and Elsina Billy's house. Indeed criticism soon mounted from more progressive elements of the population that I spent too much time among the longhouse people "down below."

My term as community worker eventually ran out, I had filed a dissertation at Yale, and anthropologists were no longer fashionable in the Indian Service. I turned to teaching, which I then thought was the way to professionalism in anthropology. I did not dare to dream of a career in research. Unbeknownst to me, Jesse Cornplanter, an inveterate letter writer, had touted my capabilities to J. N. B. Hewitt, the Tuscarora-Iroquoian specialist at the Bureau of American Ethnology, and Hewitt had shared the letter with M. W. Stirling, director, whom I met on the Plains several summers previously. Stirling was impressed because, he later told me, Indians usually complained about anthropologists.

Jesse Cornplanter (1889–1957) had been my first contact and principal collaborator at Tonawanda. He grew up on Cattaraugus Reservation during the height of the Handsome Lake religion, of which his father, Edward, was the leading preacher. Jesse knew collectors from museums, and he had developed a reputation as a boyhood illustrator of traditional Seneca activities. He was aware of his culture, and working with ethnologists was not new to him. Jesse had come to live at Tonawanda with Elsina Billy, whose house stood behind the longhouse where the Coldspring Keepers of the Faith introduced me in 1933. It mattered not that Jesse was a Snipe and Elsina a Beaver; Jesse, the resident intellectual, became my tutor on Seneca culture (Fenton 1978).

The summer of 1938 found me back at Allegany with a party of students working on ethnobotany. My Hawk clan relatives and their spouses came to our assistance as informants and interpreters. Hewitt had died, leaving a pile of unpublished manuscripts on Iroquoian topics and creating a vacancy at the Bureau of American Ethnology. As summer's end, while preparing to return to teaching at St. Lawrence University, I received a wire from Stirling inviting me to accept Hewitt's post. How soon could I report?

Saint Lawrence had promoted me to assistant professor, and I felt obliged to return for at least the first semester while the college found a replacement. After Christmas, my small family remained in Salamanca, while I finished the fall term in time for the Midwinter Festival down river at Coldspring. My wife, Olive, who by then was expecting our second child, and I commuted daily to attend the doings at Coldspring, where Olive, bundled in a raccoon coat, aroused solicitous inquiries and advice from Hawk clan matrons. We were present on the eighth day of the festival (January 31, 1939) to hear an animated discussion about adopting white people.

A Seneca tribesman had brought to the longhouse a white man whom he wished to have adopted. John "Twenty Canoes" Jacobs (Bear clan) was present to act as agent for the candidate when the way was open for giving names. However, because of the discussion that ensued, no action was taken. I was told that, at a meeting of the longhouse officers on the fifth day, sentiment had prevailed against further adoptions just then.

The speaker of the longhouse, Henry Redeye, said that he opposed giving names belonging to clans to white people. In recent cases white adoptees had claimed hunting and fishing rights on the reservation by virtue of adoption as "Indians." The longhouse officers did not wish to confer the privilege on white men. Charles Butler, who interpreted for me that morning, said he disagreed that such conveyance of status was legally possible. He had attended the meeting on the fifth day when the majority of officers opposed adoptions.

I inferred from Henry's statement that some Senecas regarded adoption, when done wholeheartedly, as conferring complete status as a member of the Seneca Nation. Still other elder Senecas opposed adoption on principle, in as much as they expected persons adopted to behave as Indians, which would imply rights to hunt and fish, privileges which they did not wish to convey. Other Senecas who regarded adoption as honorary did not expect full participation from those whom they honored, and they would confine the honor to an exclusive few persons who were genuinely interested.

That morning Chauncey Johnny John, ranking elder of the Turtle clan, arose from his seat facing the speaker and the "head ones" to comment on the speaker's remarks. He was not opposed to adopting white people as much as he opposed the way certain Indians exploited persons whom they adopted for their own personal gain. For instance, he pointed to me with the stem of his pipe, saying:

> That white man over there we adopted. He comes back here frequently. Just the other day he gave the longhouse money. He gave it here before the crowd in the longhouse. He handed the money to the head ones (the women) right here before all of us. I suppose that if he gave it to the officers outside, they would put it in their pockets and not bring it here to the longhouse. That is the way we Indians are. When we get hold of a little money, we put it in our pockets.
>
> And then there is *haowan?go:wa:* ("Big boat") [attorney Charles E. Congdon of Salamanca] whom we adopted. He always gives to the headmen.

There was some latent jealousy of the Wolf clan matron who had sponsored Congdon. She and her son lived adjacent to the longhouse. They had been censured by implication for the disappearance the previous night of firewood brought to the longhouse for heating and cooking. Others in the community resented the gains that this family made in the form of clothing and the odd dollar from this adopted person. The way that this matron and her son strained to fulfill all the perquisites of office, which few people acknowledged they were entitled to, aroused further enmity among their peers. Seneca society encourages participation, but overzealous achievement arouses resentment.

Chauncey continued his commentary: "Last summer near Corning, New York, I met a white man whom we had adopted. He has been sending money and groceries here to a certain family intended for the longhouse festivals, so he says. But we all know that it [his donations] has not been brought here. That family has kept it for themselves."

Here Chauncey paused to knock the ashes out of his pipe on the heel of his left hand, which he then brushed against his trouser leg before solemnly putting the pipe into his coat pocket. He turned slowly and walked toward the men's (north) door of the longhouse, where he paused and said, "I know who that family is, but I will let that white man come here and himself tell who the family is." Chauncey went out the door, not waiting for a rebuttal. However, he returned later for the feast.

A sense of what adoption into a Seneca clan means expanded in the 1940s when the Beaver clan gave names to my wife and children. Grandma Nephew of Quaker Bridge then presided over the Beaver clan, and on the urging of her daughters, she assigned free names taken from the roster of names released by deceased holders, or names of persons who assumed new names on passing from childhood to adulthood. We had rented a house that summer from two elder daughters of the Nephew lineage, and next door the lively children of Franklin and Mary John afforded playmates for our children. Olive and Mary John developed a real bond, and Mary and her younger sister advanced Olive with their mother, who made the arrangements with the longhouse officers to have the names announced on the third day of the Green Corn Festival. Soon, the Nephew lineage held their annual Beaver clan picnic at Franklin and Mary John's, a sumptuous feast that included the Fentons. Although affiliated with the Hawk clan in the other moiety, I soon became aware, as I talked with other men present, that functionally a Seneca clan includes a fringe of spouses—men who have married into that clan. As one of them remarked to me in jest, "We all have in common the misfortune to be married to Beaver clan women."

Wherever I went among the Six Nations,[2] people asked me, "What is your Indian name? And what is your clan? Your people are yonder," pointing with chin and lips to a particular house. That identified me and afforded a body of fictive kindred, and it decided with which moiety I should sit in the longhouse.

After a long absence, in 1988 I went up to the Six Nations Reserve in Ontario to represent the trustees of the Museum of American Indian-Heye Foundation in returning some wampum belts that were long in contention. It fell to me to make the presentation. Afterward, as the women filed by to shake the hands of the museum delegation, one matron from Tonawanda quietly greeted me, as of years ago,

"Nia:wenh ske:non Howanʔneyao," as if I had never gone away (Fenton 1988, 1989).

Following the presentation, a young woman approached me to say that she was the daughter of Theresa Snow, who was the teenage daughter of Jonas and Josephine Snow when I first slept in a tent on Snow Street. Theresa, having followed a husband to Canada, became the matron of her family; she sat quietly nearby where we chatted briefly of days at Allegany.

NOTES

1. The Seneca clan system comprises eight clans, divided equally into two moieties, or "sides," seated on opposite sides of a symbolic fire. They are:

BEAR		**DEER**
Wolf	**X**	Snipe
Beaver	**FIRE**	Heron
Turtle		Hawk

A Seneca clan is an exogamous kin group that reckons descent, inheritance, and succession matrilineally. A clan holds a "bag" of personal names that it awards at birth, changes at puberty, and confers on elevation to an exalted status. Adoption is strictly a clan function, rarely national. The moieties are primarily ceremonial units, performing reciprocal services for each other. They support each other in medicine society rites, they contest in games, they separate the community at midwinter and late summer when they contest in the bowl game, and they separate and condole each other's dead. Marriage between moieties is optional, if somewhat preferred, although marriage between clans of the same side is common practice.

2. Mohawks, Oneidas, Onondagas, Cayugas, Senecas, and Tuscaroras constitute the Six Nations Confederacy.

Fenton, William N. 1933–40. Seneca field notebooks. American Philosophical Library, Philadelphia.

———. 1936. *An Outline of Seneca Ceremonies at Coldspring Longhouse.* Yale University Publications in Anthropology 9.

———. 1972. Return to the Longhouse. In *Crossing Cultural Barriers: The Anthropological Experience,* ed. Solon T. Kimball and James B. Watson, 102–118. San Francisco: Chandler.

———. 1978. "Aboriginally Yours": Jesse J. Cornplanter, Ha-yonh-wonh-ish, the Snipe, Seneca, 1889–1957. In *American Indian Intellectuals,* ed. Margot Liberty, 177–195. Proceedings of the American Ethnological Society, 1976. St. Paul: West.

———. 1987. *The False Faces of the Iroquois.* Norman: University of Oklahoma Press.

———. 1988. Keeping the Promise: Return of the Wampums to the Six Nations Iroquois Confederacy, Grand River. *Anthropology Newsletter,* October, pp. 3, 25. Washington DC: American Anthropological Association.

———. 1989. Return of Eleven Wampum Belts to the Six Nations Iroquois Confederacy on Grand River, Canada. *Ethnohistory* 36(4): 392–410.

Swanton, John R. 1938. John Napoleon Brinton Hewitt. *American Anthropologist* 40:286–290.

4

Effects of Adoption
on the Round Lake Study

Mary Black-Rogers

When I was asked to write about how my adoption influenced my research, it seemed appealing, partly because this is a pleasant memory, partly because I'd never explored the idea directly, either in the field or in documents. A new focus on the data and the fieldwork experience could be fruitful.

From the beginning, my work in anthropology has been frustrated by the question, How can we presume to "know" and to write about alien cultures (that is, different from our own), when there is no choice but to filter our observations and inquiries through the lenses of our own culture? Focusing in now on the particular problem of differing concepts of adoption, the discovery that the Round Lake data yielded no specific insight into adoption came as a shock. How to make a scholarly paper from anecdotal memories? How to tell the personal side without this becoming a recital of "what fieldwork did to me"? How to pin down the facts of my adoption, as I perceived them at the time: the who, where, when, how, and why? What about these facts as the Round Lake people perceived them? Clearly, I needed to understand the customs and beliefs concerning adoption, as held in this community. A *what* fact would have to be added.

THE ROUND LAKE STUDY

The Round Lake Study has been a field-and-archival investigation of the Northern Ojibwa/Swampy Cree hunting people surrounding the area of Weagamow Lake (formerly Round Lake), which is located in subarctic Ontario west of Hudson Bay.[1] The study is both longitudinal and long term. It was begun in 1958 by Edward S. Rogers as a one-year field assignment. Rogers was accompanied by his first wife, Jean, and small daughter, Corinne. (Jean accomplished a linguistic account of the hybrid language spoken by Round Lakers when nearly 100 percent of the population was monolingual [J. H. Rogers 1963]). In 1968 Ed saw my dissertation and recruited me for a two-year field restudy.[2] He was then head of the Ethnology Department of the Royal Ontario Museum in Toronto.

We later worked together in the field during his sabbatical, then explored this people's history and ancestors in archives and in the literature, and hired a research assistant, eventually doing much of the work at home—having married during the 1970s. Data ballooned in every direction, continuing to extend the boundaries of the study. Our special interests and training were complementary: his was in the environment, material culture, and technology/subsistence, while mine was in cognitive culture, language as entrée to culture, and belief systems. (Both of us envisaged nothing less than complete ethnographic coverage, as a result.)

We created an electronic database with a wide array of information fields from diverse sources, including field data, government censuses and lists, fur trade documents, genealogies, vital statistics, residence mapping, recorded legends and accounts—all checked and rechecked against each other. Its initial period (1770–1970) was also being extended forward a generation. When Ed died in 1988, following a yearlong battle with cancer, our book and database were barely half completed.

THE SO-CALLED FACTS

Who

I was adopted by an elderly woman of Weagamow Lake. She had had eight children, by two marriages, and after childbearing age she had legally adopted a baby girl through the Children's Aid Society of Canada. She obviously desired children around her, and she had them until her death in 1994 at the approximate age of 91. Her name was Meme. She had become one of my favorite people long before I knew she was my adoptive mother.

Where

I was adopted while carrying out a field assignment with the Round Lake people at their boreal forest location just inland from the Coastal Crees of the Hudson Bay Lowlands. The Round Lake dialect is now termed "Oji-Cree." In 1968 the people said they spoke Cree, but the linguists said Northern Ojibwa, specifically Severn Dialect (J. H. Rogers 1963; Todd 1970; Valentine 1995). Whatever its label, no one there spoke anything else, save for the children who were learning English in school. Round Lake was still a decidedly "bush" fly-in community when I arrived that year. The livelihood was largely hunting, fur trapping, and fishing. A Hudson's Bay Company post and store had been there since 1949 and a school since 1955. There were two Christian churches (one no older than the school) and 355 people, by my count. They had signed no treaty until 1930, an adhesion to Treaty 9. These adhesions were the last of Canada's historic Indian treaties. Many people at Round Lake recalled the treaty and their life well before, when the outside world knew little about them (Rogers and Black 1976; Black-Rogers and Rogers 1978; Black-Rogers 1990a).

When

I was adopted sometime between 1968 and 1975. Even Meme's daughter Eva could not say exactly when. There had been rumors and innuendos, as well as a time when Eva's husband and I met on the path and he pointed out to me several teenagers giggling in our direction. He explained it was because we were now *ninimak* (cross-cousins of the opposite sex, in this case brother- and sister-in-law), between whom a joking relationship was expected. (The bilateral cross-cousin marriage system was still active.) But it took Meme herself to convince me. One frigid winter day in the mid-1970s, when I was back at Round Lake for a final year, accompanied by my new husband, Ed Rogers, she bundled herself up and walked to our cabin to visit. She announced, "I came to see my son-in-law, since he hasn't come to see me." We were lucky to have an interpreter for that. Two of her young grandchildren were present. They had been among my first acquaintances and coworkers owing to their eagerness to practice their English. I remember that one of them had replied to some question I'd asked him, "You decide. You're my mother." That was in 1969. I wonder now: Did

Meme already consider me part of the family? In terms of when, her close family perhaps knew before I did, although it may have been gradual for them, too. Probably only Meme herself could have said just when she decided to adopt me.

How

My adoption did not involve any public or private ritual. I am convinced it was Meme's own idea. For me, its outward manifestations came initially in the use of kinship terms. A year or two after our departure, however, another kind of event might be considered a manifestation. Ed and I were asked to act as parents of the bride when Meme's granddaughter married a white outsider at his parents' home.

Why

Meme told us why she had decided to adopt me on the day that she came to meet her son-in-law. Before her first husband died, she had given birth to a girl baby who lived only a few days. She had named the baby Mary. I was a replacement. This custom was not a surprise, although I had not heard of its taking place nearly fifty years later![3]

What

What adoption is, from my view, has something to do with a kind of "fictive" familial relationship, involving a commitment to maintain it as if real. I distinguish adoption from fosterage, generally, yet I had not done so in my study of the latter at Round Lake (Black-Rogers 1989). I had automatically applied their definition in reporting cases. My usual idea of *foster* is, basically, to take care of vital needs, often temporarily; in fact, the *Oxford English Dictionary* shows it to have derived from the word *food* (obsolete; Old English) and states that it can refer to relationships "not by blood but in virtue of nursing or bringing up" even in the sense of "incubator." The *what* fact, from the Round Lake view, is only now coming into focus from a variety of directions and data. I am fortunate to still be in touch with Oji-Cree speakers from Round Lake, as well as linguists of their language. The language question will be dealt with more fully below.

Most of the effect came after the end of field residence. The field record itself suggests that I ignored the signs, perhaps even brushed them off. (Of this I was not aware at the time. The field record is now my source for uncovering some subliminal or automatic behavior.) Perhaps I felt that acknowledging them might put at risk the validity of the data or interrupt, delay, or confuse the learning process. It is well known that becoming involved too closely with one family, especially at the beginning, can bias access and relations with the rest of the community.[4]

Yet the record also shows that I was far from avoiding this family (see my description of their trapline departure in 1969, Black 1978). During my resident years, two of Meme's grandchildren had failed to receive their parents' permission to "go out" to finish high school— that is, to leave the village of their family and live for the first time in the world "out" of the bush. (The Round Lake school at that time taught classes only through grade 8.) Both children were above-average students and dearly wished to continue their schooling, but my persuasion on their behalf did not succeed. In 1969, the boy who had just "graduated" had then asked his grandmother for permission to accept my invitation to go out with me at Christmas to visit my sister's family in California. Meme allowed the visit. There was the impression she rather ruled the roost, in her gentle and true Ojibwa manner. Perhaps the boy himself (at Meme's suggestion?) saved my neutral position in the community by asking that two other boys go along who happened to represent different local factions.

That California trip was something else! Three midteen Round Lake boys, first time out of the bush! Needless to say, it was instructive, and if Meme's approval was crucial, her perception of her relationship to me certainly affected my work.

Later, when we were working at home on our accumulated materials, more data tumbled in, from time to time, via visitors to our home, phone calls, and letters. We had begun the computerized Round Lake database, and they filled in gaps. We had audio tapes yet untranslated, on which we put them to work. The wedding role was followed by other requests and news that fit a family member—providing foster care, helping in emergencies. Thirteen years had passed this way when Ed Rogers succumbed to cancer in 1988.

Four visits between 1988 and 1994 certainly improved my knowledge of the community. They also helped to solidify the *what* question, as the following abbreviated summary will show:

> *AUGUST 1988*: Funeral service for Edward S. Rogers, "Weaga-mow Friend," and burial in Round Lake Cemetery.[5] Meme sat in church with the bereaved family. She rode in van escorting family to cemetery along with Henry, former Anglican cate-chist, now reverend, first Indian friend of "Mr. Rogers" at Round Lake in 1958. He had conducted the service in Oji-Cree, reading from a Cree syllabic Bible. The chief drove.
>
> *JULY 1991*: Brought plaque for Ed's grave. His daughter accom-panied. Meme's son-in-law set the plaque in cement. (Plaque courtesy of U.S. Veterans Administration.) Ceremony at grave, bilingual now—Henry and the young Evangelical minister (one of the three boys I'd taken to California). Exchanged gifts with old friends.
>
> *FALL 1993*: Went to Meme's "family reunion" during Round Lake's Hunters Festival. Feast at her house, all relatives helping. Fresh moose and bannock, and I brought turkey and all the fixings. An Ojibwa friend from the city accompanied me and gave Meme a very nice gift. Meme's legs ailing, hard time walk-ing, but made it to church and back alone in rain. Then she presided at her reunion, sitting on bed, helping children with their food.
>
> *MAY 1994*: Meme's funeral. I traveled fast, alone. No time for gifts. I was told my getting there was my gift. Took photos with borrowed camera. Stayed with same grandson, now 40 years old and director of education for Round Lake.

Each visit brought more closeness and knowledge. Grown-up chil-dren now volunteered comments and items they figured would inter-est me. It was good to be there again, but my mother was gone. It may be of interest that following the last trip I applied to the airline for "compassionate travel" status; in the space for "Relationship of deceased to passenger," I wrote "Mother (adoptive, by Indian custom)," and I received a refund.

THE *HOW* QUESTION REVISITED

While in the field, did I really avoid recognizing the facts of the adoption? Was it deliberate but subliminal? Since I cannot remember either avoiding or acknowledging the adoption, let us take up each side in turn.

Let's suppose it was deliberate. Perhaps I was reacting in terms of my old belief that ethnography (describing an alien culture) cannot be done from the inside. I remember my first publication (Black 1963: 1347), which pointed out that the ethnographer is there and can "use himself as a measuring device." And soon I declared that we must include the effect of the measuring instrument on the measurements obtained (Black and Metzger 1965:144). The present recollection concerns the effect on the measuring instrument as well. I remember later assigning Carlos Castaneda's first book (1968) to an ethnography class partly because I was struck by his ending. He wrote that he was forced to stop his lessons with the Yaqui Indian man of power because if he went any further into it he would have to leave his own culture.[6] Yet it is the inside view that we seek to describe. Contradictory? Probably. This is one of the difficulties in being an anthropologist.

More evidence of my avoidance: I neglected to ask how one would talk about adoption in Oji-Cree. This was truly uncharacteristic. My introduction long ago to Ojibwa belief systems was through the medium of language-revealing concepts and connections, as can be found in terminologies and classifications (Black and Metzger 1965; Black 1963, 1967, 1969, 1973).

But if I was not avoiding the issue, what was I doing? A fair bit of wondering, soul searching, and examining the record resulted in an answer that rings so true I can't help recalling Clyde Kluckhohn's "implicit" cultural rules and behaviors (1952, 1956): rules and patterns that we follow implicitly, without being aware of them (until they are violated). Someone once called it "out of awareness"—I think Dell

Hymes—to avoid "subconscious" or "subliminal," probably. (See also Black 1958:19–25, and Black 1974.)

What is adoption in Ojibwa or Oji-Cree society? Before resorting to native language definition and concepts, and a few comparative cases from other Algonquian groups, here is some insight behind the scenes of Round Lake, a closer look at Meme's own life experience.

My half-sister Eva, when asked what Meme had told her about life during her first marriage, responded that her mother had never spoken about that, since Eva's father "was always around." Later she added that her father "didn't want Job around, so his grandparents brought him up." She was referring to her half-brother Job, who was eight years old when Meme remarried. Of course! I replaced a child of Meme's first husband. My Indian stepfather needn't accept me, according to custom (and indeed he sometimes appeared not to). The *what* answer includes the idea that children become "orphans" when one parent dies and the other remarries. This is substantiated by several sources: the Department of Indian Affairs, fur trade reports, missionary registers, and field accounts. It appears to hold true for either spouse in Round Lake data. As noted, Meme's son by her first husband had been brought up by her father's household after Meme remarried, although she had raised him by herself for more than five years following his father's death (see Black-Rogers 1990b for Round Lake foster/adopt data).[7]

Other "adopt" cases that I have heard about reveal varying characteristics or properties of the broad category. The "replacement" property, though frequent and traditional, is not a necessary element. Replacement relatives could be acquired by capture; this means was also utilized for obtaining slaves. Note that the 1789 capture of John Tanner, a nine-year-old white boy, was said to be initially motivated as replacement for a deceased child. But as he was then sold to another family, it resembles the slave position. However, his relationship with the second family soon shows him as an important adopted son of the Indian woman whom he thenceforth referred to as "my mother" and her son as "brother" (James 1956).

Another study that points to captives becoming adoptees is that by

William Quinn (1993:43), in which he considers the legal status of nonmember Indians of reservation populations: "Adoption was another institutionalized form of nonmember (extra-tribal) residency among Indian groups. In the Plains as well as in the neighboring Great Lakes region, it was customary for families to adopt outsiders to replace kin who had died. Sometimes these adoptions took place in the context of sustained trading and merger relationships, but they often occurred in relations dominated by hostilities. . . . Both adoptees and 'captives' (often the two were the same) frequently were integrated in time within the kinship and social networks of their foster tribal communities." Note that the words *foster* and *adopt* are both used here. To be "adopted into the tribe" as an honorary member happens especially to well-known or powerful persons, such as Hubert Humphrey when he was governor of Minnesota. Frank Hamilton Cushing of the Bureau of American Ethnology certainly adopted himself into the Zuni Pueblo during his stay there in 1879–84, and he was initiated in 1881 into the society of the Bow priesthood (Basso 1979:14). Cushing, too, felt for a time he could no longer do anthropology after such assimilation.

To give someone an Indian name is a formal procedure that can be likened to adoption. Humphrey received his Indian name in a well-publicized public event. My receipt of such a name was done with ritual, but privately (except for my tape recorder, which I was asked to turn off for certain portions). This ritual was performed by a Minnesota medicine man who also gave me medicine for protection.[8]

In a case that sounds somewhat similar to mine, John Nichols wrote me that it was from a January 1996 Minneapolis newspaper obituary for Maude Kegg, his Minnesota Ojibwe coworker and informant, that he learned he was an adopted son, for he was named as such among her survivors.

OTHER SUBARCTIC ALGONQUIAN CASES

Other Algonquian studies have also reported the effect of adoptions on the progress of their work. MacKenzie and Clarke (1983:252–253), when trying to recruit a representative sample for linguistic variability in the Montagnais hunting community Sheshatshiu in Labrador, remarked, "Sample selection . . . proved difficult to handle, however, . . . because . . . most older people had moved around to a re-markable degree during their lives" and with regard to family groups, it "became clear that complete genealogies for all members of the community were necessary before one could confidently choose members of the same family group. . . . The situation was rendered more complex in that there is an enormous amount of adoption of children within Cree, Montagnais, and Naskapi communities. As a result, even individuals who are clearly within the genealogy of a particular family may not have grown up within that family, but have been brought up by grandparents or, indeed, any close or even distant relatives. Only a complete life history of each individual, then, could reveal the complex interpersonal relationships which exist within the community." For a language study, the speakers with whom the subject sample were "brought up" and learned to speak are obviously of great importance.

Then there is Speck's 1918 report on kinship terms and marriage systems of several northern Algonquian peoples, in which the word *orphanage* is an indicator: "A man's sister's child . . . could not come into the filial relationship by the custom of the levirate though he could by being adopted by his maternal uncle. This is the case both in social practice and in the kinship indications among the Wabanaki tribes, where the differentiation of the terms involved confirms the levirate. I think, however, that possibly the inclusiveness of this category is due to the frequency with which wholesale adoption takes place, on account of frequent orphanage." He goes on to apply this reasoning to the Timagami Ojibwas, the Montagnais, the Penobscots, and the Malecites (Speck 1918:150).

It can be seen that studies of northern Algonquian communities tend to blend *adopt* and *foster* under one term or the other in English.[9]

ANOTHER CHANNEL TO THE *WHAT* QUESTION: LANGUAGE USE

The *what* case generally implies a definition: what is adoption in the alien culture described? This in turn requires placing it in a category, in a taxonomy, in a context, in a dictionary, in observed usage. It requires contrasting or equating it with other terms. And of course it requires doing all of this in their language.

Upon finally undertaking a bit of this for the present article, I found that Oji-Cree *adopt* appears very closely related to *foster*, when pursuing concepts through terminology. In English these two can be contrasted, as in my own usage described above. Round Lake speakers had difficulty expressing a difference. A speaker could specify, in Oji-Cree, "replacing another" and then apply it to household membership (residence) or kin relationships, for example, "bringing up a child not your own" where "bringing up" can refer to any portion of a child's life. The bilingual speakers also offered phrases that they translated as "to raise a child" or "being given a child." They concluded there was no way to distinguish between the two English concepts.

I then asked Eva to describe my adoption by her mother. The phrase she offered was glossed by linguist John Nichols (personal communication) as "I take care of someone deliberately, on purpose." This seems as close as Eva came to something like "I decide to take care of someone."

A Cree dictionary then surprisingly turned up a translation for *adopt* that involves "replacing" another, with no reference to children, while giving a different Cree form for *caring for*, *fostering*, *ministering*, *supporting*, etc. There is even a Cree entry, *Tapakomewao* (in the English section "adopt"), that Cree linguist David Pentland rendered "becoming a replacement relative" (Nichols and Nyholm 1979; Watkins 1938; also personal communication John Nichols, David Pentland). Probably more thorough work with a good sample of Round Lake speakers would produce more definitive distinctions.

THE HOW AND WHAT IN ACTION

Another clue to why the situation of my adoption was difficult to define may be found by examining Ojibwa interactional behavior with respect to defining situations. How I was informed of the fact helps to explain the slow evolution and resolution of the matter. It was a distinctly Ojibwa *how*, that is, a typically indirect opening that could lead nowhere or could lead to some particular destination, depending on the response. My reports analyzed Ojibwa interactions and their implicit components (Black 1973:17; Black-Rogers 1988:47).

Pertinent here is the manner in which interactants chose to avoid defining the situation (a case of not controlling others) and thus to create an ambiguous situation. It is left open, as if to say, "You get my point, or you don't. It's your choice." This accords with an important underlying cultural rule: to respect another's individual autonomy (Black 1977). The Ojibwa tendency, or practice, of avoiding or deferring actions that define the ongoing situation had long been familiar to me—so much so, apparently, that I automatically expected it regarding the adoption. I believe now that, "out-of-awareness," I had responded in kind, returning the ball back into their court—until Meme had to come over and make the (relatively) explicit pronouncement: "son-in-law."[10]

USE OF ROUND LAKE STUDY DATABASE ON ABOVE PROBLEMS

I should like to have given sophisticated results about fostering and adoption as related to kinship and marriage, to environment, hunting territories, and subsistence/survival, to residence and household composition, rates of endogamy, and inbreeding coefficients, and what Molohon and Bisaillon (1996) have called "managed fertility." But that awaits the appearance and use of the Round Lake Study database file. Version one was completed in 1997, and an upgraded version two is nearly done, adding residence and adopt/foster information. Anonymized copies will be accessible from the University of Toronto Data Library Services, as well as the University of Alberta Archives. Grant (1991) gives a brief overview of the Round Lake Study as a whole and of the database's storage of several dozen fields of information on over 5,000 coded individuals, covering 1770–1970. (See also Krech and Sturtevant 1995.)

FINAL FACT

I have just decided to code myself into the database as adopted daughter—of Meme, but not of her second husband—on the assumption that the adoption began before the end of 1969. It might be risky to wait for the upgrade extending the file beyond that cutoff year. You see, my adoption had a final major effect on the study. It facilitated collection of field data beyond the present cutoff by two generations (so far). After all, relatives are people you tend to keep in touch with.[11]

1. In the 1960s, the community's name was officially changed, in English, from Round Lake to Weagamow Lake (according approximately to the Ojibwa *waweagamow* in which the morpheme /gam/ includes the sense of water or lake). Many people still call it Round Lake when speaking English.

2. The 1958–59 fieldwork was supported by the *Toronto Globe and Mail*. The 1968–70 work was carried out under the Canadian government Project ARDA 25075, in conjunction with Ontario's Department of Lands and Forests.

3. No idea of what we call "reincarnation" was ever implied; I have not heard of such beliefs among Ojibwas. Adoption of this kind was generally regarded as filling a vacated space or a need (i.e., a void space) in a family or household. For subarctic hunting people, a full-complement winter household was a requisite for survival.

4. There are advantages as well as disadvantages to becoming associated with one faction or family, as my friend Margaret Smith recently pointed out. She has been closely associated with a family in northern Minnesota who gave her an Indian name. This association provided an important "participant" opportunity to experience the world as the subject people do. My own Minnesota fieldwork—although supposedly a "white room" endeavor (see note 10)—had given the experience of being part of a singular "faction" in the community, thereby learning how *that* felt and how to handle "opposition" views and actions. In this case, my teachers and I shared one position regarding my learning something of traditional Indian life; the opposing view made itself known to us but did not interfere. (A hesitation to interfere in another family's affairs is characteristic.) In a sense, then, it was a form of being adopted.

5. The decision by the band to offer burial at Round Lake was a gift to me, as well as an appreciation of Ed. The chief, at the funeral service, told the congregation about that; here are excerpts in translation: "The Bible says there is another home—forever. Another better place for us. I know a lot of people knew and worked with this man. I have personally seen his work. We received a letter from

Mary regarding her desire to bury her husband here. We met three times regarding this request, as our land was designated to us and I didn't want anyone questioning our decision. We are only giving up a plot for our friend here. We came to our decision also knowing that a lot of people knew him and would like to say their farewells. . . . And as Mary said, he didn't have a plot to be buried in. And as you people here all know, the government gave us this land to do what we wanted. . . . It is not the same for white people. There is no land given for burial. When white people work, they lose almost half of their earnings paying for everything. I believe that is sometimes how they pay for land to be buried in when they die. I am not sure. . . . But according to this letter, there is no land like that. And we should say our thanks to our Lord and government for providing for us . . . [for] this is what it looks like when the government doesn't look after you." Actually, it was Reverend Henry I had written to, with no mention of land or lack of it. Rather, I asked if his son, now a pilot, might fly a Weagamow plane to scatter the ashes over Ed's beloved northern lakes and forests. My "request" had apparently been turned over to the chief, and meetings were held to resolve the issue of "scattering" remains of the dead, which offended some local feelings. Some had opposed the practice of cremation itself. The outcome of the meetings was agreement to offer to bury his remains in the Round Lake cemetery, which I accepted.

6. Little did I realize then, when assigning to students Casteneda's findings about the limits of fieldwork, that something of the same sort was to happen to me.

7. I have in mind an article contrasting the life history of Meme with that of Ellen Smallboy (Flannery 1995). Meme was born 50 years later than Ellen (1903 vs. 1853). Yet their childhood lifestyles were very similar—with the exception that Ellen and her family were more, rather than less, in contact with the Euro-Canadian world than were Meme's people. This underlines the rather large time gap between the inland Northern Ojibwa-Crees in Ontario and Smallboy's home with the more accessible Swampy Crees on James Bay, the most southerly part of Hudson Bay where European trading posts had existed since the 1660s. In fact, the historical summary by John Long (Flannery 1995:65) states, "When Regina Flannery met

Ellen Smallboy the Cree of James Bay had already experienced two and a half centuries of contacts with Euro-Canadian outsiders."

In the period between the signing of their respective treaties (1905–30), the people of the Round Lake area were remote and little known to outsiders, including governmental agents (Black-Rogers 1990a, and the unfinished book)—just as they had remained remote from fur traders in the 18th and 19th centuries (largely due to lack of waterways to their traditional interior lands). Thus, Meme was still living essentially in the old ways when Ellen was recalling them to Flannery (circa 1930). When Meme was recalling her youth to me into the 1990s, Flannery's book was published, in which the introduction says of Smallboy: "Her life history offers important glimpses into the lives of Cree women and their families in an era now inaccessible to present-day students of subarctic Canada" (xii).

It is notable, too, that the early 1930s also saw I. A. Hallowell's famous fieldwork at Berens River, Manitoba. This community, he himself soon learned, did not contain the "most remote" of Ojibwa people (a category he had sought and anticipated to find there). He soon undertook two trips north to Island Lake (one of the posts where Meme's people had traded furs in past centuries), where he found ample evidence that cross-cousin marriage systems did indeed still exist—his initial aim in going west (Hallowell 1937). Hudson's Bay Company trading post journals record Hallowell's comings and goings (HBCA B.16/a/14, 15 and B.11/a/17).

8. Alice Kehoe later told me that a person with medicine power feels obliged to protect anyone to whom he has revealed some of its secrets. Since the old belief system of Minnesota Ojibwes held that nothing is accidental, the medicine man gave me, in addition to an Indian name, some medicine to ensure that I would get safely "over the mountains" on my return flight to California.

9. Neither "adopted" nor "fostered" categories will include stepchildren. The latter can be determined from genealogical and marriage records, but fostered and adopted children cannot. Whenever the research requires actual household compositions, foster and adopt information is important but typically missing from documentary sources. For the Round Lake Study database, a good portion of the

information about adoption/fosterage came from Ed Rogers's field notes (1958–59) when he was learning from the men how or from whom they had acquired the use of their family hunting/trapping lands. Many cases were found where the territory had derived from an adoptive or foster father (Black-Rogers 1990b).

10. Talk about "white room" ethnography (Black 1963, 1965, 1967) leading to participation in applying implicit rules of behavior! "White room" referred to informant elicitation that takes place in a controlled context removed from the scene of the actions discussed. In the Round Lake action context, I received the indirect communications about my "adoption" as a proper Ojibwa person should—by not reacting directly. I had learned this cultural rule in the white room. That early work was not so much an exercise of dispassionate distancing as an experiment in getting closer to the implicit rules of interaction (Kluckhohn 1952; Black 1958), which often involve, as my professors used to call it, "the right way to do the wrong thing," usually learned not by instruction but by goofing, which happens in the white room, too. In other words, the approach was not designed to insulate oneself from ordinary interactional situations. It was a ploy to learn how to understand and engage in these more productively. It did not rule out other scenes of action but gave an entrée to them. See also Black-Rogers 1988.

11. The research papers of E. S. Rogers and M. Black-Rogers are now the property of the University of Alberta Archives, Edmonton (Canada), Accession nos. 97–15 and 97–16.

REFERENCES

Basso, Keith H. 1979. History of Ethnological Research. In *Handbook of North American Indians*, vol. 9, ed. Alfonso Ortiz, 14–21. Washington DC: Smithsonian Institution.

Black, Mary B. 1958. The Value System of the Winnebago Indians. Master's thesis, University of Minnesota.

———. 1963. On Formal Ethnographic Procedures. *American Anthropologist* 65:134–135.

———. 1965. (with Duane Metzger) Ethnographic Description and the Study of Law. *American Anthropologist* 67(6): pt. 2 (special issue). Reprinted in *Cognitive Anthropology*, ed. Tyler, 137–165. New York: Holt Rinehart and Winston, 1969.

————. 1967. An Ethnoscience Investigation of Ojibwa Ontology and World View. Ph.D. diss., Stanford University. Ann Arbor: University Microfilms.

————. 1969. Eliciting Folk Taxonomy in Ojibwa. In *Cognitive Anthropology*, ed. Tyler, 165–89. New York: Holt Rinehart and Winston, 1969.

————. 1973. Ojibwa Questioning Etiquette and Use of Ambiguity. *Studies in Linguistics* 23:13–29.

————. 1974. Belief Systems. In *Handbook of Social and Cultural Anthropology*, ed. Honigmann, 509–577. Chicago: Rand McNally.

————. 1977. Ojibwa Power Belief System. In *The Anthropology of Power*, ed. R. D. Fogelson and R. N. Adams, 141–151. New York: Academic Press.

————. 1978. Trapline Mystique. Prologue and introduction to *Weagamow Notebook*, by Sophia and Saul Williams, 1–8. Toronto: Amethyst.

Black-Rogers, M. 1988. Ojibwa Power Interactions: Creating Contexts for "Respectful Talk." In *Native North American Interaction Patterns*, ed. R. Darnell and M. Foster, 44–68. Ottawa: National Museums of Canada, Mercury Series, no. 112.

————. 1989. Dan Raincloud: "Keeping Our Indian Way." In *Being and Becoming Indian: Biographical Studies of North American Frontiers*, ed. James A. Clifton, ch. 10. Chicago: Dorsey Press.

————. 1990a. Treaty Period for the Crane Indians of Northwestern Ontario, 1905–1955. Paper presented at 1990 meeting, American Society for Ethnohistory, Toronto.

————. 1990b. Fosterage and Field Data: The Round Lake Study, 1989. In *Papers of the 21st Algonquian Conference*, ed. William Cowan, 51–71. Ottawa: Carleton University.

Black-Rogers, M., and E. S. Rogers. 1978. A Method for Reconstructing Patterns of Change: Surname Adoption by the Weagamow Ojibwa, 1870–1940. *Ethnohistory* 25:319–345.

———. 1979. Weagamow: A Representative Community of the Land and the People. *Tawow* 6 (2):12–17, 28–32.

Castaneda, Carlos. 1968. *The Teachings of Don Juan: A Yaqui Way of Knowledge*. Berkeley: University of California Press.

Flannery, Regina. 1995. *Ellen Smallboy: Glimpses of a Cree Woman's Life*. Foreword by John Long and Laura Peers. Rupert's Land Record Society Series, no. 4. Kingston: McGill-Queen's University Press.

Grant, Valerie. 1991. Users' Guide to Round Lake Study Database. In *Papers of the 22nd Algonquian Conference*, ed. William Cowan. Ottawa: Carleton University.

Hallowell, I. A. 1937. Cross-Cousin Marriage in the Lake Winnipeg Area. In *25th Anniversary Studies*, ed. E. S. Davidson, 95–110. Philadelphia: Philadelphia Anthropological Society.

Hudson's Bay Company Archives (HBCA), Winnipeg.

James, Edwin. 1956 [1830]. *A Narrative of the Captivity and Adventures of John Tanner . . . during Thirty Years Residence among the Indians in the Interior of North America*. Minneapolis: Ross and Haines.

Kehoe, Alice. 1995. Personal communication.

Kluckhohn, Clyde. 1952. Values and Value-Orientations in the Theory of Action: An Exploration in Definition and Classification. In *Toward a General Theory of Action*, ed. T. Parsons and E. Shils, 388–433. Cambridge: Harvard University Press.

———. 1956. Toward Comparison of Value-Emphases in Different Cultures. In *The State of the Social Sciences*, ed. Leonard D. White. Chicago: University of Chicago Press.

Krech, Shepard, III, and William C. Sturtevant. 1995. The Uses of Ethnographic Records. In *Preserving the Anthropological Record*, ed. Sydel Silverman and Nancy J. Parezo, 85–94. New York: Wenner-Gren Foundation for Anthropological Research.

MacKenzie, Marguerite, and Sandra Clarke. 1983. The Sheshatshiu Sociolinguistic Variability Project: A Preliminary Report. In *Papers of the 14th Algonquian Conference*, ed. W. Cowan. Ottawa: Carleton University.

Molohon, Katherine, and Michael Bisaillon. 1996. Fertility Management and Community Continuity in Northern Ontario Native Communities. Paper presented at 28th Algonquian Conference, Toronto.

Nichols, John. 1996. Personal communication.

Nichols, John, and Earl Nyholm. 1979. *Ojibwi-ikidowinan: An Ojibwe Word Resource Book*. St. Paul: Minnesota Archeological Society.

Pentland, David. 1996. Personal communication.

Quinn, William W., Jr. 1993. Intertribal Integration: The Ethnological Argument in *Duro v. Raina. Ethnohistory* 40:34–69.

Rogers, Edward S. 1958–59. Field notes, Round Lake, Ontario. Edmonton: University of Alberta Archives.

———. 1962. *The Round Lake Ojibwa*. Occasional Paper 5, Art and Archeology Division. Toronto: Royal Ontario Museum.

Rogers, E. S., and M. Black. 1976. Subsistence Strategy in the Fish and Hare Period, Northern Ontario: The Weagamow Ojibwa, 1880–1920. *Journal of Anthropological Research* 32:1–43.

Rogers, Jean H. 1963. Survey of Round Lake Phonology and Morphology. Paper 3, Bulletin 194, *Contributions to Anthropology, 1961–1962*, pt. 2:92–154. Ottawa: National Museums Canada.

Smith, Margaret. 1995. Personal communication.

Speck, Frank G. 1918. Kinship Terms and the Family Band among the Northeastern Algonkian. *American Anthropologist* 29:143–161.

Todd, E. M. 1970. A Grammar of the Ojibway Language: Severn Dialect. Ph.D. diss., University of Toronto. Ann Arbor: University Microfilms.

Valentine, L. P. 1995. *Making It Their Own*. Toronto: University of Toronto Press.

Watkins, Rev. E. A. 1938 [1865]. *A Dictionary of the Cree Language*. Ed. Ven. R. Faries. Toronto: Church House, Church of England.

5
All My Relations

The Significance of Adoption in Anthropological Research

William K. Powers and Marla N. Powers

Today, modern Lakota orators begin their speeches by saying, "Matuwe kin he slolwaye lo. Mataku kin he slolwaye lo. Tokiyaematanhan kin slowaye lo" [I know who I am. I know what I am. I know where I come from].

In keeping with this Lakota conceit, we would like to begin by saying that we know that we are white people, one of Italian heritage, the other of Irish. We are presently anthropologists, although this was not the case when we first went to Pine Ridge. We met in New York City in 1954 where we both were pursuing theatrical careers. We both live some of the time in New York, some of the time in New Jersey, some of the time in New Orleans, and some of the time in Pine Ridge.[1]

We know that we are not American Indians in general and Lakotas in particular. Nevertheless, the singular common thread that has run through most of our lives is our relationship with Lakota people. Since we began going to Pine Ridge (52 years ago for me and 40 for Marla), we do not feel that anthropological interests per se have had any major influence on our cultural sharing with Lakotas, although obviously after having become professional anthropologists some 25 years ago, we are constantly aware of a dual responsibility—one to the Lakotas and one to our discipline. But as far as our Lakota relatives and friends are concerned, they really don't care what we are so much as who we are. And since we have been going out to the reservation for so many years, they insist that we're from South Dakota.

In discussing the significance of adoption by Native peoples to anthropological research, we should say at the start that our responsibilities are rather clearly defined. We rank our responsibilities to the Lakota people first. So, for us to discuss adoption and anthropology, we must perforce look as objectively at anthropology as we look at Lakota culture. Perhaps it is safe to say that we view anthropology much more critically, if not cynically, the longer we spend time among our relatives.[2] And when we talk about advantages and disadvantages generally, we may not consider them personally as significant as other anthropologists might. We also are aware that other anthropologists, adopted or not, may not agree with our ideas about priorities.[3]

Nevertheless, when anthropologists are adopted by the people whose lives they share, advantages and disadvantages arise that ultimately affect anthropological research. Advantages include the mutual honor and respect inherent in the adoption process, the pleasurable feeling of belonging to another culture of choice, and the commensurate values that adopters and adoptees share. We express our respect for our relatives through the proper use of kinship terms, appropriate kinship behavior including what anthropologists refer to as avoidance, and public joking between certain affinal kin. Here, avoidance and respect are a single category in Lakota, *woohola* ("respect"; that is, avoidance is a form of respect), although joking is recognized as a mutually exclusive category, *woiȟaȟa* (laughter).[4]

Today, when so many people identify with New Ageism, environmentalism, or other movements, many have assumed Indian names either through adoption by Indian families or by self-appointment. We are very much aware not only of our names but of the circumstances under which we received them and the significance of the adoption process to the people who have adopted us.[5] Since 1949, I have been named and adopted twice, Marla has been named once and adopted twice, and each of our sons, Jeff and Greg, has been named and adopted once—all under differing circumstances that are worth noting.

In 1949, I was given an Indian name, Wanbli Waste (Good Eagle) at a celebration held at Oglala, South Dakota. It was my second year at Pine Ridge. In 1947, I had the good fortune of meeting several Lakota men at the International Folk Festival in my hometown of St. Louis. I attended the event at the Kiel Auditorium with my eighth grade class. Clearly thrilled with seeing "Sioux" Indians for the first time, I slipped away from my class and went backstage. Having been raised by a theatrical family, I knew how to "crash" stage doors. Putting on an air of importance incongruous with my age, I asked directions to the Indians' dressing room, and the stage doorman, preoccupied with a newspaper, waved me through. I was partly guided down the cavernous corridors by the aroma of what I later learned was sweet grass, which Lakotas used to pack their costumes in. As I approached, I was greeted with "Hau Kola" by John Colhoff, the leader of the group. He introduced me to Edgar Red Cloud, Joseph Elk Boy, and Daniel White Eyes, who apparently were accustomed to non-Indians descending upon them for a quick glimpse of "real Indians." But they were friendly at the onset, perhaps recognizing my subdued enthusiasm. I spent the next five days ushering them around St. Louis, taking them by bus back and forth from their downtown hotel to the auditorium. I remember Daniel White Eyes, a very tall man with long, unbraided hair who towered over me as I stood next to him on the bus, very proud. On the last day of the performance, John invited me to come to Pine Ridge.

My parents agreed that I could go as long as I could find a reasonable place to stay "among the Indians." And so through the auspices of the Jesuits who maintained a Jesuit Mission Bureau in St. Louis as well as a seminary in Florrisant, Missouri, plans were made for me to stay at the famous Holy Rosary Mission.

In June 1948, at the age of 13, I left Union Station, St. Louis, and traveled to Omaha by Union Pacific. There I changed to the Chicago and Northwestern Railroad to Rushville, Nebraska, where I was met by a young Jesuit scholastic who drove me over a 30-mile gravel road to Holy Rosary Mission. I don't remember his name; we stayed in touch until he left the order. I worked for my room and board hauling lumber from Igloo, South Dakota, to Holy Rosary, which the Jesuits used to construct new classrooms. I stayed in Red Cloud Hall, a massive concrete dormitory, with a handful of orphans who also worked around the mission.[6] It was a marvelous adventure. The Lakota boys and I rode horses and herded cows every day that we weren't riding in an open semi up to Igloo. We played basketball every evening in the gym, and in the communal dining room we ate food raised in the Jesuit garden and bread baked by Brother Siers.[7]

But despite the breathless beauty of the land, the sweet and invigorating fresh air, and camaraderie with new friends, I felt very isolated. After all, I had come to Pine Ridge to see Lakota culture first-hand. But the Jesuits did not look favorably on the Lakota way, attributing much of its ceremonies to acts of the devil. Today, of course, things are different: priests and nuns join in the sweat lodge, at least one priest has performed the sun dance, and another recently forsook the cassock for the medicine man's rattle and drum. But I was simply not allowed to go to celebrations or, for that matter, to leave the mission. So the second year I decided to stay in town with my first Lakota friend, John Colhoff, also known as White Man Stands in Sight, the son of a galvanized Yankee and a Lakota woman. John, who at the time was in his early seventies, and was employed as public relations director for the Oglala Sioux Tribe. He also served part time as curator at the Rapid City Sioux Indian Museum. He lived in Pine Ridge in a seven-room house and introduced me to Lakota foods like *wojapi*, a sweetened and thickened fruit dish with the consistency of gravy, and *wasna*, the Lakota equivalent of pemmican, which he collected and prepared himself. John also wrote and illustrated old Lakota stories and had a large collection of photographs and relics that he kept in footlockers. He always was eager to open them and tell me about Lakota warriors he had known. I fondly remember him sitting in a rocking chair singing old love songs and carefully explaining the words to me.

It was John who took me to the dance at Oglala where a group of old men were impressed with the fact that this white boy of 14 could sing and dance Indian. They decided on the spot that I should be given the name of a deceased Lakota warrior. Typically, among the Lakotas, names may be created for the first time as an attribute of a person's physical being or characteristic behavior, or the name may be appropriated from a living or deceased person. In the case of the former, the person who gives away his or her own name is left nameless; in the latter, the deceased person's name lives on. The procedure surrounding my naming was rather simple: a old man named Sam Helper got up and announced to everyone present the decision of the elders, that I should be called Good Eagle. There was an audible round of *hau's* after which the singers began an honor song for me using my new name, and everyone got up and shook hands with me and we danced an old Omaha dance. Of course, I was elated and proud, and John said that I could show my appreciation to the singers for singing the honor song for me by giving them a dollar, and I did. John announced my intention in Lakota, the singers struck the drum in appreciation, and the head singer got up and shook hands with me.

Later I met the other singers and dancers, including John Sitting Bull, the deaf and mute son of the famous Hunkpapa chief and spiritual leader, who was one of the last survivors of the Custer battle.

Although I was named, I was not adopted. And it should be made clear that naming and adoption are two different processes quite capable of standing on their own, even though the two, under certain circumstances, may be combined.

In 1950, I stayed with a well-known singer, Henry White Calf, in the now defunct Loafer Camp, four miles west of Pine Ridge agency. This is a beautiful area surrounded by pine-dotted buttes and rolling hills. Henry was a Roman Catholic catechist who attended St. Ann's No. 2 Chapel, located next to his log house. Another log house served as a meeting place for local parishioners and also served for indoor Indian dances in the winter. A more spectacular round dance hall was located a mile away at what was called the Y, that is, the junction of Slim Buttes Road and the local wagon trail to Henry's house. In those days a number of people lived in Loafer Camp: Gilbert White Whirlwind and his son, Leroy, Jim Grey Blanket, Mr. and Mrs. Oliver Red Cloud, Mr. and Mrs. Willie Bear Tail, and Peter Stands. But as the old people died off or moved away, all signs of the community disappeared, and today only the painted hills and traces of the old wagon road remain. Even the round house was torn down, but one can still find scraps of tin that formed its roof lying rusted in the prairie grass.

I lived with Henry for several months that year. He and Edgar Red Cloud spent countless hours teaching me Lakota. Henry and his wife, Berdina, had a large family: Belnita, Lindy, Richard, Isidore, Melbita, Billy, Bruce, Wesley, and Cynthia Ann. The younger ones spoke only Lakota, so I was able to practice with them. Henry also taught me how to sing, and my fondest recollections of Lakota culture drift back to these early days where living Indian was not just participating in dances and religious ceremonies. It was also hitching a team to a wagon and going after water two miles away, or riding double through secluded canyons along the Nebraska state line, listening to Henry's powerful voice echo off the canyon walls as he sang rabbit dance songs. It was stealing government fence posts for wood to burn in the cook stove. It was listening to stories in the dark in Henry's house while mice scampered over the roof beams. It was eating supper by kerosene lamp until the miller moths pestered you to turn down the wick.

Later Henry visited me in St. Louis. In 1951, on a return trip to Loafer Camp, he named me Kolayapi (Made a Friend) and adopted me as his son. He made a number of songs for me and always sang songs using my name in them whenever there was a gathering. Since I used to hoop dance, he made the following Omaha dance song by putting new words to a rabbit dance tune that I liked:

> Kolayapi k'un cangleška kin yuha yahi cana
> Iyokipimayaye
> Tehan yaun eyaš ohinniyan ciksuya waun welo
>
> [Made A Friend, when I see you come with the hoop
> You make me happy
> Even though you're far away, I'll always remember you.][8]

The same year, Edgar Red Cloud introduced me to Frank Afraid of Horses and Frank's son-in-law, Clarence Janis. Frank was the son of Young Man Afraid of Horses and grandson of Old Man Afraid of Horses. Young Man Afraid of Horses had two wives, and the children of one wife took the name Young Man (Youngman) while the children of the second took the name Afraid of Horses.

It was sheer coincidence that the same winter Frank, traveling with a group of show people in the St. Louis area, was stranded and contacted me. Some of my friends and I arranged to put them up in St. Louis and managed to get them safely onto a train back to Pine Ridge. Consequently, when I returned to Pine Ridge in 1952, Frank adopted me as his son.

Thus I was adopted into a rather large network of kin mainly due to the polygamous marriage. My "closest living" relatives today are Frank's daughters, Zona Fills the Pipe and Sadie Janis, whom I call *tanke* (elder sister), and my deceased brother's wife, Judge Etta Youngman, juvenile judge of the Oglala Sioux Tribal Courts, whom I call *hanka* (sister-in-law) and with whom I maintain an obligatory "joking" relationship even though our linking relative, Pugh Youngman, is deceased.

Upon adoption, Frank preferred to call me by my first given name,

Good Eagle, and so no new name was bestowed. It is the name that I currently use for ceremonial purposes.

In 1957, Marla and I were married in New York City, where we both had been employed in the theater. She knew nothing about Indians except that I had a strong interest in them, and it was not until the summer of 1958 that we traveled to Pine Ridge with a load of buckskin and beads, which we traded for finished craft products such as beadwork and quillwork. We'll never forget driving through the sun dance camps with a load of buckskin strapped to the roof of our car, following Bob Thunder Hawk, an *eyapaha* (announcer), whose clarion voice told the people that we had beads and buckskin to trade. Slowly heads peaked out of the wall tents, and soon elderly women were coming up to our car to negotiate for white elk skins and hanks of beads.[9]

Since that time we have traveled to Pine Ridge every year. We are also pleased that our Lakota relatives and friends have visited us in New York, New Jersey, and New Orleans with some frequency. However, it was not until 1961, when Jeff was two years old, that both Marla and he were adopted formally at a sun dance by Charles Red Cloud. It was at night. While the whole camp gathered, Charlie and Marla, carrying Jeff in her arms, walked to the center of the arbor. The eyapaha announced that the chief of the Oglala Sioux tribe was going to adopt this white woman and her son. He named Marla Tacanunpe Wakanwin (Her Holy Pipe) and Jeff Wicahpi Ska (White Star), names by which they are still known. Most memorable is the day following the adoption. An old man came up to our tipi and asked, "Where's White Star?" Marla and I brought Jeff out of the tipi, and the old man immediately began singing an honor song for him while we stood in place and danced.

When our younger son, Greg, first came with us to Pine Ridge in 1964, he was adopted by my father, Frank, and called Wamniomni (Whirlwind), which made reference to his characteristic perpetual motion as a child of two. He still is Wamniomni.

There was one other brief incident that was significant for Marla. An Arapaho man named Sidney Willow made a special trip from Wyoming to our house in Pine Ridge during the summer of 1966. He came to the door and said to Marla: "They said you looked like my daughter, so I am going to adopt you as my daughter." Subsequently we made trips to Wyoming and spent time with Arapahos who made frequent trips to participate in sweat lodges with their Oglala relatives at Pine Ridge.

One of the particular circumstances of our independent adoptions is that the two major families into which we have been adopted, the Red Clouds and Afraid of Horses, also are related. My father, Frank Afraid of Horses, married Marla's father's (Charlie Red Cloud) sister, Lucy Red Cloud. My sisters, Zona Fills the Pipe and Sadie Janis, jokingly refer to themselves as "double princesses" because they are born of two Lakota "royal families." Functionally speaking, however, it means that Marla and I actually have two sets of kinship terms that we may use to address our relatives on both sides of the family. Theoretically speaking, there is no way to solve this kinship dilemma. However, pragmatically, there is a tendency for Lakotas to regard us initially as if we were two people adopted before we were married. Since I was adopted first, the set of kinship terms I use to address both families tends to prevail. Hence my sisters chastise Marla for not serving me breakfast in bed and otherwise attending dutifully to all my material needs. At the same time, Marla teams up with my sister-in-law to level sometimes sharp criticisms at my uncontrollable incompetence.

Thus located firmly in the social structure of the *tiwahe* (family), *tiyošpaye* (band), and *oyate* (Oglala), we customarily treat the first with proper respect and the second with proper attendance at rituals and other forms of celebrative functions at districtwide events. With respect to our allegiance to the Oglala, we customarily degrade other less fortunate members of the Lakota Nation, such as the Rosebudders, for whom we place our garbage in see-through sacks so that they occasionally may go window shopping.

TYPES OF ADOPTIONS

There are two types of adoption procedures. The most common is the kind of adoption mentioned above in which an individual becomes part of a family either through a formal or informal procedure. In Lakota, this type of adoption is called *wokah̃nige*, from *kah̃niga* (to select). Usually, the adoptee receives a name unless he or she already has one. The relationship formed in this case is usually parent-child, though not always. For example, R. D. Theisz, professor of English at Black Hills State University, reports that he was adopted as a "brother" to an elderly man's son.[10] Although the ultimate effect is that the adoptee is automatically related to everyone in the family, frequently the ceremony places more emphasis on the adoptee as *waliyacinpi*, meaning "substitute" or "replacement" for a deceased relative. Waliyacinpi is the only form of adoption listed in the Oglala Sioux Tribal Law and Order Code. According to chapter 11, p. 260, of the code,

> Any Indian or Indians wishing to adopt an adult according to Indian custom (waliyacinpi) shall appear before the Superior Court of the Oglala Sioux Tribe with the party to be adopted and all other parties and declare their intention. The Court, if after examination, finds the person or persons requesting the adoption be made is of sound mind and that the request is free and voluntary, may authorize such adoption and make a record thereof upon the payment of a fee of one dollar ($1.00), which is to be deposited to the Court Funds.
>
> All adoptions made heretofore by Tribal custom shall be null and void unless they are renewed in the manner as above described.[11]

I have never met anyone outside the courts who was aware of this law, which is an obvious attempt to retain some bureaucratic authority over Lakota adoption procedures but with little success.

In our case, our sons were adopted logically as grandchildren.

The second type of adoption ceremony is historically known as *hunka* (making of relatives) and is derived from the Pawnee Hako, a ceremony that originally established a bond between two tribes.[12] The hunka is always formal; it takes place at a celebration, thus guaranteeing a relatively large audience, and it is presided over by a *wicaša wakan* (medicine man) or a respected elder of the tribe, male or female.

The hunka today is more frequently referred to as *caštun* (to create a name) or simply naming ceremony. The important principles in the ceremony are an elder male or female who enters into an adoptive relationship with a younger male or female creating a relationship called *hunkayapi* in which both parties subsequently address each other formally as *mihunka* (my hunka).

Although in theory a ceremony may be held for only two people (the hunka father or mother, or the hunka son or daughter), in practice hunkas are performed en masse. Sometimes as many as 20 bonds are formed at a single ceremony. Each adoptee sits on a chair covered with quilts and blankets, while the adopters stand behind them. The singers sing traditional hunka songs, after which each adoptee is given an "Indian name" while their respective adopters tie a feather—usually *wacinhin* (eagle down)—to their hair. At the conclusion, the adopters and adoptees dance around the arbor followed by as many new relatives as wish to join in. After the dance, the sponsors of the hunka give away gifts to the adopters and adoptees, and adoptees claim each gift-laden chair (as well as the chair itself) as their own.

Although not a type of adoption per se, we have occasionally met Lakota people who after our first meeting begin to address us by a kinship term, usually brother or sister. In these cases, we reciprocate with the proper terms, but no adoption has taken place. Of course, there is always the problem of determining just who relatives are because, after adoption, you maintain a relationship throughout the adopter's entire kin network. Given the benefits of kinship, one can reexamine the adage that everyone on the reservation is related. If they are, it may not be because of hereditary reasons. It may simply be because they want to be. Like other Lakotas, when we meet a Lakota person for the first time, we routinely attempt to determine if and how we are related.

Although a number of non-Indians and non-Lakotas have been adopted, we are not aware of any other anthropologists who have been adopted at Pine Ridge, probably because the trend is for anthropologists to spend no more time on the reservation than is required to witness a single event, such as a sun dance, or to conduct research for a dissertation. However, there are a number of clergy, teachers, BIA employees, and public health workers who, because of their tenure at Pine Ridge, have been adopted or have received an Indian name.

RITUAL PARTICIPATION

Long-term association means that we have become increasingly involved in family and *tiyošpaye* rituals. We have participated in the celebration of births and baptisms, and mourned the deaths of loved ones. We also have served as principals in a number of important ceremonies.

In 1983, Clarence Janis, who was my elder sister Sadie's husband and thus my brother-in-law, died after a long illness. My relationship with Clarence was never clear-cut, mainly because right before my father, Frank, died, he told Clarence that even though Clarence was his son-in-law, he respected him more as a son. I was affected by the old man's last words, and so was Clarence. Thus sometimes he would joke severely with me in true Lakota fashion, but other times he would treat me more like a younger brother. It was never clear. A year after Clarence died, Sadie asked me to serve as the announcer for Clarence's memorial feast. Being an eyapaha for such an occasion is particularly important because the announcer is required to say something to and about each person who is recipient of giveaways by the deceased's family and thus has to be knowledgeable about Lakota culture as well as the kin network. After the memorial, Sadie also asked me to accompany her daughter, Darlene (Shortbull), her eldest brother-in-law, "Boob" Janis, and the medicine man, Floyd Hand, to feed Clarence's spirit for the last time. I still have vivid recollections of that day every time I pass the old tree under which the spirit food was buried.[13]

In 1985, Tom and Darlene Shortbull asked Marla to serve as the hunka mother for their daughter, Vanessa. At an elaborate naming ceremony for Vanessa and her brother, Frank, whose Hunka father was to be Dr. Ronald Forgey, a physican from Los Angeles who had worked for the Indian Health Service at Pine Ridge, a bond was established between Marla and Vanessa that continues to be very strong today. The ceremony became the basis for Marla's book *Lakota Naming: A Modern-day Hunka Ceremony* (1991).

On two occasions, I have been asked to compose songs to honor young people. Most people who know me remember when I sang with the Red Cloud Singers at public events such as the Oglala sun dance and powwow in the 1960s and 1970s. The group was composed of Oliver Red Cloud (the present chief of the Oglala), Lymon Red Cloud, William Horn Cloud, Richard Elk Boy, Howard Blue Bird, and Tonto Black Bear.

In one case, I was asked by Mr. and Mrs. Melvin Red Cloud to compose an honor song for their daughter, Bobbie, who was leaving for the army. I changed the words slightly to a song that Henry White Calf had sung for his son, Lindy, for the same purpose. Mrs. White Calf was present at the honoring ceremony, and I asked her permission to revise the song before singing it. By extension of the original adoptions of Marla and me, Bobbie's parents are our cousins. The following year,

Mrs. Celia Martin, who had attended the honoring ceremony for Bobbie Red Cloud, asked me to compose an honor song for her grandson, which I performed publicly at the Oglala Nation Powwow.

In 1996, Brenda Youngman asked Marla and me to serve as hunka mother and father for her daughter, Cody Sarah. Brenda is the daughter of Judge Etta Youngman, my sister-in-law; however, the joking relationship does not extend to children of in-laws. As a matter of fact, the relationship between Brenda and me would be characterized as one of "extreme respect." During my joking bouts with her mother, Brenda and her siblings simply stand attentive to the discourse without ever participating. All of Judge Youngman's children call us uncle and aunt in English. However, by Lakota standards, we are their father and mother because their father, Pugh, is my brother through adoption.

We also were asked to confer a name on the child, which was the first time we had been asked to do so. For several weeks in anticipation of the ceremony, we pondered over an appropriate name. After talking with Brenda, we were struck by the fact that 19-month-old Cody already had learned to offer food and beverages to others, including complete strangers. Since generosity is such an important Lakota value, we finally decided upon the name Wacantognakawin, best translated as "Generous Woman."

The ceremony was held at the Youngman home in Oglala under an extended cook shade. About 50 people attended. The Youngman males were busy cooking soup in a large iron kettle outdoors, while women, including Marla, prepared the salads indoors. On this occasion, Marla helped make *wasna*, a sacred food used exclusively at hunka ceremonies and weddings.

After the meal was distributed, some clean tarpaulins were placed on the ground, and the family members brought out armloads of giveaway items. Five chairs were set up: one for Cody, one for another hunka, and three for others who were being honored. Wilmer Mesteth, a well-known spiritual leader, conducted the ceremony with help from two singers. Marla and I were instructed to stand behind the quilt and blanket-laden chair occupied by Cody. We were given an eagle feather attached to a medicine wheel which at the proper time we tied to the child's hair. Afterward, I was asked to give a small talk in Lakota in which I announced to the public the little girl's name, saying that from this time forward wherever she went, she would be known by this name. The relatives then got up to dance while the singers sang an appropriate song for little Cody. Each time the baby's name was mentioned in song, the female relatives gave the tremolo. Marla and I were then instructed to take the chair and its belongings as well as other gifts that had been placed behind the chair. In all, the ceremony lasted five hours.

At larger events, Marla and I are conspicuous if we do not join in either the singing or dancing. It is customary for women to wear shawls when they appear on the dance floor, and my sisters criticize Marla if she has not brought her shawl. When our sons accompanied us to the reservation, they also participated.

EFFECTS ON TEACHING AND RESEARCH

For the past 20 years Marla and I have taken more than 60 students to the field. In 1991, we established the Lakota Field School domiciled at Holy Rosary Mission. Our relationships have enabled us to place students in a variety of volunteer jobs where they get firsthand experience of living and working with Lakota people. Of particular importance is that about half of each year's cohort returns the next year and thus builds a solid relationship not only with our relations but with other individuals and families at Pine Ridge. As the Lakota are prone to tell you, a lot of non-Indians come to Pine Ridge to satisfy their curiosity about reservation life. But few ever return. Thus, when our students return, they are greeted warmly because the Lakotas appreciate their sincere interest in the people, not just in research.

Our network of relations also has enabled us to place students in many situations where confidentiality is paramount. For example, a number of our students have worked in the Oglala Sioux Tribal Courts, the social services department of the Public Health Hospital, and alcoholic treatment centers. They have also served as community health representatives, providing medical services and companionship to people throughout the reservation.

Our students attend rigorous indoctrination seminars on the importance of maintaining confidentiality, obtaining clearance from the commission on the protection of human subjects (if they plan to interview and publish), and obtaining parental consent if they wish to interview minors or tribal consent if they wish to publish works related to their volunteer jobs with the tribe or Bureau of Indian Affairs.

Most (but not all) of our contacts for student placements come from our relatives, and each year is somewhat different. Our students have mapped cemeteries, cooked meals for senior citizens, worked at the local radio station, KILI Voice of the Lakota Nation, interviewed contemporary Lakota artists, helped out in an organic garden project under the auspices of the Oglala Lakota College, and conducted historical research on Holy Rosary Mission. But it is never certain just what opportunities are available until we arrive each summer. In 1996, for example, as soon as the students arrived, they were invited to attend a buffalo hunt conducted by the Oglala Sioux Parks and Recreation Authority in the reservation preserve and to help butcher three of the animals that were to be donated to a local sun dance sponsored by the Red Cloud Family. Students also were invited to help build the sun dance shade and to attend the ceremonies later in the month.

Most of our students have responded well to the situation. Most return to their homes and universities completely changed by the experience. A minority, however, soon learn that reservation life is often hard and dreary, and the never-ending pace of the four weeks of fieldwork helps them to decide quickly whether or not anthropology is really a field for them to consider. Nevertheless, we feel that without our own lengthy tenure with Lakota people, and the graciousness of our relatives, conducting such a field school would certainly be less rewarding to our students and to ourselves.

With respect to research, our relatives have been indispensable in providing reliable cultural information. They know what we do professionally. They have read our books, and many of them are featured in them.[14]

Our long-range involvement with our relatives has resulted in Marla and me being asked to conduct certain kinds of research *because* we are related. For example, in 1978 Mary Douglas, who at the time was director of the Food and Culture Program at Russell Sage Foundation in New York City, asked us to join her research team because we already had "cultural knowledge" of the Lakotas and could assist her in developing a methodology for studying food systems cross-culturally. During the actual fieldwork and analysis, we had access to a great number of Lakotas who were willing to share with us the kind of cultural information we needed.[15]

In 1991, the National Park Service, recognizing our close relationship to the Lakotas, approached us to conduct research concerning the possible establishment of a Wounded Knee National Memorial. In about six weeks, we interviewed more than 200 Lakotas at Pine Ridge, Rosebud, Cheyenne River, and Standing Rock. We concluded that most Lakotas wanted no kind of memorialization because they thought it would offend the spirits of the deceased who were massacred there in 1890. Fortunately, our particular network of kin was ultimately connected with Big Foot, the leader of the ghost dancers who were decimated at Wounded Knee, and it was easy to interview a large number of Lakotas because of our relationship.

Although our research, both individual and collective, has led us into a number of cultural domains, we have resisted much early anthropological jargon such as "participant-observation" and characterization of our relatives and friends as "informants," because after such a long and intimate relationship, the terms and ideas they represent are, frankly, crude and demeaning to people with whom we share our lives.

DISADVANTAGES

Although adoption obviously increases the probability of access to people, places, and things within Lakota culture, this access is available only as long as proper behaviors are maintained between kin year round. From an anthropological perspective, there are disadvantages in that the adoptees become part of their adopter's social, political, economic, and religious sphere as well as their interactions with other individuals and institutions, including other anthropologists. Thus research objectives sometimes must be abandoned for the sake of the adopter's reputation and privacy both inside and outside the community and tribe.

Living with relatives, whether biological or adopted, is not all that different. Although it is advantageous to be related to the people who not only provide you with cultural information but encourage you to get it right, there are times when being related to some carries with it a burden if not a sense of futility. For example, we have become involved inadvertently in our relatives' personal and ceremonial business where we have been admonished for going to a certain sun dance or warned to stay away from certain Yuwipi men. The net result has been an abdication of research interests. We frequently are criticized by some for precisely the same things others have encouraged us to do, for example, publish photos of the sun dance, which was allowed until 1973. Some of our research has been quoted out of context by Lakotas almost as much as it has been by anthropologists. If we do not visit every relative each summer, we are subject to criticism by those whom we did not see. This requires us to make up a whole host of culturally relevant excuses not unlike the ones we make up in New Jersey or New York, where our other relatives live. We also participate in joking behavior simply because it would be unthinkable not to. Such participation in fact separates the truly adopted from the wannabes because cross-culturally what one can and must say in Lakota is prohibited, at least in polite non-Indian society—for example, responding to an in-law's criticism of an elderly sister for urinating in her pants; asking if there were any frogs available in New Jersey so that my in-law who recently suffered a stroke affecting his face could have a skin graft; answering the question whether it was me who was crawling through the tall weeds headed for the widow's house, usually at a large public gathering; asking Marla why she starves me. Unless one can become involved in such banter, one can never live up to being Lakota. Conversely, no Lakotas would involve a novice in such behavior because they are aware that non-Indians will become embarrassed or enraged at such humor. As one relative told me, "You know how those Indians are!"

Also, adoptees know all their relations. They know all the landmarks on the reservation and where everyone is buried. And heaven help you if you ever get lost. Ridicule will be heaped upon you for the rest of your days, particularly by your joking relatives.

There also are points at which Lakota philosophy and the practice of anthropology conflict. When this occurs, the concerns of our relatives must take precedence over anthropological objectives, and problems must be resolved in such a way that neither our special relationship with our adopted families nor our professional obligations are compromised.

For example, we never engage in anthropologist bashing, nor do

we defend antiwhite sentiments. Lakotas freely talk about such subjects in front of us without ever making us feel that we're white—or
anthropologists. We never argue about evolution, because Lakota philosophy does not accept its principles. I have on occasion discussed
theory with some. In fact, one became fascinated with Lévi-Straussian
structuralism and seemed to grasp it with much more enthusiasm and
understanding than some of my colleagues.

We do have lengthy discussions about language, linguistic change,
dialectology, and ethnographic semantics. Lakotas today are fascinated with etymologies, most of which are untenable in linguistic
circles, but we do not criticize them, because they represent the latest
trends in Lakota cultural expression.

However, we have had open debates in the presence of tribal council members about various subjects with which we have been involved. As we mentioned above, in 1991 the National Park Service
retained us as consultants to determine the appropriateness of their
proposed Wounded Knee memorial and visitors center. After interviewing more than 200 Lakotas at Pine Ridge, Cheyenne River, Standing Rock, and Rosebud, we agreed with the Lakotas that the National
Parks monument was undesirable because of a fear that it would disturb the spirits of those massacred there. Furthermore, it would require condemning 1,800 acres of private and tribal land to accommodate the monument. We presented our findings to the tribal council,
who opposed the project despite the National Park Service's determination to build it anyway.

Earlier in 1978–81, we both were active in attempting to prevent the
production of the film *The Mystic Warrior*, a made-for-television version of Ruth Beebe Hill's *Hanta Yo*. The Black Hills Treaty Council,
comprising several elderly men from all the Lakota reservations as well
as independent women, argued that the book was insulting to the Lakotas, particularly Lakota women. Younger men, however, argued that
the tribe would make money on the film, since it was proposed that it
be filmed at Pine Ridge and surrounding venues in South Dakota. We
know many of the people supporting the film, but at the request of the
council we debated the issues in public. Taos, New Mexico, was re-
portedly the second choice for filming if the Lakotas refused. Since we
were headed in that direction, the Treaty Council asked us to deliver a
message to the Taos Tribal Council on their behalf. The Taos were sym-

pathetic to the Lakotas, although they were puzzled over why the Lakotas sent two white people as their messengers. The film ultimately was produced in Mexico, and long-range promises to the Lakota people were predictably broken. However, it was years before we could reconcile these differences from those who were once our friends but also supportive of the film.

Of equal importance are problems associated with our relatives' perceptions of acceptable and unacceptable behavior from unrelated Lakotas as well as anthropologists and other outsiders. In the wake of the recent inundation of Pine Ridge reservation (and others) by New Agers, wannabes, and other American and international aficionados, there has occurred a rash of antiwhite sentiment that often must be addressed and defended by both adopters and adoptees. For example, Lakota persons who do not know us may make racial slurs against me, and Marla has on occasion been criticized for trying to pass as white. Usually, a quick recitation of our genealogy satisfies a stranger that we are somehow different than most whites. If the stranger is a Lakota speaker, a response in the native language is sufficient. However, today young Lakotas who do not speak the language are frequently intimidated by a white man speaking Lakota, and I have been criticized accordingly.

Furthermore, just as elders express concern over the younger generation losing its language and culture, we are sometimes questioned about our own continued participation in Lakota culture as well as our possible disaffection with it. Elders sometimes ask me, "Naȟanhci Lakol iyaya he?" [Do you still talk Indian?] And I reassure them by answering, "Hau. Nahanhci" [Yes. Still].

However, the success of adoptive relationships ultimately depends on the continuous sincerity expressed between kin, one expected in any consanguineal or affinal relationship, and the ability for both the adopters and the adoptees to express mutual respect, affection, and concern without which the anthropologist forever remains a perpetual stranger or an uninvited guest.

At any rate, thanks to *mitak' oyas'in* ("all my relations"), as the ritual formula goes, we know who we are, and what we are, and where we come from, and are continuously honored by the mutual choice that we and the Lakota people have made.

This paper has been revised substantially since it was first presented at the 1995 AAA session, "Native American Adoption/Naming of Anthropologists."

1. Marla's mother and father, Jean and James Rossi, owned a glove factory in Gloversville, New York. They are retired on a farm outside Gloversville. My father, William V. Powers, was a well-known dance director at the Roxy Theater in New York City as well as on early television. My mother, Mildred Ruth Burkhardt, was one of the original 16 Ambassadorables, who danced at the St. Louis Ambassador Theater. The line of girls later became internationally known as the New York City Roxyettes and then as the Radio City Music Hall Rockettes.

2. As much as we would like to view this tenure as the longest longitudinal study in anthropology, the plain fact is that we enjoyed 20 years of "fieldwork" before becoming credentialized. In a very early publication (Kemnitzer 1970), W. K. Powers appears as an informant.

3. Some of the reviews of our work by colleagues suggests that they exhibit a rather supercilious attitude toward our longtime and intimate association with Lakota people, a little like the general attitude border-town whites exhibit toward Indians.

4. Sometime we hope to compare the reality of Lakota kinship with their respective anthropological models. To that end, Marla has collected genealogies for the past 25 years focusing mainly on our kinship network.

5. Today, many non-Indians identify with Lakota culture resulting in their being ostracized from some religious events such as the sun dance. In July 1995, the Three Mile Creek sun dance was abruptly terminated when the land owner complained that there were too many whites dancing. The same dance resumed in 1996 but at a different venue and with more rigid restrictions governing actual participation. Because of the high visibility of New Agers, their particular form of dress, and their physical behavior during ceremonies,

Lakotas are perplexed over what appears to be a fine line between emulation and mockery.

6. Unfortunately, the Jesuit razed this historic landmark in order to sell off the iron contained in the infrastructure.

7. At that time, Holy Rosary Mission was self-contained with its own cattle ranch, herd, gardens, and various shops that attended to vocational and domestic instruction.

8. It is customary to compose songs with new words inserted into old melodies.

9. Marla's parents were instrumental in helping us obtain large white elk skins through their glove business.

10. See Young Bear and Theisz 1994.

11. See chapter 11 of the Oglala Sioux Tribal Law and Code, p. 260.

12. For early descriptions of the hunka see Densmore 1918 and Walker 1917. For a more recent description see M. Powers 1991.

13. This event is part of a piece I published in French in 1992 but that has not yet been translated.

14. A list of our most significant publications to date appears in the bibliography.

15. This research, which lasted for four years, resulted in a number of publications and presentations, particularly in Douglas 1984 and Powers and Powers 1984, 1990.

BIBLIOGRAPHY

Densmore, Frances. 1918. *Teton Sioux Music*. Bulletin 61, Bureau of American Ethnology.

Douglas, Mary, ed. 1984. *Food in the Social Order*. New York: Russell Sage Foundation.

Kemnitzer, Luis. 1970. The Cultural Provenience of Objects Used in Yuwipi: A Modern Teton Dakota Healing Ritual. *Ethnos* 1:4.

Oglala Sioux Tribe. 1937. *Oglala Sioux Tribal Law and Order Code.* Pine Ridge SD.

Powers, Marla N. 1980. Menstruation and Reproduction: An Oglala Case. *Signs* 6:54–65.

———. 1986. *Oglala Women in Myth, Ritual, and Reality.* Chicago: University of Chicago Press.

———. 1988. New Perspectives on American Indian Women. *Revue Francaise d'Etudes Americaines* 13(38):350–356.

———. 1988. Symbolic Representations of Sex Roles in the Plains War Dance. *European Review of Native American Studies* 2(2):17–24.

———. 1990. Mistress, Mother, Visionary Spirit. In *Religion in Native North America,* ed. Christopher Vecsey. Moscow: University of Idaho Press.

———. 1991. *Lakota Naming: A Modern-day Hunka Ceremony.* Kendall Park NJ: Lakota Books.

Powers, William K. 1977. *Oglala Religion.* Lincoln: University of Nebraska Press.

———. 1980. The Art of Courtship among the Oglala. *American Indian Art* 5(2):40–47.

———. 1982. *Yuwipi: Vision and Experience in Oglala Ritual.* Lincoln: University of Nebraska Press.

———. 1986. *Sacred Language: The Nature of Supernatural Discourse in Lakota.* Norman: University of Oklahoma Press.

———. 1987. *Beyond the Vision: Essays on American Indians.* Norman: University of Oklahoma Press.

———. 1990. *Voices from the Spirit World.* Kendall Park NJ: Lakota Books.

———. 1992. Les Premieres Contacts entre les Francais et les Sioux: Temoinage d'un Ethnologue Adopte par les Indiens. In *Destin Croises: Cinq Siecles de Recontres Avec les Amerindiens,* ed. Joelle Rostkowski and Wilcomb Washburn, 249–261. Paris: Editions Albin Michel and UNESCO Press.

Powers, William K., and Marla N. Powers. 1984. Metaphysical Aspects of an Oglala Food System. In *Food in the Social Order*, ed. Mary Douglas. New York: Russell Sage Foundation. Also published as *Sacred Foods of the Lakota*. Kendall Park NJ: Lakota Books. 1990.

———. 1986. Putting on the Dog. *Natural History* 95(2):6–16.

———. 1994. Lakota: A Study in Cultural Continuity. In *Portraits of Culture: Ethnographic Originals*, ed. Melvin and Carol Ember. Englewood Cliffs NJ: Prentice Hall.

Walker, J. R. 1917. The Sun Dance and Other Ceremonies of the Oglala Division of Teton Dakota. *Anthropological Papers* (American Museum of Natural History) 16, pt. 2.

Young Bear, Severt, and R. D. Theisz. 1994. *Standing in the Light: A Lakota Way of Seeing*. Lincoln: University of Nebraska Press.

6

Naming as Humanizing

Jay Miller

Before the age of ten, I had lived among Native peoples of the Northeast and Southwest, fascinated by their differences and outlooks. Bolstered by family ancestry among the Lenapes (Delawares), I decided on a career in anthropology. By conscious choice (and lack of full-time teaching), I have always availed myself of any contacts with Native Americans in whatever locale I happened to be.

Although I might have joined any number of scholarly organizations, I soon realized that meeting more and more anthropologists, particularly non-Americanists, would drain energies from more rewarding pursuits. This attitude became entrenched after I met Viola Garfield, who informed me that her lifework among the Tsimshians, Tlingits, and by extension other American Natives "was not fashionable anymore in anthropology." Disparaged by a smug if global anthropology, what follows will require some effort and obfuscation to satisfy cross-cultural considerations of privacy, shame, and secrecy.

After decades of research, I now realize there is much more to naming than just names, which remain intensely personal. Instead, nicknames, anecdotal references, and kin terms are more likely to be used and heard in conversation or address, depending on the people and places involved. Nor, of course, are any of these usages fixed. A proper human should and will have available a series of these cross-references over time, as long as life is lived with vigor and prestige.

In my own case, my names have not so much changed as they have accumulated. While it may appear an embarrassment of riches, my adoptions, indicated by four Native names and two kinship statuses, actually represent limited responses, based on notions of our common humanity, to a variety of situations and contexts.

From earliest childhood I have never been without a Native name, although the bestowals became much more public and formal as I grew up. In every generation, Natives are dismayed again to discover that they have been "rediscovered" by anthropologists and others who thought that Natives were somehow "all gone." These adults only came to realize that Natives still lived, and even thrived, after taking college courses or being exposed to local reservations. While elders may be amused by their repeated "discovery," they are nonetheless also astonished that anyone would have the poor manners to admit to such ignorance in public.

Indeed, Native and mainstream networks are often so distinct that individuals can grow up near a Native community but have no awareness of its members. I well recall a Jesuit, who served several decades in Native churches, declaring that he grew up near a huge reservation but, for all he knew as a child, "Indians might as well have been on the moon." By contrast, the only professionals I know who grew up knowing about Indians were members of scout troops who earned merit badges in the subject. A few who lived near reservations might actually visit, with mixed results, or get help from nearby elders when making their powwow outfits for these badges.

I never was in such a situation, always living near and with Native peoples. My family lived in the mainstream but insisted on an all-consuming tolerance. Thus, as a babe in the Hudson Valley, it was not particularly amazing that my first informal Native name was Mohawk, even though my family sympathies are with the Lenapes (Delawares), who never were kind to the Iroquois.

I received my name from a Mohawk woman who ran a store where I bought craftswork and supplies. She wanted to encourage my ongoing interests. Once she was visited by Tuscarora chiefs who were trying unsuccessfully to prevent the flooding of part of their reservation near Buffalo by a New York utility company. They were remarkably kind to me.

Later, in New Mexico, my nickname, derived from Spanish, referred to my eyes, which sparkled in greater intensity whenever people delighted me with joking anecdotes about tribal traditions. Having heard about the "job" from family members, I always wanted to be an anthropologist because they were "concerned with" Native peoples, but as an undergraduate I had trouble deciding whether I wanted to be an archaeologist, a linguist, or an ethnologist. Of course, at that time, professors teaching about Pueblos, especially Florence Hawley Ellis, did all this and more, so I was initially encouraged to generalize to the best of my ability.

Unfortunately, specialization has since led to fragmenting provincialism, cutting southwesternists off from the unified (once professional as well as native Pueblo) tradition that had kept that region in the forefront of Americanist research. Somehow, I became a symbolic anthropologist, concerned with both artifacts and ideas. But my dissertation was a synthesis of the published record, not based on sustained fieldwork.

I gave my first professional paper in Long Beach, California, where I happened to sit next to a linguist who had just finished his own dissertation on Delaware grammar. He told me that the premier Delaware speaker would shortly be in New Jersey, where I was then finishing graduate school (Miller 1974b, 1979). As a strong upholder of Lenape culture, she was also one of the few remaining name givers, sanctified to do so by a series of visions.

DELAWARES

A few weeks later, I went to the conference where she was a featured guest and waited for a chance to speak with her. As I leaned against the wall, someone in the mob surrounding her asked for a particular Lenape word, which she spoke but claimed to be unable to write. I walked over and offered to do so, based only on my linguistic classes rather than any knowledge of Algonquian. There were people at the conference who could have done the transcription, but they were not present at that moment.

When she thanked me, I gave her greetings from the linguist I had just met in California, further convincing her of my seriousness. When I asked to work with her on "ethnoscience" paradigms of the Delaware cosmos, she agreed and gave me directions to where she was staying. Moments later I met other members of her family, who took requests for such interviews as expected, based on her fame and dedication. For several nights thereafter, I began collecting data that later appeared in publications. At the end of that conference, she conferred a name on a man who had been visiting and writing to her as he finished a massive history of the Delawares. During one of our nightly sessions, she took time to describe how and why she qualified as a Delaware name giver and told me what was required to receive a name from her, along with membership in her own Wolf clan if the person did not already belong to a clan. When I was collecting kinship schedules, she insisted that the word for friend be included because, over time, a good friend became a relative; there was no middle ground.

Under her direction, the three Delaware clans whose emblems were Wolf, Turkey, and Turtle began to make sense to me. Since the 19th-century writings of Moravian missionaries like John Heckewelder and a complicated list of 34 "clans" and "invented" marriage data given to Lewis Henry Morgan, Delaware ethnography has been confused. Localized and named lineages within a clan-owned town, to judge from comparative northeastern data, characterized their homelands, yet all were subsumed under the three animal categories also shared by Mohawks, Oneidas, and Mahikans (Miller 1973a, 1973b, 1974a, 1974b, 1975b). Fortunately, for my own future scholarship, the Wolf emblem was one of the most widely known.

As I was moving to a job in Seattle, I stopped off in Oklahoma to continue my research, then returned for several summers thereafter. Whether or not I had funding, I always helped out with food and labor. When her new HUD house was being built, I joined with family members to do "sweat equity" to help make up her share of the purchase price.

In all, then, my naming and adoption were predisposed on the basis of both natal and personal inclination along with existing cultural rules. What distinguished it from others, handled more informally with a dinner and brief ceremony around an outside fire, was that she had invitations typed out in Lenape for a family party that specifically mentioned my naming. Afterwards I was given the firestick used during my naming as a solid token to serve as a reminder.

Each Delaware name is only first announced in public at its bestowal so there seems to be no preparation or instruction involved. Yet once I heard my new name and its translation, I realized from which of her visions it had come. Nothing was ever said in explanation, but

I did hint at what I understood. Certainly, the high regard we had for each other and the kinds of information she was willing to share with me, sometimes specifying that it not be published, indicate our degree of kinship.

My "clan mother" was a bright and talented woman who would have gone to an Ivy League college if the Indian agent had not denied her access to her own funds. For years she had been helping scholars work with her well-informed, fluent parents and other elders. Unfortunately, these were mostly historians who were asking for clarifications about names and events in the past. I was interested in what she knew and went about it in a thorough fashion. She delighted in giving declensions and conjugations because she liked things orderly, so ethnoscience appealed to her (Miller 1975c, 1977). Later, when I focused on the Gamwing, Big House Ceremony (Miller 1980, 1991a, 1991b), the major historical beacon for Delaware identity, she was delighted to share a joint publication of her own memories of this important rite (Miller and Dean 1978).

Of note, Delaware personal names were only said in public during the special summoning rite within the Gamwing; otherwise they were rarely mentioned and known only to immediate family and close friends. Indeed, close kinship within a matriline was based in part on knowing the names that had been given to its members. So closely linked were names and identities that its misuse was the primary focus of malevolent sorcery. Delaware names remain closely guarded and private, ready to be changed when danger threatened that person (Miller 1975a; Weslager 1971).

TSIMSHIANS

My Tsimshian name, as described (Miller 1984) for a brief time when it "should be mud," was given in recognition of goodwill badly expressed. While an undergraduate in New Mexico, I had taken classes using Tsimshian examples, before married friends went off to do fieldwork on this language in British Columbia. Later, in Seattle, Viola Garfield, who had made the Tsimshians her life work, became a friend. Thus, it was fairly easy to ask for and receive a letter inviting me to visit one of the more remote villages, where I began fieldwork while living in the home of a chiefly family who worked as local schoolteachers. Kind hosts very concerned with education, they gave me much help and direction (Miller 1997).

For several years I came to the village during the week between Christmas and New Year when all of the feasts of the three resident crests (matriclans) were concentrated, staying in their sometimes crowded home. I helped out as much as I could, mostly with house-keeping, although we did go clamming by lanterns one pitch-black night, traveling on a fishing boat in conditions that could have been terrifying if I had allowed a little imagination to intrude.

Because Viola, Franz Boas, and others had researched in the trad-ing and mission communities that attracted Native people from all over, I was anxious to work in the village of a single tribe where tradi-tions would be less confusing. This decision proved correct when it became clear that the Tsimshian four crests (Orca, Raven, Wolf, and Eagle) which seemed to set them apart from the moieties (Raven/ Eagle-Wolf) of the neighboring Tlingits and Haidas did not occur in this village. Instead, there is a more moiety-like system of Orcas/ Eagles, with the Ravens more like in-laws and the Wolves virtually absent.

In my eagerness to please my hosts, I made an innocent mistake. On my way out of their home to the community hall for a Orca feast, I came upstairs through the kitchen at the moment when one of the glass cups of junket (Jell-O in America) proved to be more than the tray could hold. I scooped it up and offered to take it to the hall, feel-ing that I was doing my part as a guest.

When I got to the hall, however, the formal ushers who guided people to their seats thought otherwise. The cup was obscured, tucked into my hand, as I carried it to the table where the wife in the house where I was staying would be hostess. I set it down, but it was the lone cup of junket on the table. Because I was "safe" as a visitor from an-other country miles away, I became an example in the moral respon-sibilities of hosts and guests. By bringing my own "desert," I was act-ing like a host and not like a guest. At the end of the evening, my bad behavior was singled out in a speech (Miller 1984).

Mortified, I chose to respond by supplying the next year's feast with quantities of Jell-O mix, sent carefully across the border, since it was a white powder in six-pound cans.[1] The weather was bad, so I could only fly into the village on the day of the feast, when everyone was unusually reserved. Later, during the feast, my name was bestowed by the chief assisted by the local nurse and a visiting linguist.

The name was not a traditional one; rather, it was a word for a kind of person that was mentioned in the text of a famous Native song in which a chief longed for someone to write down his tragedies and triumphs. The song belongs to the Eagles, who loaned the name to the Orcas, since it was appropriate for my activities as a frequent scribbler. The actual form of the name seems to have shifted, since the term I wrote down at the time "constantly writing" has become variously "stick that marks, pencil, writer, historian," which is much better known and easier to pronounce. However, with the publication of my single volume on the Tsimshians (Miller 1997), the original full form has come back into use.

My prior Delaware name was not taken into consideration, but in the North Pacific region, wolves and orcas (also called blackfish or killer whales) "go together." In legends, the same being takes the form of a wolf on land and an orca in the water. Since both are social carnivores in packs or pods, this makes good biological sense. Moreover, this equation gave me insight into the nature of Tsimshian semi-moieties of Orca-Wolf or Raven-Eagle that allowed them to be matched with the moieties of Haidas and Tlingits (Miller 1978, 1981a, 1981b). In regional context, John Dunn (1984), also well known in this village, further explored this matching to show a Macro-Crow system for the whole northern coast.

It is noteworthy that, though remote, this village remains widely known for its friendliness and economic success. Its educated elite have welcomed scholars from all over the world. Those outsiders who marry in and have children acquire proper hereditary names from their house of adoption, while others, like ministers, teachers, and the crew of a missionary ship, have also been thanked with impromptu names.

Other anthropologists who were at that winter feast have treated, in print, my atonement and naming as a staged entertainment. "The joking relationship with outside observers at the feast creates a friendly edge around the community" (Seguin 1985:88). Yet the chief, who assumed full responsibility for the bestowal, and other families continue to treat it seriously (Miller 1997). I send yearly donations for the feast hosted by my crest clan and have helped perform its songs and dances with other members in public gatherings. Most important, since I received the name, my fieldwork has been curtailed to an interesting extent. I no longer have total access to the community because I am now identified with one of the four crests (the largest, though), its leaders, and its concerns. My appearances in public, on the boardwalks that serve as streets, on the beach, and in offices are unobtrusively monitored by other clan members to head off any possible "shame."

Before my naming, I would take buckets of empty shells or slops to the beach to be removed by the tide, making my unsteady way over obstacles. After my naming, I am carefully instructed in the best route to take and often sent along with a child to cover any mishap. Were I to fall in public, a feast would have to be held to help people forget my clumsiness. If I got seasick on a crowded boat or otherwise shamed myself, compensation would have to be made for my failings.

In all, by receiving a name, others have acknowledged taking some responsibility for me or at least my actions in public. I continue to help out in the house, on fishing boats, and in preparing food for storage, but I do so with an awareness that others are watching my movements with a certain sense of dread because I am not as well informed or coordinated as I should be.

Now, as a result, I learn more quickly from my mistakes. They have barely been committed before someone, often a tactful clanswoman, explains what I could do in the future to prevent a repetition. While people remained stoic and silent in the past, crest members now feel free to utter the single syllable (*la!*) meant to convey dismay at my feebleness.

My contacts remain best with the family of my hosts, but since they are well informed and well connected, this has been to my advantage. In fact, during a visit to another town with a dubious reputation, my host left a public message to indicate that I had friends nearby.

While a mixed blessing in terms of community access, my Tsimshian naming has allowed others to formally take me under their "fins," which is very beneficial when living in a coastal community and traveling by boats in a climate where the weather and the sea can quickly conspire against life.

Warned by my Tsimshian experience, I have maintained a very flexible stance among the confederated tribes of the Colville Reservation of north central Washington (Miller 1990). I keep close ties to the Miller family there, along with a few others, but I never received a name or special kinship status, in large part because I never expressed specific interest and, accordingly, have moved freely among several antagonistic families. Those Jesuits who have asked for Native names have received them, devised from Interior Salish compound words rather than passed down from particular families.

When I first went to Colville, I played a sensitive role as fieldworker and mediator between the Army Corps of Engineers and the tribal council. Researchers had been scarce for twenty years, so when I began to ask the oldest elders about specific people long dead, they had several discussions among themselves to figure out who or what I was. Several simply assumed that I was some kind of reincarnate coming back to check up on things, while a few merely regarded me as the guy who paid them for reminiscing. If these discussions had gone on, I am sure that the woman I was closest to, the grand dame of the community, would have found some way to provide a name that resolved all the ambiguities swirling around my status as a newcomer strangely familiar with their distant past.

Instead, what settled out was a status which Colvilles and other Plateau communities have developed over the past century. Most are Catholics tended by Jesuits with a fine sense of intellectual commitment and community involvement. In response to these priests and long-lasting friendships with Jesuit volunteers, Colvilles feel they have a special obligation to those outsiders who leave home to help them, especially under religious or church auspices.

Elders say they have to take care of such people because "their families gave them up" to a life of service in the missions. Since they have, in effect, no family in any sense meaningful to the Native community, these elders have a special responsibility to provide them with something like family support and encouragement. They feed, gift, clothe, and shelter such visitors whenever they can. Rather than being uniquely Catholic, this status blends Native concerns with the connectedness of kinship and religious desires to "do unto others." Elders write and phone absent parents, celebrate birthdays, and attend, when possible, the funerals of those kin for whom they have been stand-ins at Colville.

While not all of the elders who shared with me have been Catholics, the ones who have been most helpful have been active in the Church as deacons and prayer leaders. Thus, by foregoing a name in lieu of an immediately available position based on mutual respect and helpfulness, I have drawn upon community sources of information and insight. Most recently, when I testified for this reservation in federal court, I found that such broad-based experience also served well for dealing with the tribal council and its political contexts.

CREEKS

My Creek (Mvskogi) name came as a result of professional friendships in Chicago just before the Creek doctor of philosophy among us was to marry. An anthropologist specializing in Creek and Seminole politics had already been named at the ground, and he had been participating in the Green Corn Ceremony (known in the language as *Busk* from a term for purification) for several years. Fascinated by a chance to witness a rite perpetuated by descendants of a town mentioned in the 1540 Hernando de Soto chronicles, we agreed to meet in Oklahoma at the square ground. In particular, the other anthropologists among us were concerned to have our friend named so he could enter marriage as a full adult. His family belonged to a Christian church and had avoided contact with the traditional religion.

The Creeks, along with the Cherokees, Choctaws, Chickasaws, and Seminoles (who were a Creek offshoot), had been forced to Oklahoma by President "Old Hickory" Andrew Jackson in the 1830s during the federal versus states' rights conflict in Georgia and the Old South. The actual history was much more complicated because advance parties, often wealthy Native owners of plantations with black slaves, had settled in Arkansas and Oklahoma decades before to avoid exactly this kind of racism, factionalism, and governmental pressure. They had, of course, moved onto lands already owned by tribes such as the Osages and Wichitas, further muddying the waters. The Cherokees, in particular, held a series of meetings with these long-resident tribes to smooth things out, which is more than U.S. officials ever did later on.

In their homeland in Georgia and Alabama, the Creek confederacy comprised city-states like the polis of the ancient Greeks. Each of these towns, called an *italwa*, was headed by a *mikko*, called a "king" by the British, with a staff of officials and advisers that were hereditary in certain matriclans. Everything was in turn divided into red or white halves, moieties representing war or peace. A white town was so painted and served as a refuge for all who could reach its shelter. Towns were ranked in terms of satellite hamlets, towns, and a "mother" red or white capital town.

As luck had it, when we were introduced to the Mikko, he too became concerned that our Creek friend was about to be married yet still had the uninitiated status of a child. To be fair, the functions of these traditional towns have been perpetuated among Creek Christians by membership in a Baptist or Methodist church, which included a camp for revivals and other gatherings that looks and acts like the family camps around the perimeter of the arbors and open square of each ancient town. Long active in Oklahoma Native affairs, our friend mentioned relatives, friends, and allies well known to the Mikko.

Finally, after some reflection and much talk on my part about "respect" for traditions, the Mikko decided to name and initiate the rest of the contingent visiting from Chicago. It was a kindness on his part to realize that we were close friends, so initiating only half of us could have been adverse to our bond. Once he decided, moreover, as novice members of the ground, we had to prove our own dedication by getting to work, along with all the other men, renewing the sacred precincts, rebuilding the fresh willow-roofed arbors, and adding to the town mounds, all with very little sleep. Meanwhile, women were cleaning their camps and cooking for all those who would attend as singers, spectators, dancers, or visitors.

Thus, on the strength of one member, three more of us were named and initiated on the very same day that we arrived. Other anthropologists had also been named at this town, some of them ill-behaved, along with other non-Creeks who had served faithfully.[2] In other words, the Mikko and town remained open to a somewhat diverse membership provided that those named behaved properly.

After receiving a name at a town, there is a probationary period of four years before full membership is given. Thus, every year until disrupted by internal dissention about the Mikko succession, we have fasted, danced, and feasted at the Green Corn Ceremony, contributed money, and gotten legal and tribal advice on various matters. Attending the Busk has become an annual homecoming to Oklahoma for all of us, based on an emotional bond blending suffering with service.

TEWAS

My most recent naming involved three of us, administrators at a library who provided the funds to bring Pueblo musicians to an exhibit opening on a cold January night in 1992. I quickly realized, based on childhood experience, that one of them was a Native priest, who always made offerings from any food he was given. I warned my colleagues that we had a Native priest among us, but being urban cynics and historians, they remained obtuse to his special requirements. I had taken classes from a Tewa anthropologist and so had a limited vocabulary that included some esoteric terms. As I led them through the building, arranged for their needs, including white cornmeal for making offerings, and chatted about life in the Pueblos, we developed a friendship. Among the library holdings are a collection of watercolors done by a man from their own Pueblo, which I showed them while using correct Tewa terms for some items.

I do not know when it was decided to give names to the woman who coordinated the trip and provided the funds, to the man responsible for the overall project, and to myself. As luck would have it, the woman had been raised Catholic and so had a proper appreciation of ritual. The man, on the other hand, later held up the ear of corn used in his naming and asked, "What do I do with this?" Like the firestick from my Delaware naming, I treasure my own ear of corn, and I periodically feed it cornmeal, as expected.

These namings were held as part of the exhibit opening, at the bottom of the grand stairway surrounded by hundreds of guests from the Chicago Native community and others. All names referred to winter conditions, while mine also used part of the name of the Tewa artist whose drawings I had shown them, leading me to realize that the names had been bestowed because a ritual namer happened to be among the musicians and we were being reminded to "take care" of the Tewa items in our collection. It was a gesture that was not taken very seriously, except that when I later visited this Pueblo during a public dance, one of the musicians greeted me by my Tewa name and invited me to his home for a meal.

What was especially fascinating about this situation was that another Native man from a displaced Pueblo town had befriended these visitors, driving them around Chicago until he felt comfortable enough to ask if they would give him a name. His own ancestors had gone south with the Spanish after defeat in the 1680 Pueblo Revolt, yet they too were Tanoans. The visitors liked him because he was indeed kind and unassuming, but they said that he had to come to New Mexico before they would name him. Clearly, they held him to a more rigorous standard than those of us already protecting Tewa heritage in Chicago.

SKAGITS

Lastly, it should be noted that my closest working relationship, with the Lushootseed Salish of Puget Sound (Miller 1999), transcends the need for a name. Among my Skagit family, kinship terms are used, along with special designations, sometimes insulting, that vary by project. At first, I was "youngest child" in that family, then when I employed its elder while acting director of an American Indian studies program, I became "brother" or "little, younger brother," using proper Native kinship terms instead of English. When I have need of a Native name, I use my Tsimshian name, since, as another Northwest Coast nation with great prestige, Lushootseeds can appreciate my good fortune, even as they begrudge often invidious comparisons made by journalists with "those northern people."

The relationship is much more free flowing, especially since it has involved periodic disagreements and disruptions, than more formal fieldwork. I once went an entire year without contact because I was so enraged by their dismissal of a need for proofreading and scholarly rigors, yet I have also moved in with them when I was working very intensely on a project involving their own traditions (Miller 1988). Because I was there, answers came automatically and delays were minimized. My status may be attenuated at times, but, at its best, my membership is clear whenever something I have just learned was "only for the family to know" and thus unpublishable as such.

What is particularly fascinating about this cooperation is our different perceptions of what is important and constitutes "the best." For me, it is preserving a record, but for the grand dame of the family it is passing on traditions. She has moved from print to video because she knows tapes will more readily find a place in Native homes. Whenever new materials are found, she looks first to see if any names are mentioned, feeling that these are the most significant and useful parts of any text. Since names belonging to families are passed on in each generation, returning forgotten names to proper families is vital to her work. Indeed, at most gatherings, someone will stop her, explain who their ancestors are, and ask for any names that she may have on record. She supplies these to the family, calling it "archiving," because she believes that Native traditions are best preserved by sharing them along many appropriate channels (Miller 1985).

Naming is foremost a recognition of common humanity and kinship. Families name and rename their members, as do communities. By including someone neither born nor married into that family and community, naming indicates that that person is, in some sense, a kindred spirit (Miller 1992). Above all, it suggests that they conform to Native ideals about conduct and personality extolling those who are quiet, patient, respectful, and willing to be involved. By working in the native language, participating in native rituals, and helping as much as possible, a fieldworker can become identified as a sustainer of traditions, a resource for the community. Eventually, this support will be confirmed by adoption, either as outright naming or by professed kinship, to indicate mutual responsibility in an ongoing relationship, bolstered by contributions of money, labor, and time.

Sometimes virtually automatic mechanisms exist for taking in outsiders as new members, much as the Seneca Hawk clan has been adopting anthropologists since Lewis Henry Morgan or Colville Catholics replace the family that gave someone up to church service. Among the Mescalero Apaches, Claire Farrer (1994) reports that the more intensely she worked with their head shaman, the more that family indicated that she had to become either an affine or a sibling. In all cases, the insistence is that someone be fit into the existing system.

In the case of academics who have been adopted, there is also the intention that involving a Ph.D. in their activities and membership adds luster and public approval in ways understandable to mainstream society. Moreover, adoption involved the explicit obligation to "take care" of information, objects, and relationships in the same or a better manner than those doing the adoption. Indeed, the further removed from family or tribal control, the more important such adoptions are for the welfare of all. Thus, at the Chicago library, people who had already shown concern and some appreciation were taken into the fold as a courtesy and as a safeguard of Tewa materials already there.

Moreover, adoption need not be one way. As recognition of what the larger society thought was "proper" behavior and dedication, my Delaware clan mother had plaques and certificates from the governors of New Jersey and Pennsylvania naming her a "goodwill ambassador," my Skagit sister received an honorary doctoral degree and became a National Heritage Fellow (American "Living Treasure"), and several elders were elected to local and national historical societies. By helping others, they received symbolic tokens of their like-mindedness from various appropriate organizations.

In all, naming and adoption constitute a formal recognition of shared sentiments, along with a way of rendering other humans manageable and trustworthy. In close and caring societies where only your immediate kin can be fully trusted, while others are under suspicion for potential sorcery, you need all the relatives you can get.

NOTES

1. When I innocently went to mail these cans to the village, I was given a customs declaration that the postal clerk refused to accept. Who would mail that much Jell-O? A week later, academic friends from Canada took the cans across the border and mailed them to the village, where they arrived long before I did. While I waited for clear weather to get a small plane into the village, the "old ladies" took pity on me to make up cups of my offering.

2. In the most notorious example, a newly named anthropologist had taken a nap during the all-night green corn dance when sleep or rest is strictly prohibited. Rather than revoke the name, thereafter,

members of the ground watched this man to make sure he was always in view, awake, and alert for the entire final night.

REFERENCES

Dunn, John. 1984. International Matri-moieties: The North Maritime Province of the North Pacific Coast. In *The Tsimshian: Images of the Past, Views for the Present*, 99–109. Vancouver: University of British Columbia Press.

Farrer, Claire R. 1994. *Thunder Rides a Black Horse: Mescalero Apaches and the Mythic Present*. Prospect Heights IL: Waveland Press.

Miller, Jay. 1973a. Delaware Clan Names. *Man in the Northeast* 6: 57–60.

———. 1973b. Triads in Delaware Culture. *Bulletin of the Eastern States Archaeological Federation*.

———. 1974a. Why the World Is on the Back of a Turtle. *Man* 9(2):306–308.

———. 1974b. The Delaware as Woman: A Symbolic Solution. *American Ethnologist* 1(3):507–514.

———. 1974c. The Unalachtigo? *Pennsylvania Archaeologist* 44(4): 7–8.

———. 1975a. Kwulakan: The Delaware Side of Their Movement West. *Pennsylvania Archaeologist* 45(4):45–46.

———. 1975b. The Cultural View of Delaware Clan Names as Contrasted with a Linguistic View. *Man in the Northeast* 9:60–63.

———. 1975c. Delaware Alternative Classifications. *Anthropological Linguistics* 17(9):434–444.

———. 1977. Delaware Anatomy: With Linguistic, Social, and Medical Aspects. *Anthropological Linguistics* 19(4):144–166.

———. 1978. Moiety Birth. *Northwest Anthropological Research Notes* 13(1):45–50.

———. 1979. A "Struckon" Model of Delaware Culture and the Positioning of Mediators. *American Ethnologist* 6(4):791–802.

———. 1980. A Structural Study of the Delaware Big House Rite. *Papers in Anthropology* 21(2):107–133.

———. 1981a. Tsimshian Moieties and Other Clarifications. *Northwest Anthropological Research Notes* 16(2):148–164.

———. 1981b. Moieties and Cultural Amnesia: Manipulation of Knowledge in a Pacific Northwest Coast Native Community. *Arctic Anthropology* 18(1):23–32.

———. 1984. Feasting with the Southern Tsimshian. In *The Tsimshian: Images of the Past, Views for the Present*, ed. Margaret Seguin, 27–39. Vancouver: University of British Columbia Press.

———. 1985. Salish Kinship: Why Decedence? *Proceedings of the 20th International Conference on Salish and Neighboring Languages*. August 15–17. Vancouver BC.

———. 1988. *Shamanic Odyssey: A Comparative Study of the Lushootseed (Puget Salish) Journey to the Land of the Dead in Terms of Death, Power, and Cooperating Shamans in Native North America*. Anthropological Papers 32. Menlo Park CA: Ballena Press.

———. 1990. *Mourning Dove, a Salishan Autobiography*. Lincoln: University of Nebraska Press.

———. 1991a. Delaware Masking. *Man in the Northeast* 41:105–110.

———. 1991b. Delaware Personhood. *Man in the Northeast* 42(fall): 17–27.

———. 1992. A Kinship of Spirit: Society in the Americas in 1492. In *America in 1492*, ed. Alvin Josephy, 305–337. New York: Knopf.

———. 1997. *Tsimshian Culture: A Light Through the Ages*. Lincoln: University of Nebraska Press.

———. 1999. *Lushootseed Culture and the Shamanic Odyssey: An Anchored Radiance*. Lincoln: University of Nebraska Press.

Miller, Jay, and Nora Dean. 1978. A Personal Account of the Delaware Big House Rite. *Pennsylvania Archaeologist* 48(1–2):39–43.

Seguin, Margaret. 1985. *Interpretive Contexts for Traditional and Current Coast Tsimshian Feasts.* National Museum of Man, Mercury Series, Canadian Ethnology Service, paper no. 98. Ottawa: National Museums of Canada.

Weslager, C. A. 1971. Name-Giving among the Delaware Indians. *Names* 19(4):268–283.

7
Adopting Outsiders on the Lower Klamath River

Thomas Buckley

A friend thought her life was a mess and tried a little psychotherapy to straighten it out. She only went once. "He didn't have any stories!" she exclaimed indignantly. "How can anyone even live their own life if they don't have any stories?"

The Yuroks and their close Indian neighbors (Karuks, Hupas, Tolowas, and others) do not practice the elaborate public adoptions and name-givings of the farther Northwest Coast. There are neither clans nor lineages in the formal, structural senses usually intended by anthropologists (although extended families are sometimes called "clans" locally). There are no hereditary crests, and names tend to be a private matter. The very existence of a "Yurok Indian Tribe" was not accepted by most "Yuroks" until the 1990s when it was forced upon all by the federal government. No one has been "adopted into the tribe" in any widely meaningful way. There are, however, relatively enduring, loose associations of bilateral families, often intertribal, centered around ancient ceremonial districts: intricate networks that can have deep but fluid histories. Adoption of outsiders (whites or Indians, anthropologists and linguists or more innocent friends) happens within these fluid domains, and forms of adoption are suitably nuanced, processual, and outwardly informal.

Individuals adopt other individuals as relatives that they feel they need, to express shared sentiments and to achieve personal ends. Brothers, sisters, nephews, nieces, grandsons, and granddaughters and their reciprocals are often created in this way, but these adoptions do not necessarily generate wider kin ties.

At another level, however, an outsider can be brought into a residential group as a family member—a daughter, perhaps, who then has sisters and brothers and so on in that house, in addition to her adoptive mother.

Finally, a person might be adopted into an extended family. The adoptive daughter now has uncles and aunts, grandparents and nieces, nephews, and many cousins in addition to her kin in her adoptive mother's residential group.

The first two kinds of adoptions are sometimes extended, incrementally, the first to the second, the second to the third. Like adoption, marrying-in can create a broad, third-order web of extended kinship (which might extend to reciprocal uncle-in-law/niece-in-law relationships, for instance), but divorce can rend this web irrevocably and overnight.

The wonder of it is how widely and how rapidly the depth and breadth of a particular adoption becomes known throughout the far-flung Native community. There may or may not be a family gathering to announce an adoption (or a marriage). Simple public use of kin terms may suffice. Adoption is a process that radiates outwards from its center in individual sentiments to generate a consensus generally respected by the wider community. I think that this is part of what people mean when they say, "There's no love like Indian love."

One could go on about the many intricacies of Yurok adoptions— their implications for inheritances, for instance, or the ways they can interface with the ownership and dancing of ceremonial regalia. While I have said a bit about kin terms in the stories that follow, I don't intend these narratives to cover all possible ethnological topics arising from a scholarly consideration of adoption. They are, as much as anything, fragments of a still unwritten autobiography.

These stories are about three interlinked adoptions at three levels of the social system. At the end of the 19th century, Robert and Alice Frank were adopted into a large, widely extended family, the Spotts. Harry Roberts was adopted into a smaller residential group of Spotts in the village of Requa, California, in the early 20th century. I was adopted by Harry, as an individual and as a nephew, toward the end of that century. These three adoptions cover the range of possible Yurok Indian adoptions that I know about.

Captain Spott of Rek´ʷoy and Omen Hipur was an ambitious man of no mean talents, with the high self-regard of a real gentleman, *numi pegerk*, "an independent man who others can depend on." His enemies said he was *syałew*, "just rich," but no one could deny that he was a boss, *poyweson*, and however they felt, he was indeed learned, *teno·wok*, well educated in ancient ways. It is uncertain just when the Captain was born, but it was a few years before the California gold rush brought a massive and sudden influx of white men into the Klamath River drainage.[1] Captain Spott's father was from house Haʔagonor at Omen Hipur, downstream at the Tolowa end of the world, and his mother was a doctor from house Wonau, in Rek´ʷoy. Like this town poised on the north bank of the mouth of the Klamath River, on the Pacific Coast, a crux of the world, the Captain could have expected to be of some consequence among both Nrʔrnyrs and Puliklahs, coastal people and people of the lower Klamath. But there was a problem.

His father and his mother came from respected houses, and by the time they wanted to marry, his mother had enhanced her own prestige considerably by becoming *kegey*, a doctor. Being a doctor is a two-sided thing, however. Her lover from Omen Hipur could not pay her bride price—or perhaps her father would not accept any offer—because her earning potential as a doctor made her too valuable to her father's family. The doctor and the man from Omen had a baby anyway, and the child was born disgraced—*ka·mu·ks*, a bastard. He lived at house Wonau in Rek´ʷoy, with his mother's family.

The baby grew up to be the Captain, not one to let the circumstances of his birth get him down. He was determined to work his way back up. He was ambitious, and by the time he was seven, I've heard, he had made a small bow, shot birds for their feathers, and put these feathers away carefully in a wooden box. He was already a hunter and, as far as hunting went, was recognized as a man, *pegerk*, at an early age.[2] He needed wealth, especially in its traditional forms—the scalps of pileated woodpeckers, obsidian blades, dentalium shells, rare hides, and so on, *oʔlekʷoh ci·k*, "Indian money," but also the gold pieces and silver coins that were increasingly recognized as wealth by the 1860s. White man money, *wo·gey ci·k*, was valuable in itself and good to buy dance regalia with respectable wealth. The young man from Wonau didn't turn it down. He started a freight service between Rek´ʷoy and Crescent City, 20 miles to the north, transporting the white men and their goods—and Indian customers as well—back and forth in heavy seas, running an oversized redwood river canoe with a partner, singing his ocean songs.

There are many stories about this time. One day when he had already established his leadership in Rek´ʷoy he was on the Crescent City docks and met the master of a coastwise packet from San Francisco. The white man introduced himself as "Captain Spot." The canoe stern-man, learning English, said "I am a 'Captain Spott,' too," and so Captain Spott he was, from then on. I don't know if this story is true.

Needless to say, the Captain was set on paying full bride price for his own wives. In time he became a rich man and increased his prestige further by dressing dance teams for the great dances. He could completely outfit a side of dancers at two jump dances going simultaneously in two places, upriver and down: an outstanding feat. He was a boss and a devout man. He played important ritual roles in the dances himself, but only to the extent that his low birth formally permitted: he had principles. He also had "a devil" they say, *ʔumaʔa*, "the mysterious thing," to defend himself against jealous rivals.[3]

Captain Spott married his first wife early, but it was only after struggling for six more years to accumulate the necessary wealth—clean money, not from blood money or gambling—that he was able to marry his second wife, Mary Ann, a high family young woman from house Wogwu (In The Middle) at Weċpus, a powerful town at the junction of the Trinity and Klamath Rivers. They were full-married but, alas, could not have children.

ROBERT SPOTT

Mary Ann had a brother, Weitchpec Frank, who had married a woman from a fine family at house Otsu, also in Weċpus, in a display of his own power, unafraid of being accused of marrying a relative. They had several children, including a daughter, Alice, and a slightly younger son, Robert Frank, born in 1888. Captain Spott adopted both of these children, and in 1903 they went downriver to live with him and Mary Ann in Rek´ʷoy, which by then was called Requa. Robert called the Captain his father.

Robert Spott, as he was called, became well known among whites after the First World War (in which he fought with distinction in France) as a spokesman for the welfare of the Yurok Indians in government dealings and as the anthropologist A. L. Kroeber's final great Yurok informant. Kroeber wrote of Robert Spott in the preface to *Yurok Narratives*, a volume that they published together in 1942,

> More than making Robert an heir, Captain Spott and [Mary Ann] exerted themselves to give him a thorough Yurok education in addition to the American one which the government provided at the Hoopa Indian School. Their efforts fell on fertile soil. Robert is endowed with an excellent memory, his natural inclinations are intellectual, and above all he is possessed of extraordinary sensitivity to the value of his native culture. . . . He knows as much, on the whole, of old Yurok ways and beliefs as the men of his father's and grandfather's generation. (Spott and Kroeber 1942:vii)

Undoubtedly, family solidarity and responsibilities played a strong role in these adoptions, but Captain Spott and Mary Ann's efforts didn't necessarily "fall" on arbitrary actors in a social structure. They put them out on purpose. It seems most likely that the Captain adopted Alice and Robert in part *because* he recognized them as "fertile ground" and because he needed heirs (by 1903 the Captain was already at least 60 years old) suited to inherit all of his wealth, the regalia, and the knowledge that went with it. Extraordinary himself, Captain Spott must easily have "spotted," as they say, these two other extraordinary beings. Adopting these children of real insiders, the Franks, people of good births and good marriages, also brought the Captain, an outsider by birth, a bit more inside and cemented trade connections at both ends of the river, at Wečpus (by that time, "Weitchpec") as well as Requa. The new family was closely bound by affection and respect as well.

True to the Captain's expectations, Robert Spott became *teno·wok*, a "well educated one," too: a "high man," very active in ceremonial and political spheres and "the most Yurok-religious of men," as

Theodora Kroeber called him (1970:157). But whether it was because of the indelible stain on his adoptive father's escutcheon, or because of his wealth and that which he had a right to borrow from upriver, or because Robert had problems with his sexual identity (though just whose problem it was remains unclear), or a combination of all of these, Robert was both respected and suspect, both inside and outside, like the Captain himself.

Whether Robert chose to remain largely chaste, as many of the old-time high spiritual people are said to have done, or whether (as an elder who had known him told me) he was, "well, homosexual," is a complex matter and especially hard to figure given the cultural presuppositions underlying the question itself. However so, in Requa and Weitchpec alike, Indian Time seemed to be coming to an end, ruptured by the white invasion and occupation and the tortuous dilemmas posed Native peoples by European mores and power. Just what should be presupposed, in the interests of survival, was no longer clear. Robert, like the Captain, was a man of archaic principles. He was exacting and made concessions to no one. He knew what he knew.[4]

What he said was that there were no longer any women in the world able to meet his standards for a wife, which he claimed were the standards of all real men since the beginning of Indian Time. Unmarried and without a direct heir, Robert came to be in somewhat the same situation that Captain Spott had faced and for a parallel reason. The Captain addressed his outsider's problem by adopting the children of insiders, for all that he may have chosen Robert more for this new heir's own outsider's gaze than for his insider's credentials. Robert did much the same. He adopted the son of a member of the élite. By now, however, in 1915, there had been a profound change in who held the wealth (increasingly, "white man money," wahgay cheek) on the Klamath: in who were the bosses. Robert adopted the son of an accountant at the salmon cannery in Requa as his nephew, wekcum.

KIN TERMS: AN ANTHROPOLOGICAL INTERLUDE

This term, *hekcum*, is referentially equivalent to the English word *nephew*, denoting the son of a sibling or spouse's sibling. In the same way, the Yurok *cimos*, "uncle," denotes a father's or mother's male siblings or the husbands of their female siblings. Traditional Yurok and contemporary Euro-American kin term systems are similar in these regards.

Captain Spott was Robert's *cimos*, uncle—his father's sister's husband—and Robert was the Captain's *wekcum*, his nephew. But the relationship became more complicated through the Captain's need for an heir which, in keeping with the high family ideal to which he aspired, would best be served by a first generation patrilineal descendent, a father's son. This was the formal adoptive arrangement agreed upon by Captain Spott and Weitchpec Frank, Robert's biological father.

The Spotts and the Franks remained close kin, friends and allies, and Robert remained attached to both families. Weitchpec Frank was not an anonymous progenitor but the scion of a great house, Wogwu, which remained Robert's house. While referring to Captain Spott as "my father," in English, Robert took Wogwu as his public Indian name, and correctly so. These relatively familiar complexities took, however, a less familiar twist.

Captain Spott and Mary Ann adopted Robert and his sister, Alice, in part so that they could transmit to them the cultural knowledge that they commanded, the survival of which they feared was jeopardized by the increasingly necessary acculturation of surviving Yurok people to white ways. However, there is an old pattern in Yurok society of uncles teaching their nephews, after puberty, rather than fathers teaching sons. People say that fathers are too emotionally attached to their sons to exercise the necessary stringency. In actuality, Captain Spott *was* Robert's uncle and an appropriate teacher for him, as well as his sociological father by adoption.

All of this is suggested, somewhat, by Robert's concrete grave marker above the old Spott house site in Requa. It reads, Spotts Robert Frank.

HARRY ROBERTS

The accountant's son whom Robert Spott adopted was christened Harry Kellett Roberts and when he met Robert as a young boy he took to him. Robert, perhaps recognizing Harry as another extraordinary one, paid Harry's father one Chinook salmon of remarkable quality for the privilege of adopting Harry as his "nephew." Much later I asked Harry why his uncle, Robert Spott, was buried as "Spotts Robert Frank."

"Was the Captain's name really Spotts?" I asked.

"Oh, that's easy," said Harry, who had adopted me as his own nephew. "When Robert was in the army, he got used to hearing last names first—'Spott, Robert.' The people who made that marker didn't know punctuation. There should be a comma after Spott."

"But it isn't Spott," I reminded Harry: "it's Spotts."

"That's what I told you," Harry said. "They didn't know punctuation. There should be an apostrophe in it, because Robert belonged to the Spotts."

Did he belong to the Spotts or with the Captain? Or both?

Probably the inscription was intended as "Spott's Robert Frank." There are precedents for this, like the name "Tom's Pete," a young warrior who accompanied Captain Spott and 17 other Yurok men when, in 1889, they went to the Indian Service Station in Requa to complain about their treatment by a non-Indian entrepreneur (Sgt. La Foret to commanding officer, Ft. Gaston, May 8, 1889, U.S. Army Archives, Carlisle PA. Courtesy of Sally McLendon). But the Spotts are a family, not just an individual, and no doubt the first name on the marker has been read as "Spotts'" by some, as well as "Spott's."

Harry was Spotts Robert Frank's, Robert Spott's, Wogwu's spiritual heir (this hardly exhausts the names Robert Spott bore). Harry's biological father, Harry C. Roberts, was as Irish as they come (despite the persistent rumors of some connection with the Franks, of Weitchpec). His mother, Ruth Kellett, never acknowledged her Seneca maternal grandmother who seemed best forgotten in Ruth's pursuit of respectability in turn-of-the-century Bay Area society, around San Francisco, where being any part Indian was not a paying proposition. Harry, their only child, was probably born in 1906.[5] He had bright red hair, which led the Indian workers in his father's cannery to call him *kokonew*, "woodpecker," and to let him hang around, to bring them gambling luck. His playmates in Requa called him Hr´k^{w}r, "rabbit," word-play on "Roberts," but his uncle Robert Spott called him "Harry" and, when gravity demanded it, "nephew," which he pronounced "naaphew." Harry, in his turn, was to call me "naaphew" and, on occasion, "son."

The Roberts family had become close friends with Robert and Alice Spott and old Mary Ann, who survived the Captain by many years. They went to dances and camped together. Robert was a foremost spokesman in labor's dealings with management at the cannery, and Ruth and Alice did long and productive service together securing Yurok welfare both on the Klamath and in the Bay Area, where people from the river went to work and to appear in federal court regarding land allotments. Harry called Mary Ann "grandmother." Robert Spott was a natural "uncle" to Harry, as I called my own biological parents' best friends "uncle" and "aunt" as a child. But there was far more to it in Robert and Harry's case.

When Harry was a boy, he heard the First People making the Rek´ʷoy jump dance while he was playing beneath the rock *oregos* at the mouth of the river.[6] The spirit people were singing. Harry stayed until dark, learned the song, and then—after some careful thought—went to sing it for Robert Spott. Robert recognized it immediately. Although the dance had not been given in his lifetime, Robert had been trained as a jump dance medicine man and hoped to see the dance revived. They had been talking about it in Requa, but no one had gotten around to it, which is why the First People were making the dance themselves on the beach. As Captain Spott had recognized Robert Frank as "fertile ground" in which to sow the seeds of elite Yurok knowledge, so Robert now recognized Harry Roberts as a suitable heir to his own spiritual and intellectual heritage, according to Harry.

Robert needed an heir for various reasons. He had been put outside of the circle of real respectability by changing sexual mores. Again, putting his perceived homosexuality aside, at that difficult time there were not many young Indian men eager to work for the knowledge that Robert Spott commanded or whose survival-minded parents would allow it (remembering that these youngsters were to become the "shorthair" or "missing generation"). And Robert had the highest standards—was, like his adoptive father, a man of strict principles. In light of all of this, Robert had been unable to find a suitable student to teach what he had learned from the Captain and the other old notables of his boyhood, real men like Old Kerner and Sregon Jim who "thought and thought" about things and knew what to say if a young man came to ask a question.[7] While Robert had found some satisfaction in trying to teach the ethnologists who came up from Berkeley— A. L. Kroeber, T. T. Waterman, E. W. Gifford, and the others—he had found them to be slow learners. When young Harry Roberts came to him singing a jump dance song in spirit language, Robert understood that the solution was at hand. He liked Harry, and so much the better if, like the "white doctors," Harry was an insider to the emergent power structure.[8] He was the son of well-to-do, respected people, as Robert himself had been. As Captain Spott enhanced his prestige by adopting up, as it were, so did Robert, securing new ties with the dominant houses, which were now the houses of white people.

Again, of course, there was a distinct difficulty. Harry's being for all intents and purposes white placed him outside much as the Captain's illegitimacy and Robert's perceived homosexuality excluded them from the highest ranks of the Yurok elite. The house name to which Robert clung, Wogwu, "In the Middle," was both a claim to spiritual attainment and a statement of unrealized social aspiration as much as a birthright. By the same token, Harry's training under Robert Spott was to leave him, not in the middle of society, but in between white and Indian worlds, an outsider to both, as perhaps Robert knew it must. To whatever extent, Robert recognized Harry as one who could stand the loneliness that was the price of his inheritance, a born outsider like the Captain and like Robert Spott himself.

Robert trained Harry seriously for about 15 years, until the mid-1930s, when Harry left Requa to seek his fortune in the Bay Area—a move that many Indian people were making at that time, too. By then Harry, the anthropologist Dale Keith Valory wrote, had become "the last to be formally trained and initiated as a high class Yurok man" (1968:2). It is a statement that is somewhat misleading, having been written in 1968 when talk of the last this and the last that was still common among anthropologists and the fantasy of the White Indian was newly popular. However off the mark Valory's claim may have been, there is no doubt that Harry Roberts became an "all-grown-up man" like Robert and like the Captain before him, and well educated, too, with a thorough Yurok education.

Like all "real men," Harry was both independent and dependable. He was deeply spiritual in his orientation to the world and commanded great traditional esoteric acumen, though Harry was actually less an intellectual, like Robert, and more a man of action, like the Captain. Perhaps it was the solidarity of alternate generations. Along with his high, spiritual medicine and his knowledge of Indian law,

Harry was a warrior and could move, as the old-timers said, "just like lightning."

MYSELF

Now, moving like lightning is not something that you can fake. I only saw Harry do it once—when he was an old man on crutches, by the way—but that was because I was only with him in a situation that called for it once. I know that he could have done it anytime, "every time, on purpose," as he said a real man did everything that he really knew how to do. I know that he did have that old-time Yurok knowledge, too, because I spent many years going around to other elders checking out Harry's information. And I know that he was spiritually a profoundly developed man, although this is by far the aspect of my understanding of my late uncle least subject to empirical verification. Harry had learned from Robert Spott and others; he was indeed new "fertile ground" for a Yurok education.

At the time I met Harry Roberts in 1970, 30-some years later, he was living in poverty with a young wife, his fourth. He had had a long and rousing go of it after leaving Robert and Requa, making a living as a logger and commercial fisherman, a heavyweight boxer, precision machinist, ballroom dancer, horticulturist, and just about everything in between. By 1970, though, he had had a run of bad luck and was ill and isolated and, not so much for his own sake as for his new wife's, looking for a way back in among people who might appreciate his knowledge and experience, and looking for an heir, his two sons having moved away from him.

This was a moment that found Native California poised on the brink of a great and lasting renaissance of Native ways that built during the mid-1970s, came into flower in the 1980s, and today bears rich fruits. The Native children of the short-haired generation have come home to claim their own ancient world, reinventing it when necessary. But 1970 was too early. Ten years later, Harry probably would have found more than one dedicated Yurok Indian student among the many younger people who became determined to reclaim their heritage, in the 1980s, and began seeking out the few remaining elders who had hung on to old ways during the hardest years. As it was, Harry ended up with me.

At the time I was working in San Francisco as a writer and photographer and studying Buddhism under my first teacher, the late Sunryu Suzuki. I heard about Harry through a mutual friend and went to visit him where he was living then, in Sonoma County. He asked me what I wanted and I told him that I wanted to "go home." We understood each other pretty well from that first day on and, in a way that would probably not be made any more clear by explanation, understood that we belonged together, though I had not thought much about American Indians one way or another before then. After Suzukiroshi died in 1971, Harry adopted me as his nephew and my son as his grandson, and began teaching me in earnest.

I studied with Harry until his death in 1981. In fact I continue doing so, listening for his voice within myself when I'm considering a difficult question, much as Harry used to listen for Robert's voice during the long nights we spent together, smoking tobacco and studying "the law" and the world, "creation." (Like everything, Harry taught, independence has two sides.)

He had moved back up to the Klamath River 1972, going home. It was Harry who sent me off to finish college and become an anthropologist, "to set the record straight on the Yuroks," he said, and to get me away from the mouth of the river where I had beached after a stormy divorce and was probably headed for more trouble—yet full of *hauteur*.

"Why don't you become a bishop?" he asked one day, laughing.

"But, Harry, I'm not a Christian."

"Well, then, be a professor. That's about the same, and you seem like you might be a teacher, to me."

"What would I teach?"

"Why don't you become an anthro? You like Indians." Just then a rich uncle, my deceased father's eldest brother, died and left me enough money to go back to school.

Of course, by the time I finished my bachelor's degree in 1975, married another good woman in 1979, and got my Ph.D. in anthropology in 1982, writing a dissertation on Yurok worldview change, the postmodern critique (to which I was to contribute) was suggesting in no uncertain terms that setting ethnographic records "straight" was not at all the self-evident task that A. L. Kroeber—the last anthropologist to try it in the Yurok case—had assumed. Meanwhile Harry Roberts, whom I had loved as the father I had lost too early, had died in 1981. A new generation of Yurok and Hupa, Karuk, and Tolowa Indian intellectuals and artists and spiritual people had begun restoring the great dances (including the Yurok jump dance at Pecwan) and were also publishing books, holding symposia, curating museum shows, and generally taking charge of their own cultural affairs again. Usually I find a warm welcome among them.

Like the Captain, Robert, and Harry, however, my welcome is a bit constrained: the Captain a bastard, Robert a "two-spirit," Harry a white man and me, not only white but an anthro. Yet even anthros can have families, lineages that soften sharp boundaries across time, voices to listen for and smile to hear. When it's time for people to think about a tombstone for me, I'd just as soon they'd let it read, "Roberts Thomas Buckley." No apostrophe.

NOTES

1. The first three months of 1850 saw a sudden influx of 10,000 whites into the Klamath River drainage. A. L. Kroeber put Captain Spott's birth "around 1844," whereas Arnold R. Pilling placed it ca. 1821— a considerable difference (Spott and Kroeber 1942:147; Pilling field notes, 1968). Pilling gave 1911 as the year of the Captain's death, which is accurate, and people had told Pilling that the Captain was about 90 when he died; certainly he seemed older than 67 and, in terms of cultural change during his lifetime, he was. Still, Kroeber's birthdate is probably the more accurate.

   For more on Captain Spott, an outstanding man of his generation, see Spott and Kroeber (1942:144–152) and Kroeber (1976: 419–420).

2. Here and below, Captain Spott's story bears striking similarities to the Yurok myth of "The Inland Whale." I don't know whether Robert Spott's definitive rendering of the narrative in English (Spott and Kroeber 1942) reflected his adoptive father's life, or whether the various renderings of that life I draw on here reflect the myth, or to what extent both of the above are true. But the similarities are obvious (see also T. Kroeber 1959).

3. This mysterious thing, ʔumaʔa, a "devil," is putatively a small kit of

miniature poison arrows with which a sorcerer, or "devil" (also ʔumaʔa) introjects a telogeł, "pain," into the body of his victim from a distance, "deviling" him. These arrows are associated with obsidian, rattlesnakes, and fire. The bundle itself may blaze with mystic heat, seem unnaturally heavy, and stink. A person who owns one is said to "have a devil." Some say that Captain Spott's adoptive daughter, Alice, threw his ʔumaʔa away in disgust after his death and that it was enveloped in a fiery ball as she did so.

4. Same gender sexual and affectional preferences were certainly known among Yuroks in the past as they are today, although the English term *homosexual* carries cultural connotations that do not necessarily represent Yurok individuals with these preferences accurately.

    There were largely celibate "priests," some of whom may have had, nonetheless, same-gender sex. (Such men were also known to act as secondary inseminators of pregnant women, however.) There were certainly transvestite men, *wrgrn*, who did women's work, like basket weaving. Some but not all *wrgrn* were "homosexual"; some are known to have married women. Whatever the intricacies of sexual identity in the past, in the 20th century homosexual men have been controversial figures—indeed, they are sometimes referred to as "controversials" today. Robert Spott was caught up in this controversy, the more so because he was knowledgeable about basket weaving—women's work.

    At the same time, "high men" like Robert were expected to command a considerable amount of women's knowledge, as female doctors and other female sociological "men," *pegerk*, commanded considerable male acumen. Alice Spott, Robert's sister, who had several husbands and many children, was highly respected as *numi pegerk*, "very much a gentleman." She was a hunter, canoe handler, and trained warrior.

    A full discussion of Yurok gender would be a large undertaking. In lieu of it, I choose to leave Robert Spott's sexuality ambiguous, as Harry Roberts did in our many conversations about his uncle.

5. Harry may in fact have been born in 1905, the date of his birth being advanced within his natal family to conceal a certain awkwardness in the date of his parents' marriage.

6. "First People" is a modern equivalent of the Yurok *wo·gey*, "ancient ones." These spiritual beings were here during the mythic time of creation; when they "went away," "Indian Time" began. (It ended with the gold rush of 1849.) These first people have many English names: "angels," "unseen beings," "immortals," "Little People," "the spirituals," etc. Seeing or hearing them is not always profoundly portentous but it was in Harry's case—a sign that he had a "natural calling" to spiritual experience, the highest calling, more powerful than an inherited calling or one obtained by sheer will, through training.

   The Yurok lexical item *wo·gey* also came to mean "white man" after contact, as in *wo·gey ci·k*, "white man's money," United States currency.

7. In the early 1930s Robert Spott told A. L. Kroeber's student, Sylvia Beyer, that Sregon Jim (Yurok) had told him about the difference between a rich and learned man and a poor man lacking in the self-control that brought wealth: "Not every old man could tell [what Sregon Jim told me]. Some of them have been poor all their lives. All such men know is how to eat. When they have eaten enough, they go to sleep. In the morning they get up and want to eat more. That is how some of them do all their lives. Other men are not like that. They think and think, and want to know what they ought to do. If there is a boy in the house, they know what to tell him" (in Sylvia Beyer, untitled ms. on Yurok Indian doctoring, Kroeber Papers, carton 7, Bancroft Library, University of California, Berkeley, 1933–34).

   Robert Spott's identifying Sregon Jim as an "old man" is significant. Yurok men like Sregon Jim (or Captain Spott) did not customarily begin teaching younger men in a concerted way until they were in their mid-fifties, more or less. Boys and men trained hard from just before puberty until they were about 20, and then devoted themselves to family life and to making reputations in trade, politics, and ritual. The fruits of their training paid off when they were older and began attracting wealth through their earlier austerities (and through both inheritance and the bride-wealth paid for their daughters). It was at this time, in the general model, that their wis-

dom ripened and their teaching—often of adoptive nephews—
began in earnest.

Captain Spott, adopting Robert and Alice Frank when he was 59,
seems to have followed this pattern, as did Harry Roberts in adopting me when he was in his mid-sixties. Robert Spott's adoption of
Harry Roberts when Robert was only about 30 was unusual in
terms of this old pattern. Various matters seemed to have contributed to his decision.

First, Robert—as an intellectual, sexually ambiguous, and already having come into his inheritance from Captain Spott, in 1911
when Robert was 23—largely omitted the wealth-questing and
reputation-building segment of most men's lives. Second, the Captain, Robert's primary teacher, was gone and Robert alone, experi-
encing himself as the last of a line, was responsible (at however
early an age) for passing along the Captain's teachings.

8. The late Mrs. Florence Shaughnessy (Yurok) from Requa, where she
was Robert Spott's neighbor, called Kroeber and the others "those
good white doctors from Berkeley."

REFERENCES

Kroeber, A. L. 1976. *Yurok Myths*. Berkeley: University of California
Press.

Kroeber, Theodora. 1970. *Alfred Kroeber: A Personal Configuration*.
Berkeley: University of California Press.

Spott, Robert, and A. L. Kroeber. 1942. Yurok Narratives. *University of
California Publications in American Archaeology and Ethnology* 35(9):
143–256.

Valory, Dale K. 1968. Ruth Kellett Roberts, 1885–1967. *Kroeber Anthropological Society Papers* 38:1–9.

8

Tell Your Sister to Come Eat

Anne S. Straus

Making relatives is a common, creative activity in American Indian communities. It is important work because one's family is one's foundation, one's wealth, one's power, and a person without relatives has no "home," no secure place in the community. Marriage and childbirth are but two of the many ways in which relatives may be made. In English, we classify all the other ways of making relatives as "adoption," but adoption is not a unitary phenomenon. Minimally, adoption in Indian communities must be distinguished as tribal or familial, formal or informal.

On every reservation and in every Indian community, non-Indians as well as Indians from other tribes/communities have married into the community, had children, and raised their children as community members. There is no "pureblood" Indian community. Likewise, in every Indian community, "outsiders" have become relatives through adoption. These are not rare or surprising occurrences, nor are they recent or even postcontact phenomena: the process of turning strangers into relatives has been going on a very long time in Indian communities (Hall 1997).

Adopted members of a tribe or community may become key players in that community. During my early (1970s) fieldwork on the Northern Cheyenne Reservation, Teddy Wooden Thigh made this abundantly clear. Mr. Wooden Thigh was a respected elder in the tribe. He lived on the reservation and was married to a tribal member; he had children and grandchildren there. He spoke the old Cheyenne language, with little or no inclusion of English, and he was widely recognized within the tribe for his knowledge of Cheyenne history and traditions. He was a singer, a handgame player, and a "traditional" man. He was also white. According to the story, he was left in the proverbial basket at the door of the St. Labre Mission some 75 years ago, adopted by the Wooden Thigh family in accordance with long-standing tradition, and raised as a tribal member.

Teddy Wooden Thigh's adoption was a tribal adoption and must be distinguished from the kind of adoption experienced by anthropologists on the Plains. Formal adoption by the tribe must be sanctioned in the tribal constitution and determined by the tribal government. Such adoption confers enrollment and thus the legal and moral rights and responsibilities of tribal citizenship as well as "Indian" status vis-à-vis the federal government. Tribal adoption allows Indian communities to recognize legally those who have lived as members of the community but do not meet the "blood quantum" requirements of the tribe. It should perhaps be noted here that, despite *Santa Clara v. Martinez* (Supreme Court of the United States, 1978, 436 U.S. 49), which affirmed tribal jurisdiction over membership, the federal government has typically taken a pretty dim view of adoption clauses in tribal enrollment articles, refusing in at least one clear case (Grand Traverse) to ratify a tribal constitution because it allowed for the adoption of resident Native members of that community. Formal adoption by a tribe is politically charged, motivated, and mediated. It is an arduous process, unusual for Indian people and extremely rare for non-Indians. Teddy Wooden Thigh is the solitary exception in my own experience.

The adoption of anthropologists into Plains Indian families is specifically *not* tribal adoption; it does not grant formal tribal enrollment or Indian status. Those of us with extended family on some reservation or in some urban Indian community are not now and will never become "Indians" as a result of those relationships. Some of us have certainly suffered the throes of wannabe fantasies. Most of us have recovered. Perhaps the most common adoptions into Indian families are those which function to fill a void: a mother has lost her son in Vietnam and she adopts his best friend to fulfill his role and perpetuate his place and his memory; a child is orphaned by a car wreck and becomes "child" to his mother's sister and her family. Adoption of anthropologists into Indian families occasionally follows this pattern, but it is understood by everyone that the anthropologist is not really equal to the job.

Anthropologists working in Indian communities, at least since the late 1960s, have done so with a good deal of trepidation and a burdensome self-consciousness regarding their outsider status. We are already—as anthropologists—self-selected marginals. We arrive in the field, especially in the first fieldwork experience, very worried. The weight of history and political conflict sits heavily upon our backs, and the Great White Guilt envelops our souls. We are lonely because of this and almost expect to be treated poorly. We are grateful, extremely grateful, for any friendly overture. This preexisting alienation probably contributes to the intensity of connection and commitment that some of us develop with particular individuals, especially those who affirm the value of our own work and contribute significantly to it. In some sense those individuals liberate us from our own internal oppression, validate us, and give us back ourselves. Some such relationships become gradually acknowledged by and incorporated within the local family; some of those may result in adoption. Announcement by crier and a giveaway at some community gathering may formalize such an adoption, but the adoption itself is performed by the use of kinship terms.

In my own case, one afternoon, no different from any other afternoon, Josephine Sooktis, senior woman in the Lame Deer, Montana, household in which I lived and the mother to my close friend and colleague Rubie, simply instructed me, "Go call your sister to come eat." She didn't ask me if I wanted her daughter as my sister (and she already had two). She just decided it was time to acknowledge the bond between us and sanction it within the family.

I was, frankly, stunned. I neither sought nor anticipated having Indian relatives, and suddenly, in the space of that one word, I found myself with a whole new family. Stunned, of course, was not an appropriate reaction to express. I simply called Rubie to come eat. At that point, she did not even know that my own life had just changed.

I was "reinvented." I was a different person in some sense, because I now had a "sister" in Lame Deer. I had a family and thus a "place" in the community. I had agreed to do something—without being asked—and I did not even really know what it was. My life had changed. That much I did know. It was, as Harvey Markowitz (personal communication) says of his own adoption into the Horse Looking family of Rosebud, South Dakota, a life-defining moment. My future changed. Kin relations are for life and for the lives that come after. They may become burdensome, negative, or quiescent, but they cannot really be "unmade" once they are made. It was wonderful and frightening at the same time.

The ramifications of that moment are still presenting themselves some 25 years later. What, for example, about my relationship with the rest of Rubie's family, and what about her relationship to my family? My experience in this regard seems similar to that of others. Members of Rubie's extended family make occasional and what Joe Maxwell (1974) once called "tactical" use of kin terms. It is as though they have the option and certainly they have the initiative in evoking the relationship, and it is done rarely by most and irregularly by few. The greatest impact has been within the immediate household. In regard to my own biological family, my parents, now used to my strange ways, happily acknowledge my "family" in Lame Deer, but they have very little occasion to activate any relationship on their own. None of my three brothers has any real connection to or interest in my relationships on the Northern Cheyenne Reservation: one of them actively rejects any such notion. My husband is tolerant. He welcomes Cheyenne people into our home, and he visits Lame Deer with me, behaving himself appropriately and well. But his connection is always secondary, a derivative of my own. My children have all spent time in Lame Deer. They know and respect Rubie's parents, siblings, and nieces and nephews. My oldest child, Kala, takes those relationships quite seriously and has chosen to activate her own "family" ties. Her efforts have been reciprocated: her school picture lies alongside those of all the other nieces and nephews, and all the adults and elders in the immediate family have participated in her upbringing and have supported her in times of trouble. She has chosen to take the relationship seriously. In return, she is taken seriously and afforded a place in the family. My other children could do the same, but they have not as yet chosen to.

It seems that for other relatives in both families, there is no necessary relationship implied in the one I have with the immediate family. What is established is potential: there is no requirement for more than that. Recently, a young Menominee man in Chicago, son of the director of the Indian Center, announced to me that he had taken Kala as his sister. So my daughter has made relatives or has been made a relative as well. That has certain implications for me and for his parents, in regard to each other and our other children, but they are implications of potential and will be irregularly activated.

The network of my own relatives through adoption extends into the Chicago Indian community, even past the Menominee family. For more than twenty years, I have participated in various ways in that community and have informally established kin within it. In this case, it was I who "made" those relatives. I have many close friends in the community, but only one family with whom I have a negotiated kin relationship. One day, in frustration over my failed relationship with one of my natural brothers, I complained to Kermit Valentino, an Oneida man with whom I had a valued friendship, about that relationship and asked him if he would be my substitute brother. He agreed, which was especially generous for a guy who already has four sisters. Slowly, we have investigated and experimented with what that might mean. There was no defining moment, no conversion reaction, no new concept of myself here. The circumstances were different; the meaning is also different.

I have noticed that, as with the Sooktises, Kermit and I use kin terms in reference only. I have introduced Kermit to my Hyde Park neighbors as my "other brother." I introduced his wife to Ray Fogelson as my "sister-in-law," but I would not really think of addressing either of them using a kin term. Kermit occasionally refers to my kids as "his kids." He tolerates my referential use of kin terms in regard to himself and his family, but I am not sure I have ever heard him refer to me as his sister. It is likely he has not.

Now, as I have Indian relatives in two Indian communities, is there any relationship presumed between the members of those families? I do not know the answer to this as no Sooktises and Valentinos have ever met—at least to my knowledge. I have talked to Kermit about Rubie and her family, but I have not really talked much to Rubie about the Valentinos. I am not sure why, but it has something to do with the older and more firmly established relationship I have with the Sooktis family. Rubie will visit me in Chicago sometime and meet Kermit. Only at that point will I have any sense of whether they will feel any connection to each other. Again, there is a precondition, a possibility, but presently there is no more than that.

What about the impact of that defining moment on fieldwork? For those of us who consider ourselves Action Anthropologists in the tradition of Sol Tax and his students, fieldwork is community service as well as research. In this kind of fieldwork, there is always a kind of dynamic tension between the action work and the academic work. One does support and inform the other, but that is in the long term while, in the short run, you make daily decisions about how to spend your time, energy, and other resources (car, food, money). For me, at least, the acknowledgment and promise of long-term relations within the community strengthened my commitment to action, to the people. The "adoption" changed my feeling of connectedness to the community and, as such, my research interests and energies.

In some sense, although I did return to Chicago, I have remained "in the field." I have kept in close contact, and I visit regularly with the Sooktises. In Chicago, I did what many relocated Indians do, I guess, and found a kind of substitute community of urban people. The length of my "fieldwork"—that is, the endlessness or open-endedness of my fieldwork—is certainly part of the impact of the "adoption" upon me.

It is also clear to me that my close ties with the Sooktis family positioned and continue to position me within community politics. This position necessarily frames and limits my understanding of community issues and interactions. Actually, that was true before I called my "sister" to come eat: we all worked hard on the coal issue. In some sense, we won: there is no coal development on the Northern Cheyenne Reservation today. And the Sooktises are still paying the price with joblessness at best, violence at worst. The tribe was indeed between a rock and a hard place, and many people were in favor of development (Straus and Sooktis 1981). Factional differences established at that time are still recognizable today. In general, as Jeff Anderson (1994) has so cogently pointed out, the community splits along family lines on each and every issue. I have an expected position: if I happen to disagree with it (which is unlikely because the incoming information is filtered through the same network), I simply remain silent on it, at least outside the family; if I agree, I can do whatever I think of or am called upon to do to advance a position.

Clearly, this positioning influences what I experience and understand about the community. The tribal history I know best is the Dull Knife family version, because Josephine Sooktis is granddaughter to Dull Knife/Morning Star. Little Wolf family stories are different, although the tragedy of the trek from Oklahoma back to the Northern Plains is everywhere acknowledged. The sacred traditions I am most familiar with concern the Sacred Hat, as Rubie's father served for a while as its keeper. In regard to recent controversy concerning the proper care of the Sacred Hat, I, of course, understand the situation from what I have known to be his perspective, though the current keeper was also a friend of mine when he was a student at the St. Labre School. In this case, the extended family itself is divided, the family of Rubie's aunt on the one side, and that of Rubie's mother on the other. As these are not matters for public consumption, the people who talk to me about the disagreement and so condition my understanding of it are mostly Sooktis family members. What I know, then, and how I see things is framed and limited by my relationships to this family.

The particular instance of division within the family deserves further mention because it introduces a surprising possibility in regard to the adoption of anthropologists. While I am "positioned" as I have described, there is another "adoptee" differently positioned. Father Peter Powell, the remarkable historian and anthropologist who has been involved with the Northern Cheyenne people for much longer than I have, and who has written extensively on their sacred history and traditions (Powell 1969, 1979), has supported the current Sacred Hat keeper in many ways and has been a great source of strength to him. That is important for the whole tribe, whose well-being, as Father Powell himself has so eloquently demonstrated, depends upon the Sacred Hat. Two years ago, when the current Sacred Hat keeper and various other Dull Knife descendants sought the return of the skeletal remains from the Smithsonian, the Sooktis family and various others opposed the return. As they understood it, the particular remains were from the Ft. Robinson massacre of 1879, when Dull Knife's band of Northern Cheyennes broke out of their barrack/prison and continued their trek north in the middle of winter after having been deprived of food, water, and firewood. Most of the people died there at the fort. It seemed right that these remains should be brought home to the community and reburied there. However, in the Sooktis family view (which does not accord with the records), the victims whose bodies had been sent to the Smithsonian had been beheaded at Ft. Robinson, and the skulls remained in Nebraska.[1] To Josie and various others, it seemed unethical to rebury those bodies in Lame Deer, knowing they were incomplete. They sought to reunite the various remains and, failing that, not to disturb them. I was asked to look into the legal process of enjoining repatriation. Meanwhile, Father Powell was asked to play an important role in the ceremonies surrounding the return and the reburial.

None of this is unusual or especially relevant to our present concerns, although it does emphasize the point that your family affiliation always frames your understanding, and it suggests that those with greater independence might have a more measured view of the whole process. What is, to me, unusual and especially interesting in this network of relationships is that Father Powell and I have known each other since before I went to Montana. We respect, appreciate, and like each other. We have recognized our differences in these matters and addressed them ever so gently. In a strange way, we may provide a more positive link between the two branches of a family divided. It may be that this is the one and only time when such a configuration of relationships will obtain, and so it neither sets any precedent nor has any significance beyond our immediate situation. But it is certainly an interesting sequela of the adoption of anthropologists into Indian families.

I have tried, in this essay, to make a few points. First, adoption into a family is different from formal, legal adoption into a tribe. Adoption into a family always begins with and centers on a strong relationship between two individuals that is gradually sanctioned by the Indian family. As families are the basis of Indian communities, adoption into a family gives one a place in the community and a position with regard to community issues. Anxiety and alienation probably contribute to the emotional intensity of the adoption experience, which may become a life-defining moment. Adoption into a family certainly impacts fieldwork, leading to a shift or a clarification of purposes and priorities in "the field." The relationship between research and political action becomes very important as you seek to understand and express your commitment to the family and the community of which you are a part. Fieldwork is redefined. It is no longer a year or two in a long career. Now it is the career. You may move around and live somewhere else, but you never really leave the field. This is certainly a peculiarity of anthropology among Native North Americans, as it depends heavily on proximity and common experience of the anthropologists and the Natives.

Ethnographic perspective is both broadened and narrowed by adoption into a family. You are likely to learn things you would not otherwise learn, especially in regard to competing claims within the community, but you will learn them from your adoptive family and thus from a particular perspective. There are varying degrees and conditions of adoption, and the implications of adoption beyond the focal relationship vary widely. It is possible for the same person to experience different adoptions and different kinds of adoption, and it is possible that an independent relationship between different adoptees may impact relationships between two families or between two parts of the same family.

Finally, adoption into an Indian family, while it may be a seminal, life-defining experience for the individual anthropologist, is not a prerequisite to good fieldwork. It is also not the only sign of community acceptance or overall "good guy" status. Indeed, the non-Indian anthropologist who accomplished the most for Indian communities and sustained the strongest "good guy" image in Indian country, Dr. Sol Tax, was never adopted into any Indian family, although he had some very close relationships with Indians. Clearly, then, adoption must not be seen as either a prerequisite to or an emblem of effective research, action anthropology, or relationships with Indian people.

NOTE

1. The fact that the Ft. Robinson massacre took place only a decade after the 1867 surgeon general's order leading to the decapitation of hundreds of Indian skeletons for research purposes is relevant to this apparent misunderstanding.

REFERENCES

Anderson, Jeffrey. 1994. Northern Arapaho Knowledge and Life Movement. Ph.D. diss., University of Chicago.

Hall, Robert L. 1997. *The Archaeology of the Soul: North American Indian Belief and Ritual.* Urbana: University of Illinois Press.

Maxwell, Joseph. 1974. The Evolution of Plains Indian Kin Terminologies. Master's thesis, University of Chicago.

Powell, Peter. 1969. *Sweet Medicine: The Continuing Role of the Sacred Arrows, the Sun Dance, and the Sacred Buffalo Hat in Northern Cheyenne History.* 2 vols. Norman: Oklahoma University Press.

———. 1979. *People of the Sacred Mountain: A History of the Northern Cheyenne Chiefs and Warrior Societies, 1830–1979.* New York: Harper and Row.

Straus, Anne S., and Rubie Sooktis. 1981. Between a Rock and a Hard Place: Mineral Resources on the Northern Cheyenne Reservation. *Chicago Anthropology Exchange* 14(1–2):27–35.

9

Friendship, Family, and Fieldwork

One Anthropologist's Adoption
by Two Tlingit Families

Sergei Kan

ADOPTION OF EURO-AMERICANS: A HISTORICAL OVERVIEW

In the late 18th century, when the Tlingits first came in contact with Europeans, their social and ideational life was already ordered by the fundamental principles of moiety exogamy and the solidarity of matrilineal descent groups (clan, lineage, house). Among the various tangible and intangible possessions shared by clan relatives was a stock of names or titles solemnly bestowed on new recipients in the memorial feast (potlatch, _koo.éex'_) honoring the recently deceased previous owners of these names. So important were these divisions in their social universe that the Tlingits tended to divide the world of the non-Tlingits into those people who had clans and moieties and those who did not. Whenever they tried to establish an alliance with a group in the latter category, an attempt was made to assign its members to a clan and a moiety (de Laguna 1972:17–21). Usually when a non-Tlingit Indian married a Tlingit, he or she was assigned to the clan belonging to the moiety opposite that of the spouse and given a name owned by the adopted clan.[1]

To some extent this was also true of the first Europeans with whom the Tlingits came in contact. Although we lack solid evidence of Europeans being formally adopted into Tlingit kinship groups, we do know that nicknames as well as high-ranking titles were given to various newcomers, from the head of the Russian-American Company (Alexander Baranov) to fur traders and even missionaries (Kan 1999:67).[2] In some cases, these acts were clearly aimed at recruiting a powerful non-Native ally; in others they were expressions of friend-ship or gratitude.[3] In most instances it does not seem likely that the adoptee was expected to perform all the duties of a Tlingit clan member, especially to participate in potlatches. After all, this important Tlingit ceremony had been under attack by American missionaries, teachers, and government officials from the 1870s to the 1950s (Kan 1989a, 1999). At the same time, an adopted minister or storekeeper would clearly have been expected to feast his new relatives or offer them special gifts and services.[4]

Since the end of the 19th century, anthropologists have also been adopted by the Tlingits. The Krause brothers, who wintered among the Chilkat Tlingits in 1881–82, report having been adopted by the head of a powerful local clan, the Kaagwaantaan, who acted as their host and protector (Krause 1993:147). George T. Emmons (1852–1945), who studied Tlingit culture for several decades, beginning in the early 1880s, and who developed a close rapport with many Tlingits, was adopted and given a Native name, even though the identity of his adopted clan remains unknown.[5]

It seems that usually those anthropologists who carried out extensive field research in southeastern Alaska and kept visiting their Tlingit friends and informants (for example, Olson, de Laguna) were given names, while those who either made only a brief visit to a Tlingit community or stayed on its margins (Swanton, Oberg) were not. Adoptions before 1960 tended to be informal—that is, not part of a memorial potlatch—and involved no distribution of gifts. Here, for example, is how Ronald Olson, a University of California anthropologist who spent several seasons in southeastern Alaska between 1933 and 1954, described his adoption, which took place in the early 1930s:

> I was a member of Tlingit society by adoption. This was done,
> without any formality, by Mrs. John Benson of Klukwan, a
> high caste member of the G̲aana̲xteidí (Raven moiety) clan.
> She simply stated that I was now her grandson and that she was
> naming me Yetkadinakeh [sp.?]. This was a name of fairly high
> rank and derived of course from her family line. . . . The Tlingit
> from that time on treated me more or less as one of themselves.
> By using kin terms, in obtaining informants and so on, I was
> able to secure information which otherwise might have been
> withheld.[6]

In the last 30 years, the number of Tlingit adoptions of Euro-Americans has increased significantly. On the one hand, Tlingit-white intermarriage has become quite common, with the in-marrying non-Tlingit spouse usually being adopted and given a name. This is particularly important if the spouse is female, because the act of adoption ensures that her children have a legitimate place in the Native sociocultural order. On the other hand, with the weakening of Euro-American antipotlatch attitudes and the rise of political activism and ethnic pride among Native Alaskans, the memorial _koo.éex'_ has become a much more public institution (Kan 1989a). This has meant that the adoption of Euro-Americans often takes place within the context of this ritual, which makes the adoption and the naming much more public and legitimate. In addition to non-Tlingit spouses, whites who perform valuable services for the Tlingit community (priests and ministers, lawyers, doctors, schoolteachers, museum curators) or who are being courted as potential influential allies (the governor of Alaska, David Rockefeller, Jimmy Carter) have been adopted as well.[7] Sometimes the adopted person is simply a close friend or coworker.

This proliferation of adoptions has also had a lot to do with the fact that after World War II, ties between matrilineal relatives have weakened. As a result, many individuals no longer feel obligated to consult their lineage or clan kin before adopting a non-Tlingit and bestowing a valuable name.[8] This has led to some conflicts and resentment, especially if the given name is particularly prestigious. At the same time, with intermarriage and other close social ties between Tlingits and non-Tlingits increasing, more Euro-Americans are now invited to take part in the memorial _koo.éex'_ and other religious and secular Tlingit activities, not only as guests but as hosts as well, which means that they are expected to contribute labor and money to the ceremony (Kan 1989a).[9]

The degree of each adoptee's involvement in the social, political, and ceremonial life of the adopted clan and community varies from minimal to very high. Thus a number of men and women married to a Tlingit and adopted into his or her clan have taken a very active role in potlatching. A few non-Tlingit women have even tried to learn the Tlingit language and have encouraged their children to do so.[10] Generally speaking, Euro-Americans residing in a Tlingit community are more likely to fulfill the obligations expected from a clan member.

Thus when a high-ranking head of one of the Angoon clans died, a Euro-American physician whom he had adopted contributed a very generous sum toward the cost of the memorial potlatch. Some adopted persons leave the community, however, without any intention of maintaining ties with their adopted family, matrilineage, or clan.

There is another reason why the number of adoptions of non-Tlingits has been increasing over the past few decades. While having an "Indian name" has always had a certain romantic appeal to the American public (P. Deloria 1998), it has become especially attractive to Euro-Americans since the 1960s.[11] The Tlingits are well aware of that and are willing to bestow clan-owned names on non-Tlingit friends, relatives, and allies as a demonstration of their generosity and a certain superiority. After all, in the traditional _koo.éex'_, the hosts (= givers) have always assumed a superior position to the guests (= receivers). The "Indian name" and the right to take part in traditional Native ceremonies may be one of the few gifts the Tlingits can bestow on Euro-Americans without the latter being able to reciprocate with a gift of equal value.

MY OWN FIRST ADOPTION

When I arrived in Sitka in August 1979 to begin a year of ethnographic and ethnohistorical research aimed at collecting data for my doctoral dissertation, I had no idea that in eight months I would be adopted into a Tlingit clan and given a Tlingit name in the context of a memorial _koo.éex'_. In a way, it all happened by accident. My original research topic was not traditional ceremonialism, which I ended up writing my thesis about, but the history and current form of Russian Orthodox Christianity among the Tlingits. Having been born and raised in the USSR, I was familiar with the basic features of Orthodoxy and could read missionary literature without difficulty. Being Jewish, however, I had not been baptized, and I had only occasionally visited an Orthodox church, partly out of curiosity and partly to do something of which my schoolteachers would definitely not approve. I also got a taste of Russian peasant Orthodoxy from conversations with my pious nanny, Anna Andreevna Parshina, who came from a peasant family.

After leaving Russia in 1974, I completed my undergraduate education at Boston University and went on to do graduate work in anthropology at the University of Chicago. I had long been interested in the ideational culture of indigenous northern peoples, but I realized that I would not be able to conduct fieldwork in Siberia, so I began developing a research project dealing with one of the Native Alaskan peoples. Encouraged by both my undergraduate and graduate mentors to read Boas and Lévi-Strauss, I developed a strong interest in the cultures of the Pacific Northwest Coast. Given these two areal interests, plus the fact that my research could utilize a large body of Russian-language documents, it was natural that I would choose to focus on the Tlingits. Besides the numerically small Eyaks, they were the only Northwest Coast people who maintained an intense interaction with the Russians during the "Russian America" era, 1790s–1867 (Grinev 1991; Kan 1999).[12]

During a brief preliminary research trip to southeastern Alaska during the summer of 1978, I learned that, while the Russian cultural legacy in that part of the state had almost entirely disappeared, many of the northern Tlingits—in communities such as Sitka, Juneau, Angoon, and Hoonah—had remained Orthodox despite the fact that the Russian Church had, until fairly recently, experienced severe financial problems and a shortage of clergy. I also got the impression on that trip that traditional ceremonialism—that is, the potlatch (anthropologists' favorite topic!)—was still alive. However, in the atmosphere that existed (or was believed to exist by some of my mentors and fellow students at Chicago) following the publication in 1969 of Vine Deloria's *Custer Died for Your Sins*, I decided to stay away from the more traditional and somewhat more hidden or controversial aspects of Native culture and concentrate on Tlingit Orthodoxy, which could be documented using archival materials and observed in the more public domain. My nervousness about imposing on a small Native American community accounted for my decision to conduct fieldwork in the large multiethnic community of Sitka rather than in a small village consisting almost entirely of Tlingit people.[13]

To collect the data for my project, I began attending the weekly mass ("divine liturgy") at St. Michael's Orthodox Cathedral, along with weddings, baptisms, funerals, and memorial services. The latter two types of rituals took place particularly often that fall, with several of the recently deceased men belonging to the same house group (K̲óok

Hít), lineage or subclan (Ḵóokhittaan), and clan (Kaagwaantaan). While I was initially reluctant to take part in the funeral and memorial services of people I had not personally known, their relatives and other parishioners saw my presence as a sign of "respect" for the departed men and their families (Kan 1987, 1989b, 1999).

It happened that several of the men who passed away just before or soon after my arrival in Sitka were close matrilineal relatives of Charlotte Elizaveta Littlefield Young (Tlaktoowú) (1916–82).[14] Besides being the head of the parish sisterhood, Charlotte Young was married to its president (*starosta*), Thomas (Foma) Young Sr. (Ḵaajeetguxeex),[15] a respected traditionalist elder. She was also closely related, bilaterally and matrilineally, to several other active and influential members of the Orthodox parish. Because of my frequent participation in church services in general and the death-related rites of her close kin in particular, Mrs. Young took me under her wing, and we began to spend a fair amount of time together, talking about the history of the local parish, Tlingit Orthodoxy, and the relationship between Christianity and what the Tlingits of her generation called "the old customs" (pre-Christian religious beliefs and rituals).

Like most members of St. Michael's parish, Charlotte assumed that my regular attendance at church services and attempts to sing along with the choir meant that I was Orthodox. The fact that I was born in Russia and spoke Russian further supported that impression. I neither confirmed nor denied that I belonged to the Church, but I did not partake of the sacraments or perform other acts appropriate only for one who has been baptized.[16] Thus I had to turn down one Native family's request to serve as a godfather to its newborn, even though this seemed to be a wonderful opportunity to establish a strong bond with members of the Tlingit community. Luckily, Orthodox Tlingits never directly questioned me about the extent of my membership in their church or tried to draw me further into Orthodoxy. The local parish priest, Father Eugene Bourdukofsky, an Aleut man proud of his Russian ancestry, and the Russian-born bishop of Alaska, Gregory Afonsky, showed similar tact and never questioned me about my religiosity.

It should be pointed out that, despite the fact that in the pre-1867 era the Tlingits had their share of violent confrontations with Russians, most of them now look back at that period as a time when they were free of non-Tlingit domination. Thus they tend to distinguish Russians from other whites, especially Americans, who are seen as the much more oppressive colonizers of Tlingit land and the expropriators of Tlingit resources (Kan 1999:534–536). After a few months of residence in Sitka, several elderly members of the Orthodox parish began referring to me amicably and somewhat jokingly as "the Anóoshi" (the Russian) and spoke of pre-1867 Russians as "your folks" when telling about some episodes in 19th-century Sitka history.

Charlotte Young turned out to be an excellent consultant. On the one hand, she came from a traditionalist family whose members did not abandon the memorial _koo.éex'_, even when many other local families did. From her mother and maternal grandmother (the latter belonging to the generation that matured during the 1880s, an era of massive Tlingit conversion to Orthodoxy) she had learned a great deal about this ritual, as well as various indigenous beliefs dealing with death, dreams, ghosts, reincarnation, and other subjects that I was interested in. On the other hand, Charlotte was a very devout Orthodox Christian, whose worldview, like that of many traditionalists of her generation, combined Orthodox and pre-Christian beliefs into an ideology that I have labeled "Tlingit Orthodoxy" (Kan 1999). In fact, she and her husband belonged to the last generation able to speak Tlingit fluently. Their worldview was still heavily influenced by traditional concepts and values, and they saw little or no contradiction between this and Orthodox Christianity (cf. Dauenhauer and Dauenhauer 1994; Kan 1999).[17]

Actually, Charlotte was slightly younger and somewhat more devout than the other traditionalists by whom I was eventually befriended, which meant that she would occasionally criticize a certain pre-Christian belief or practice as "old-fashioned" or not fully compatible with Christianity. Charlotte, unlike some of her contemporaries, had fairly pronounced Caucasian features and was proud of her Russian (and English) ancestry. She seemed more gentle and forgiving than some of the other older Tlingit women I met. The fact that she reminded me of elderly Russian women I remembered from my childhood, including my nanny, must have also contributed to our friendship.

Looking back at our relationship, I think that Charlotte's being in mourning for her three brothers and a maternal uncle had a lot to do with her willingness to talk to me, a newcomer with time to sit and listen to her memories of her dead relatives and her feelings about them. I was able to share my translations of documents dealing with her ancestors, which I found in the local Orthodox parish archive, and this further strengthened our friendship. I had something to give back to her (and several other Orthodox parish members), and our relationship became a little more reciprocal than it had been initially. It is also possible that as head of the parish sisterhood, she felt obligated to take me under her wing, just as her husband, the parish warden, found it necessary to offer me explanations of the local style of worship and the traditional protocol of life cycle rituals involving the Tlingits, which he presided over. Another thing that must have contributed to my adoption by Charlotte was a delicious Russian dinner that my wife, Alla, prepared for her and her husband.

Despite the fact that the Sitka Tlingits have been living side by side with a Euro-American community for over a century, Tlingit traditionalists still did not socialize much with non-Tlingits, so an invisible barrier divided the two communities.[18] Charlotte and her husband clearly enjoyed visiting our home, and they showed their appreciation and desire to reciprocate (a key principle of the Tlingit sociocultural order) by bringing a set of ceremonial regalia (*at.óow*) belonging to Thomas Young's house and lineage and asked us to try them on while he photographed us. At the time, I did not know how to interpret this action, but looking back, I now see it as a preview of our adoption.

Most crucial for my ultimate adoption by Charlotte was my participation in several funerals of her close male kin and a "40-day party" that she and her relatives organized in the winter of 1979–80 to memorialize them. This ritual, which includes a memorial mass conducted on the 40th day after a person's death, as well as a meal, originated with the Russian Orthodox Church but has become heavily Tlingitized and is now perceived by many of younger Natives as an "old Tlingit ceremony."[19] As Charlotte told me, "Since you have been with us during my brothers' and my uncle's funerals and 40-day parties, you ought to be invited to the memorial party or pay-off in honor of these men." She also asked me to bring my wife along.

To my surprise, in the course of that memorial *koo.éex'*, I was officially adopted into Charlotte's house group and lineage and given the name Shaakundastóo, which had previously belonged to Edward

Littlefield (1919–80), one of Charlotte's recently deceased brothers. The naming was performed with the traditional protocol—that is, with some money being rubbed on my forehead and then given to a guest and my new name being repeated four times by all the participants. Several young members of the host clan and two Euro-Americans who had married into it were named as well. While the new names given the Tlingit youngsters could imply reincarnation of the deceased ancestors who had been their previous owners, my adoptive name did not carry such an implication. The only explanation for Charlotte's choice of name was that I reminded her of her deceased brother, who "was also interested in education and learning." In fact, Edward Littlefield's son's son, born not long before his death and named Edward, was also given the name Shaakundastóo at that koo.éex'.

In the aftermath of this adoption, Charlotte and her family began treating me and my wife as relatives. Soon after the potlatch, the Youngs invited us to their house for dinner, at which time they officially introduced us to several of their children and grandchildren. Not long thereafter, Thomas Young, who had become an important source of information for me on the old customs and Tlingit Orthodoxy, announced that he was adopting my wife into his own clan and giving her his deceased sister's name, Aandax̲jóon. Such an act makes a lot of sense, since it gives an adopted person's spouse a proper place in the social and ceremonial system—that is, now that I was expected to attend the potlatches sponsored by Charlotte's clan, I could bring my spouse with me as other Tlingits did. In fact, at Charlotte's potlatch, my wife was given a few presents and treated as a member of the guest moiety. To confirm his intention to adopt my wife, Mr. Young invited us to a restaurant and there, in the presence of his wife and a few other relatives, presented Alla with a locally made silver bracelet depicting the origin myth of his house group's crest, a giant wood worm. He then spoke about the history of the name he was bestowing upon her.[20]

After the 1980 potlatch, the Youngs began inviting me to their house more often, and they became even more willing to share information on Tlingit culture and history. I, in turn, began to feel much more a member of the community and less hesitant about dropping by their house to chat. I finally felt comfortable enough to explain to Charlotte that I was not only a "historian" researching the history of the Russian Church among the Tlingits but also an anthropologist equally interested in the memorial _koo.éex'_. A few weeks later, I began involving Charlotte in more formal ethnographic research when I asked her to translate the speeches of the potlatch participants I had recorded. She seemed to enjoy the work and offered interesting comments on each of the speakers, their motivations, the history of their relationship with her and the deceased, and so forth. Besides being able to intensify my work with the Youngs and their immediate kin, I was now able to use my newly acquired identity to develop closer ties with other Tlingit elders inside and outside of Sitka. I am convinced that without my adoption, I would not have been able to develop such good rapport with so many Tlingit people, old and young.[21]

I was able to collect a great deal of data not only on Tlingit Orthodoxy but also on the memorial _koo.éex'_, the most important indigenous Tlingit ceremony and one which has remained significant in their lives to this day (Kan 1989a; 1999:541–543). My data formed the basis for my dissertation (Kan 1982) and a monograph (Kan 1989b). Because I participated in the 1980 _koo.éex'_ and several subsequent ones not as an outsider but as a member of the hosting group, I was able to observe important aspects of the ceremony—preparation, behind-the-scenes negotiations among the various participants, and its subsequent analysis by the hosts, something rarely commented upon by earlier anthropologists. In addition, being close to the hosts, who were also the chief mourners, I developed greater appreciation for the ceremony's emotional dimensions than most of my predecessors did. As I have been told by a number of Tlingits, I was thus able to produce a more nuanced and sensitive description and analysis of the ceremony, which gave equal weight to its sociopolitical, religious, and psychological (in their words, "emotional") aspects (see Hope 1990). Similarly, my status as an adopted Tlingit and my closeness with the Youngs enabled me to obtain information on native interpretations of Orthodoxy and indigenous beliefs and practices that differed from those introduced by the Church. This data has been incorporated into several published articles (Kan 1985, 1987, 1991a, 1991b, 1996) and is central to an ethnohistorical monograph on Tlingit Orthodoxy that I recently published (Kan 1999).

The sad part of this story is that I never saw Charlotte after we left

Alaska in August 1980. Between that time and her death two years later, she and I exchanged telephone calls, letters, holiday cards, and gifts. Gift-giving turned out to be a particularly effective and meaningful way to maintain and strengthen ties with my Tlingit kin. It made sense to them in terms of both the traditional ethos and the Christian-American ideology they share with the rest of our society. While I was unable to attend Charlotte's funeral, my condolence letter to her family was published in the Sitka newspaper. I was pleased to see that I was listed as Charlotte's younger brother in the obituary prepared by her family. In 1984 I attended the _koo.éex'_ organized by Charlotte's family and matrikin in her memory. I was treated as one of the hosts who, like everyone else among the local K̲óokhittaan, had a job to do.

At the potlatch proper, my 1980 adoption was ritually reconfirmed when the chief spokesperson for the host side, Charlotte's lineage uncle, Charlie Joseph Sr. (K̲aal.átk') (1895–1986),[22] turned to Charlotte's children and grandchildren and announced, "This man is now your maternal uncle!" To further confirm my status as a full member of Charlotte's matrilineal group, I was given blankets and other gifts to take to my absent wife (the adopted sister-in-law of the deceased).

While attending this ritual, I found myself torn between my professional determination to record and remember as much information as possible and my emotional reaction to the loss of a dear friend/relative.[23] Charlotte's family, however, simply appreciated my presence and saw it as confirmation of their mother's decision "to adopt a good person into the family."[24] When I left Sitka the day after the memorial, I carried with me a large box of dried fish and deer meat put together by my nephews and nieces.

Since 1984 I have continued to maintain ties with my adopted family through phone calls, letters, gift-giving, and several return trips to Sitka. Thomas Young Sr., who took Charlotte's death very hard and has aged a great deal in the last decade, is no longer a consultant of mine, although I visit him whenever I am in Sitka. However, conversations with several of Charlotte's children, men and women in their forties and fifties, give me a good opportunity to study the "middle-aged generation" of the Tlingit people. I have become particularly close to Charlotte's oldest daughter, Freda, who is much like her mother and has taken on the role of senior woman in the Young family. I am also very close to one of Charlotte's sons, George (Lawrence), who has studied at the Russian Orthodox seminary in Kodiak and serves as a church reader. Over the years I have also developed warm and friendly relations with my deceased namesake's widow, Mrs. Monte Littlefield, and her children and grandchildren, particularly her son, John, and his wife, Roby, who have been instrumental in establishing a summer camp for Tlingit and non-Tlingit youngsters, where traditional subsistence activities and lore are taught, and have been for years actively involved in various other projects aimed at preserving the Tlingit heritage and passing it on to the younger generation (Kan 1979–97).

The memory of Charlotte remains an important link between me and a number of Tlingit people. Every time I come to Sitka, several members of her family join me on my visit to her grave, where I leave some flowers. We also attend church services together and purchase candles, which we light in her memory and place in front of icons. Shared grief, memory, and nostalgia for the days "when Mom was still alive to keep us all together"—sentiments central to Tlingit culture as well as to my own Russian-Jewish culture—unite us.[25] Holiday cards and telephone calls help keep me abreast of the doings of this large family. News about St. Michael's parish and life cycle rituals that members of my adopted family have gone through also provide rich topics of conversation. It is my impression that the family considers me a member of their church, although the extent of that membership is never discussed. Actually, some of my Tlingit relatives drift in and out of active membership in the parish, so my marginal Orthodoxy does not surprise them.

While rarely letting go entirely of my ethnographic agenda, I enjoy my visits with the Youngs, just as I enjoy spending time with Russian-Jewish relatives in Boston and New York. In addition to several nephews and nieces, many of Charlotte's grandchildren and great-grandchildren are being taught to call me Uncle Sergei. The fact that I am an only child contributes to the enjoyment I experience at Young family dinners and picnics.

In the fall of 1988 the permanence of my ties to the family was illustrated when Thomas Young, having heard about the birth of my daughter, Elianna, from one of his children, announced that, since the baby had to belong to the same clan as her mother, he was giving her a Gaanax̱teidí name, Shaawát Katlein.

Whenever I am in Sitka, I also spend a great deal of time with another close friend and adopted relative, Mark Jacobs Jr. (Gooshdeihéen) (b. 1923). Aside from several amateur and professional Tlingit researchers, most of whom are my friends, he is the only Tlingit who fully understands and supports my anthropological work. He is someone I can call my true consultant-teacher-collaborator.

Mark comes from a high-ranking house group (lineage) (Kéet Hít) and clan (the Dakl'aweidí of the Eagle moiety). Both his parents were born in a conservative village of Angoon, but Mark has spent his entire life in Sitka. From his parents and grandparents he learned to speak proper Tlingit and acquired a great deal of knowledge about the old customs, including ceremonial protocol. However, because of his family background, he used to feel something of an outsider in Sitka, and only in the last decade or so has begun to be fully appreciated there as a highly knowledgeable elder (tradition bearer). As a boy, Mark spent his time in subsistence camps and rowed a canoe for a grandmother who spoke very little English. He graduated from Sheldon Jackson High School in Sitka, served in the Pacific during World War II, and even attended law school for one year in the "Lower 48."

Mark was employed for most of his life as a highly skilled road construction worker. In his spare time, he pursued subsistence activities and engaged in local and national Indian politics. After his retirement in the mid-1980s, he became more involved in Indian politics and spent a great deal of time attending regional and national meetings and conventions.[26] Mark is a true Tlingit intellectual. He has been working for many years on a manuscript that combines his autobiography with historical and ethnographic data. While very interested in learning about the old customs and maintaining some of them (especially the koo.éex'), he has been a member of the Assembly of God for over 40 years and is very devout.[27] I can think of few Tlingits of his generation who are fully bilingual/bicultural and comfortable in both the Native and non-Native sociocultural universes. This and the fact that he is willing to look at his own culture critically and unapologetically makes him an excellent consultant.[28] Mark's thoughtful answers to my questions are full of valuable information on traditional Tlingit culture, but they are also a good reflection of the worldview of a person of his age and cultural orientation. My close ties with this man have made me much more aware of and interested in the relationship between a person's life (biography) and his or her culture, an issue that has once again become central to our discipline (cf. Blackman 1992; Cruikshank 1990; Dauenhauer and Dauenhauer 1994). I have been particularly interested in how Mark has tried to accommodate his traditional values and his Christianity (Kan 1991b, 1999).

As both an intellectual and a deeply religious person, Mark has tried hard to reconcile Tlingit values with Christianity. While his Christian faith prevents him from accepting all indigenous beliefs, still subscribed to by some of the older, more traditionalist elders (such as reincarnation), he is convinced that the essence of the traditional social order and the memorial _koo.éex'_, which he sees as "the foundation of Tlingit law rather than religion," have to be maintained for the survival of the Tlingit nation (Kan 1989a).[29] Putting together a detailed and accurate record of the key aspects of Tlingit culture is, in his view, a task that he and other elders must carry out in cooperation with interested members of the younger generation in conjunction with a few trusted non-Tlingit scholars.

After Mark and I were first introduced in the winter of 1979–80, he quickly became my main teacher/consultant. He seemed to thirst for serious attention and was willing to discuss controversial topics that other Tlingit tended to avoid. In fact, early in our relationship, Mark (who may have been stimulated by our reading of Swanton's 1908 ethnography of the Tlingits) told me that it was for me to obtain "the most accurate information possible" to correct the errors he found in the works of previous ethnographers and other "fly-by-night observers." My adoption by the Ḵóokhittaan and my rapport with the Young family and other elders in Sitka and Angoon must have influenced Mark's decision to make me "his" anthropologist. Thus he often cites my "properly carried out" adoption and my "sensitivity to Tlingit ceremonial protocol and emotion" as the main reasons for his decision to work with me. Over the years he has turned down a number of interview requests by other anthropologists or has given them information only on Tlingit economy, while reserving the discussion of such complex topics as social organization and religion for me.[30]

It is interesting that empathy and compassion have played an important role in the development of our close ties, just as they were crucial to my friendship with Charlotte Young. As Mark wrote to me on October 20, 1984, "You are the very first person [anthropologist?] I know who is willing to be part of us, to know our feelings and participate in all of our ways. It is easy to sense that. I am sure that is the reason you have been fully adopted into one of our clans. My family and some other elderly relatives who have met you commented on how well you understand our customs. This understanding is not possible by observation only; you must feel the strong emotions, the deep feelings and their expressions in order to understand them well."

Although Mark helped me make sense of the two potlatches I attended in Sitka in 1980 and gave me other valuable ethnographic and historical information during my first field season, our relationship really flourished after I left Alaska. Since that time we have corresponded frequently. In his letters Mark has provided me with valuable historical data as well as up-to-date information on the life of his community, describing in detail everything from the latest potlatches to current political issues and controversies. He has enabled me to monitor fairly closely the Tlingit social and ceremonial life from the 1980s to the present. Some of the information he has shared with me is sensitive, but he trusts me and feels it is important that I "get the record straight." Without ever having read Max Gluckman or Victor Turner, Mark has concluded that crisis situations and local dramas provide an excellent window on Tlingit culture and society and should be shared with an anthropologist so that he or she has a better understanding of the inner workings of that society. (Of course, he always reminds me to conceal the names of participants and to omit some of the details of these dramas in my published works.)

Mark's detailed answers to my questions have been incorporated in most of my publications, from a 1985 translation of a late 19th-century Russian missionary's ethnography of the Tlingits (Kamenskii [1906] 1985) and a 1989 monograph on the potlatch (Kan 1989b) to a recently published ethnohistorical study of Tlingit Orthodoxy (Kan 1999). If being adopted by Charlotte gave me an opportunity to participate in potlatches, the information provided by Mark enabled me to get a much clearer understanding of a complex history and the current state of interpersonal and intergroup relations that underlie and are symbolically played out in these rituals (Kan 1989a). Similarly, his impressive knowledge of the names and group affiliation of many Orthodox

Tlingits, from the 1900s to the present, played a key role in my reconstruction of the history of Tlingit Orthodoxy. With his help (as well as that of a number of other knowledgeable elders), I was able to analyze this phenomenon from the point of view of kinship groups and cohorts as well as from the point of view of individual actors (Kan 1985, 1991b, 1996, 1999).

It is clear that Mark enjoys our intellectual exchanges and that our relationship has stimulated his own research and writing. As he put it in a letter dated September 8, 1981, "Please, don't apologize for the questions you ask. I really enjoy them; they refresh my mind. You are asking about the things that have kept our culture alive. Many times you have asked me questions that really got my mind working.... Your questions also help me think of things I would not normally be thinking of. If I can't answer them, I can seek others who can and in the process I'll learn, too." In a way, our dialogue has turned Mark into an amateur ethnographer and tribal historian, encouraging him to spend more time with the dwindling group of traditionalist elders and to compile detailed accounts of the traditional rituals (especially potlatches) he takes part in. In addition, our relationship has stimulated him to compile a more systematic and detailed record of his own life history, which he intersperses with ethnographic and historical data.

Exchanging letters with me has clearly become an important part of Mark's life. In his letters he often shares his intimate thoughts and describes events that happen in his family. He seems to have a strong need to communicate with a distant friend and colleague who knows a lot about his community but is not involved in its daily trials and tribulations. Mark begins to worry whenever I take too long to answer a letter; as he phrased it in one of his own letters, "Please feel free to write often; your letters are the first thing I ask about when I get home from my trips."

Being proud of "his anthropologist," Mark is concerned about helping me maintain rapport with his community. In his very first letter (December 5, 1980), he informed of the death of a prominent Sitka Tlingit we both knew and recommended that I send a letter of condolence to his family: "As you have learned, words and expressions of concern are highly respected by the Tlingit people." When he introduces me to another Tlingit, Mark always offers a very positive evaluation of my research. The same is true of the public introductions he gives at ceremonial and secular gatherings of "his younger brother, an anthropology professor from Dartmouth."[31] At the same time, Mark wants to make sure that I am not misled by what he sees as inaccurate information offered by other Tlingits. This explains why his letters often contain refutations of public statements made by others or accounts of violations of ritual protocol which illustrate a lack of understanding of the "old customs."[32]

Over the years, my professional cooperation with Mark has evolved into a deep friendship. One manifestation of this development has been my willingness to discuss my Jewish identity with him, a subject that has almost never come up in conversations with other Tlingit friends and acquaintances, for whom Jews are simply not a significant social category.[33] Like a number of other Tlingit elders who are well versed in the Bible, Mark has a special interest in and identification with Old Testament Israelites, and he likes to compare their customs (for example, levirate) with those of the old-time Tlingits.[34] His fundamentalist Christianity also contributes to a sympathetic attitude toward modern-day Jews and the state of Israel. In addition, Mark is fond of comparing his own people and the Jews, pointing out that both have been victims of oppression and prejudice. The one important difference he sees between the two peoples is the fact that the Jews were able to establish their own state and the Tlingits have not.

In 1984, Mark gave my name to the organizers of the annual convention of the Alaska Federation of Natives (AFN) as a possible keynote speaker. The AFN was interested in having a speaker who could discuss the survival of Judaism and the Jewish people as a model for Native Alaskans. To Mark's deep disappointed, a rabbi from Los Angeles was chosen, but he and I periodically return to the subject of Jewish ethnic survival in our correspondence and conversations. In one of his 1989 letters, Mark told me about an encounter with a Jewish couple visiting Sitka. He said he felt a sense of kinship with them even before they revealed their identity. In subsequent letters, Mark often stated his belief that "according to the biblical prophecy, the Lord would always punish those trying to destroy the Jews, his Chosen People." When I was denied tenure at the University of Michigan in 1988, he interpreted this as a manifestation of anti-Semitism and compared it to his own encounters with anti-Indian prejudice. In 1994, Mark stayed at our house in New Hampshire, and I was finally able to reciprocate his efforts to include me in Tlingit ceremonial life when I invited him to join our weekly Jewish family ritual (the lighting of the Sabbath candles followed by a Sabbath meal). Mark was visibly moved by the experience, and he often mentions it in his letters.

In contrast to my relationship with Charlotte, where our shared Russian heritage and participation in Orthodox Church services played a key role in bringing us closer, Mark's fundamentalist Protestant Christianity is peripheral to our interaction. I never openly admitted to Charlotte that I was not even marginally Orthodox.[35] I was candid about my Jewishness with Mark, and his respect for it has helped us to stay very close.[36] This man is probably the only Tlingit friend/consultant with whom I can freely discuss many aspects of my life and identity, and he is as interested in my culture as I am in his.

Given our special relationship, it was not surprising that for quite some time Mark had been planning to adopt me into his house group and clan. One of the first hints he gave me of his plans was at a 1983 _koo.éex'_ given in memory of his deceased brothers and a maternal uncle. While neither I nor my wife were able to attend this ceremony, she was treated as a guest and sent a nice gift in the mail. In other words, Mark, who organized the ceremony, placed her among his "opposites"—his paternal and affinal kin. The fact that my wife had already been informally adopted by Thomas Young Sr. into one of the clans of the Raven moiety undoubtedly helped Mark make this decision. After this _koo.éex'_, Mark began signing his letters as "your brother," "your tribal brother," or "your Indian brother," instead of "your friend" or "your Tlingit friend," although he still did not specifically mention any plans to adopt me into his clan.

In 1991, a _koo.éex'_ was organized for Mark's high-ranking senior clan relative, Jimmie George Sr. (Wóochx̱ Kaduhaa) (1889–1990), who had passed away a year earlier (see Kan 1999:541–543 for details). Like Charlotte in 1980, Mark took this opportunity to incorporate my adoption into the ceremony, planning to make it a surprise to me. In his invitation to the memorial, he asked me "to stand with my fellow-Eagles" (that is, members of his and related Eagle moiety clans). He wrote that he planned to introduced me by my K̲óokhittaan name and hoped that I would say a few words to the guests about the deceased man, whom I had known well and who had been one of my major teachers/consultants in Angoon.[37]

To Mark's great disappointment, just before that potlatch he came down with a serious illness and was unable to attend it. To uphold his status within the Da_k_l'aweidí clan, his son Harold (_G_ooch Shaayí) spoke and performed Mark's ceremonial roles. It was Harold who announced during the naming ritual that I was to be given the name of his deceased paternal uncle, _G_unáak'w (James Ernest Jacobs) (1929–75). The fact that I had already been adopted by another clan of the Eagle moiety, with which Mark's clan has had its share of disputes in the past, must have given Mark pause when he contemplated making me his brother; in fact, he had sometimes felt the need to apologize to me for criticizing my adopted clan. Perhaps the fact that Mark himself had been given a Kaagwaantaan name at a *koo.éex'* held in Sitka in the 1940s suggested the precedent for my adoption by two related clans and receiving two Tlingit names.[38] During a tribal conference in Sitka in the summer of 1995, Mark was finally able to personally confirm and publicize my adoption to a large Tlingit audience gathered for a banquet, speaking about my new name and the reasons for giving it to me, and concluding with a standard potlatch ritual of rubbing some money on my forehead.[39] Thus, in addition to having numerous relatives among the Kaagwaantaan, I now have an older Da_k_l'aweidí brother and a number of relatives in southeastern Alaska, Anchorage, and Seattle.[40]

My adoption into the Killer Whale House of the Da_k_l'aweidí was further made public and confirmed in the course of a major memorial *koo.éex'* given by Mark's house group in cooperation with other house groups of his clan in November 1997, which I attended and contributed money to. From Mark's point of view, this was a particularly important ritual for two reasons. First, he and his sister gave it in memory of their beloved mother, a well-known Da_k_l'aweidí matriarch, who passed away in 1989. Second, the ceremony gave Mark an opportunity to display several precious regalia (*at óow*) repatriated by his house group from the Denver Museum of Natural History.

Being adopted by two influential traditionalist Tlingit families has been a boon for my research. Despite the factionalism that has always been present in Tlingit society, I have been able to maintain good relations with a substantial number of people and kinship groups outside the two families that have made me one of their own. Whenever

I arrive in a new Tlingit community, I introduce myself as an adopted Ḵóokhittaan/Kaagwaantaan and Dakl'aweidí and explain who I am related to; almost invariably this helps to break the ice and open new doors for me. In my writing, I have had to be careful not to mistake my adopted families' and clans' positions on certain issues with those of the Tlingit community in general. In my ethnohistorical writing (Kan 1999), I have also tried not to idealize or take the side of my adopted families and matrilineal groups.[41]

Some of the sensitive information about my Tlingit kin or people they have told me about has remained hidden in my field notes. At the same time, having been involved with the northern Tlingits for 20 years, I am more willing to defend my adopted families against criticism by other Tlingits. Although I am aware of disagreements that my adopted relatives have had with certain individuals and families, this has not harmed my work in any serious way. After all, the Tlingits are great diplomats who would cooperate with their most bitter rivals if ceremonial protocol or political expediency required it.

Looking back, I would venture to say that the two adoptions changed the nature and style of my fieldwork in a very dramatic way. I was initially reluctant to impose myself on a group of people, many of whom hold negative (or at least skeptical) views of anthropologists, and I chose a low-key and informal style of interviewing, rarely using a note pad or tape recorder. It was with my adopted families that I was finally able to overcome my "professional shyness" and begin to feel comfortable about recording their words verbatim. Eventually I was able to conduct more formal interviews with other Tlingits. At the same time, after my adoptions, I was able to become more of an engaged participant and less of a distant observer. This has been particularly important in a place like Sitka, where key aspects of Native life (particularly ceremonialism) often take place behind closed doors and are not easily observed by an outsider.

My two adoptions have had a very strong influence on my ethnographic and ethnohistorical research. They have helped me gain a deeper and much more nuanced understanding of Tlingit culture, past and present, and they have enabled me to pursue important topics I had not planned to research. Without the adoptions, it is unlikely that I could have offered a new interpretation of the memorial potlatch, especially its religious and emotional dimension (Kan 1982,

1989b). Similarly, my analysis of Tlingit Christianity would have been confined to the study of a "system of symbols and meanings" and would not have examined the more personal level of religious experience, the meaning of the new religion to individual men and women (Kan 1989a, 1991b, 1999). Most important, my involvement with the Littlefield/Young and the Jacobs families is largely responsible for my interest in the relationship between an individual and his or her culture. This issue will be the focus of my work when I begin to help Mark edit his autobiography for publication.

My relationship with these two families will also make it possible for me to maintain ties with younger generations of Tlingit people, even after the elders who have been my main informants pass away. I anticipate, for example, that my friendship with Harold Jacobs, who is better versed in the old customs and is more involved in the traditional ceremonial system than most members of his own generation and even some of the older people, will be very important in any future studies of contemporary Tlingit politics and ideology that I might undertake.[42]

In terms of personal experience, being adopted has made fieldwork much more pleasurable. With most of my professional life spent in an academic community and my circle of relatives and friends being fairly circumscribed, I am drawn to a community whose lifestyle, values, and concerns are in many ways different from those of the people around me, and I find a special satisfaction in being able to share food, laughter, and tears with the members of that community, particularly those who call me uncle or younger brother. This may sound like an alienated urban intellectual's desire to be accepted by a romanticized "Other," but there is much more than that involved in my relationship with my adopted Tlingit families. As time goes by, I find that my personal ties with the Littlefields/Youngs and with Mark Jacobs are beginning to overwhelm my scholarly interest in their history and culture (cf. Straus, chapter 8). One could say that by adopting and naming me, the Littlefields/Youngs and the Jacobses have put a permanent claim on me as "their" anthropologist.

In closing, I would like to point out that my case is not unique. Several other ethnographers (for example, Kenneth Tollefson, Kristin J. Barsness, Tom Thornton, and Daniel B. Monteith) who have worked among the Tlingits in recent years have also been adopted.[43] As the articles in this volume demonstrate, adoptions of anthropologists occur in other American Indian societies, many of which have a social structure very different from that of the Tlingits. And as long as kinship remains the central idiom of social relations in Native American communities, anthropologists will continue to be adopted. Unless the society they are working in is so deeply factionalized that adoption would make them totally unacceptable to a large segment of the Native community, adoption should help their research. It is reasonable to assume that some of the more nationalist Indian people will continue to object to the adoption of non-Indians, but the politics of Indian-white relations would probably not prevent individual Native American families from adopting and giving names to favored Euro-Americans, including anthropologists.

In addition to allowing access to sensitive topics, establishing ties of friendship and quasi-kinship with informants offers ethnographers an opportunity to gain a much deeper understanding of these people's life, especially its private and emotional aspects. And by acting like relatives—people who have hearts and not just minds, people who are generous with their time and resources—ethnographers might help to mend ties between their community and Native American communities, which have sometimes been strained or called into question by radical Indian "anthro-bashers" and some postmodernist anthropologists (see V. Deloria 1969; Biolsi and Zimmerman 1997). Despite the argument made in some quarters against non-Indians continuing to conduct ethnographic research in Indian communities, I am not prepared to quit, and I do not believe that our Native American colleagues, friends, and adopted relatives want us to. The ethnographic, historical, and linguistic information we collect is of much interest to many of them. Like my older brother (*ax húnxw*) Gooshdeihéen, I believe there is still a great need—practical as well as intellectual—for careful, honest, and sensitive ethnography, as long as it is made available to the Native community.[44]

APPENDIX

In the summer of 1995, on the day I was leaving Sitka to return to New Hampshire, Mark gave me a package of smoked salmon. For some reason, he was concerned that the airport personnel might question me about the contents of the box, and he gave me a letter I could show to them. Since it captures Mark's view of "his" anthropologist so nicely, I reproduce it here with his permission.

> *To Whom It May Concern*
> August 13, 1995
>
> I, Mark Jacobs Jr., of 108 Kelly Street, Sitka, Alaska, have supplied my friend, Mr. Sergei Kan, with a small package of traditionally smoked salmon for his personal use. Mr. Kan is an associate professor of anthropology at Dartmouth College in Hanover, New Hampshire. He is accustomed to this delicacy. I am pleased to be able to share this finished product with him. It is a traditional custom. I have, in accordance with the Tlingit Law, adopted him as my younger brother [and] named him G̲unáak̲'w, [making him] a namesake of my deceased natural brother.
>
> *Mark Jacobs Jr.*
> *Gooshdeihéen*

NOTES

The first version of this essay was presented in a session of the 1995 annual meeting of the American Anthropological Association dealing with American Indian adoption of anthropologists. It benefited greatly from the insightful comments by Raymond Fogelson. Its expanded and modified version was presented in a panel on anthropology and Jewish identity at the San Francisco Jewish Museum in 1996. Dvora Yanow, the panel's organizer, deserves my special gratitude for her detailed written comments on the essay's second draft. I would also like to thank Tom Thornton for an equally thoughtful and critical reading of the latest version of the piece and for sharing with me his own recent experience of being adopted by a Tlingit elder.

1. Members of related Tlingit clans belonging to the same moiety also frequently gave prestigious names to each other. For example, a man could give a name owned by his clan to his son's son.

2. A nickname given to a Euro-American often reflected occupation or another characteristic perceived by the Tlingit to be most essential. Thus, drawing on the traditional system of teknonymy, the

Juneau Tlingits named a popular Jewish merchant who purchased furs from them "Father of Mink" (Kan 1979–97).

3. Thus, for example, when the southern Tlingits living in the vicinity of Wrangell requested in 1879 that American Presbyterian missionaries establish a church and a school in their community, they invited several leading Presbyterian officials to a grand feast. In the course of the celebration, which included a lavish banquet "in the white man's style," Rev. Sheldon Jackson, Rev. S. H. Young, and Rev. Lindsley were given high-ranking names belonging to their hosts, the leaders of the so-called Christian faction (Jackson 1880: 104–114, 234–239). As in a traditional potlatch, old-style songs and dances were performed, but only as entertainment and with an added message that the hosts were about to abandon these "old-fashioned ways" and turn to "Christianity and civilization." John Muir (1988 [1915]:28–30), who accompanied this missionary delegation, was also feasted and given a name (see also Kan 1999: 208–209).

4. It is possible that the Tlingits interpreted their baptismal names or the last names bestowed on them by missionaries, schoolteachers, and employers as a gift from the whites. On some occasions a disgruntled Tlingit would claim the Euro-American name of a person who had offended him or had not paid him properly for services offered. Thus, when a Chilkat man who had served as one of the packers for Lieutenant Schwatka during a 1885 military reconnaissance in Alaska decided that he had not been adequately paid, he appropriated the name Shwatke as his own and passed it on to members of his clan (Kan 1979–97; Schwatka 1900).

5. In a 1903 letter (cited in de Laguna 1991:xvii), Emmons stated, "I have made a study of their history, and I have lived with them on the most intimate terms, until they have given me one of their family names and look upon me as one of themselves." Given Emmons's close friendship with members of the Shotridge (Shaadaxícht) family in Klukwaan, it is quite possible that he was adopted into the Chilkat branch of the Kaagwaantaan clan (cf. Low 1991).

6. Frederica de Laguna (personal communication, 1995) was never formally adopted either, but she was given a Tlingit name by an

elderly female member of the Kwaashk'i̱kwaan clan of Yakutat (the village where de Laguna conducted her research in 1949–54), who said that she did it because she hoped that the anthropologist would someday be of help to her people.

7. In the early 1970s, for example, Willie Marks (Kéet Yaanaayí) (1902–81), a traditionalist house leader and a well-known Juneau carver, adopted the postmaster general of the United States into his own clan, the Chookaneidí, when the postmaster was being officially received in Juneau. In return, the postmaster gave Marks a set of commemorative stamps (Dauenhauer and Dauenhauer 1994:461).

8. Similarly, a small group of closely related matrikin is more likely today to bestow high-ranking names on its infant members without consulting lineage or clan relatives who might have much stronger claims to them.

9. A memorial ḵooéex' for a respected Tlingit elder that I attended in the late 1980s was financed primarily by his well-to-do Euro-American sons-in-law rather than by his Tlingit lineage relatives.

10. Several of these women are more interested in and committed to traditional ceremonialism than their Tlingit husbands. Their zeal and their devotion to their adopted culture is reminiscent of that exhibited sometimes by women who marry Jews and convert to Judaism.

11. An American sociologist who conducted research in the southern Tlingit community of Wrangell in the early 1950s reported that a number of whites in that town requested Tlingit names for themselves or their children and gave gifts to members of the Native community when these requests were granted (Scott 1953:506). While such requests may have been made during my time (1979–97), I am not aware of any.

12. The first detailed ethnography of the Tlingits was written by a Russian missionary, Father Ivan Veniaminov ([1840] 1984).

13. I must admit that I also chose Sitka because I wanted the fieldwork to be less of a culture shock for my wife, Alla, a true urbanite who

was not terribly enthusiastic about spending a year in Alaska in the first place and especially in a small village.

14. Harold Jacobs, one of my main Tlingit friends and consultants, recently suggested that the spelling of Charlotte's Tlingit name, which I had learned from her and her relatives, is actually incorrect. Instead he proposed to spell it as Laakhdu.oo.

15. Thomas Young (b. 1906) is head of and caretaker (*hít s'aatí*) to the Frog House of the Klukwaan Gaanaxteidí. For his biography, see Dauenhauer and Dauenhauer (1994:607–611).

16. My Jewish background had a lot to do with my behavior. I would probably have had no qualms about participating in a non-Christian (or non-Islamic) religious ritual. For a rather different experience of a Cuban-born American Jewish ethnographer working in a Christian community, see Behar (1996).

17. As Dauenhauer and Dauenhauer (1994:611) point out in their biography of Thomas Young, for people of his cohort, "traditional Tlingit and traditional Christian spirituality are not in conflict with each other, but are in conflict with a secular worldview that undermines both, denies spiritual reality, and results in loss of identity . . . and the ultimate loss of spiritual life itself."

18. The local Euro-American community, while basically not hostile to the Tlingit one, showed a surprising ignorance about its way of life. Of course, Tlingit reluctance to reveal the more traditional aspects of their lives to outsiders was partly responsible for this ignorance.

19. While the Orthodox Church only requires that a special memorial mass be said for the recently deceased person on the 40th day after his or her death, the Tlingits have added a banquet, ordered to a significant extent by the structural principles and ideological postulates of the indigenous sociocultural order (Kan 1987, 1999; Dauenhauer and Dauenhauer 1990:32–36).

20. My wife's adoption has never been formalized simply because Mr. Young has not given a *koo.éex'* since 1980. He now resides in a nursing home in Sitka.

21. In fact, there was only one Tlingit elder who disapproved of my adoption by the Ḵóokhittaan and refused to speak to me; his attitude was determined by a strong ambivalence about Euro-Americans in general and anthropologists in particular, rather than by animosity toward me or my adopted family.

22. For a biography of Charlie Joseph Sr., see Dauenhauer and Dauenhauer (1994:321–364).

23. One of the most memorable moments of that event occurred the night before the potlatch, when I sat with Charlotte's family and participated in deliberations about the ceremony. Hearing her relatives address the practical, ideological, and emotional topics in the same breath gave me a new insight into the memorial koo.éex'.

24. One of Charlotte's daughters wrote to me soon after the potlatch, "Mom must have had a good reason to adopt you—she knew you would not forget us in our times of sadness."

25. Charlotte's family was delighted to see my new book (Kan 1999), which is dedicated to her and contains a 1980 picture of her with me and Thomas Young Sr.

26. These trips have enabled Mark to visit me on several occasions in both Ann Arbor, Michigan, and Lebanon, New Hampshire.

27. Mark, whose parents were staunch Russian Church members, was originally baptized Orthodox, but he changed his church affiliation after marrying a Tlingit woman who belonged to the Assembly of God.

28. As he wrote in an early letter to me, "Don't get the idea that I'm trying to say that the Tlingit were always nice; on the contrary, they were tough and at times cruel and belligerent." Very few Tlingits I know would make such a statement to a non-Tlingit.

29. Mark is fond of quoting his late father, who foresaw the important role of knowledge about the indigenous social and ceremonial systems in the pursuit of land claims settlement in the early 1970s. Mark Jacobs Sr. often said, "Our custom is our law and will someday be the survival of our people."

30. On several occasions, visiting anthropologists (including a Russian) and other researchers have been told that Mark was working with an anthropologist from Dartmouth and that the information he was sharing with him "was being copyrighted."

31. One benefit of having befriended an anthropology professor that Mark definitely enjoys is the opportunity to speak to college students about himself and his culture. He did that with gusto during a visit to Dartmouth in the fall of 1992.

32. It is my impression that Mark's statements about Tlingit history and interclan relations tend to be somewhat more accurate and less self-serving than those made by some other elders I have known. In the modern context, where the number of persons knowledgeable about the "old customs" has become rather small and where the traditional mechanisms of conflict resolution and social control have declined, it has become easier for an individual to make exaggerated claims about his own or his matrilineal group's rank and status, especially when addressing a non-Tlingit audience. While Mark is more modest than some of the Tlingit elders I have known, he does use his impressive knowledge of the "old customs" to bolster his status and prestige in the community as well as in the eyes of the non-Tlingits. This is not an entirely new phenomenon, since a Tlingit's rank and status have always depended on his or her knowledge of ceremonial matters and clan history (Kan 1989b:77–102; 1989a).

33. During 20 years of intermittent fieldwork in southeastern Alaska, I have never heard any anti-Semitic remarks. It seems that Boas's experience among the Kwakwaka'wakw (or their subsequent recollections of that experience) was different (see Boas 1966:xxv–xxvi).

34. Another deeply devout Presbyterian Tlingit elder I have known, Andrew P. Johnson, was very fond of referring to the Tlingits as one of the lost tribes of Israel (cf. Dauenhauer and Dauenhauer 1994:304–310).

35. Since my relationship with Charlotte was cut short by her death in 1982, it is difficult to say whether my not being Orthodox Christian would have become an issue for her or not. I suspect that as long as

I continued to go to masses and feast day celebrations with the Youngs, this issue would not have been raised.

36. The fact that Mark has never asked me to attend Assembly of God services with him has helped me avoid some of the problems I faced in St. Michael's Cathedral.

37. After spending ten months in Sitka in 1979–80, my wife and I lived in Angoon for two months. There I developed a rapport with Mr. George and his kin as well as several other Orthodox Tlingit families. For his biography, see Dauenhauer and Dauenhauer (1994: 193–206).

38. While Mark continues to treat my adoption by the Kookhit-taan/Kaagwaantaan with utmost respect, in the last few years he has begun to suggest in his letters that my adoption into his own lineage is somehow more significant.

39. While the event was not a memorial koo.éex' at all, the conference organizers wanted to use traditional ritual protocol to give it a stronger Tlingit flavor. One evening of the conference was devoted to the Raven moiety members' memorializing their deceased kin and another one to the Eagle moiety doing the same. Since this memorialization included donations in honor of the departed relatives whose names were being invoked, this was a clever and culturally meaningful way to raise money for the conference (Kan 1979–97).

40. One close matrilineal relative of Mark's whom I have become good friends with over the years is his younger sister, Bertha Karras, who with her husband, Pete, owns and operates a lovely bed and breakfast in Sitka where I have been staying since the late 1980s.

41. The danger of idealization is obvious. See, for example, a critical review by Boelscher (1985) of Blackman's biography of her Haida informant and adopted grandmother (Blackman 1992). See also Straus (this volume).

42. Harold Jacobs has been one of the leaders in a new and interesting movement, the repatriation of the Tlingit ceremonial regalia

(*at.óow*) to their respective matrilineal groups. This is a topic that I would like to address in one of my future research projects.

43. I have discussed their adoption with each of these four scholars; in addition, I have consulted Barsness's doctoral dissertation (1997:6).

44. Collaborative projects carried out by ethnographers and their adopted American Indian relatives may be one powerful answer to critics. See, for example, Cruikshank's recent work (1990), annotated biographies of three elderly Native women from the southern Yukon Territory.

REFERENCES

Barsness, Kristin J. 1997. A Tlingit Community: A Century of Change. Ph.D. diss., Bryn Mawr College.

Behar, Ruth. 1996. The Story of Ruth, the Anthropologist. In *People of the Book: Thirty Scholars Reflect on Their Jewish Identity*, ed. Jeffrey Rubin-Dorsky and Shelley Fisher Fishkin, 261–279. Madison: University of Wisconsin Press.

Biolsi, Thomas, and Larry J. Zimmerman, eds. 1997. *Indians and Anthropologists: Vine Deloria Jr. and the Critique of Anthropology*. Tucson: University of Arizona Press.

Blackman, Margaret. 1992. *During My Time: Florence Edenshaw Davidson, a Haida Woman*. 2d ed. Seattle: University of Washington Press.

Boas, Franz. 1966. *Kwakiutl Ethnography*. Edited by Helen Codere. Chicago: University of Chicago Press.

Boelscher, Marianne. 1985. Review of *During My Time: Florence Edenshaw Davidson, a Haida Woman*, by Margaret Blackman. *Anthropos* 80:1–3.

Cruikshank, Julie. 1990. *Life Lived like a Story: Life Stories of Three Yukon Native Elders*. Lincoln: University of Nebraska Press.

Dauenhauer, Nora M., and Richard Dauenhauer. 1990. *Haa Tuwunáagu Yís, for Healing Our Spirit: Tlingit Oratory*. Seattle: University of Washington Press.

———. 1994. *Haa Kusteeyí, Our Culture: Tlingit Life Stories*. Seattle: University of Washington Press.

de Laguna, Frederica. 1972. *Under Mount Saint Elias: The History and Culture of the Yakutat Tlingit*. 3 parts. Smithsonian Contributions to Anthropology 7. Washington DC: Government Printing Office.

———. 1991. Introduction to *The Tlingit Indians*, by George T. Emmons, xvii–xxv. Edited by Frederica de Laguna. Seattle: University of Washington Press.

Deloria, Philip J. 1998. *Playing Indian*. New Haven: Yale University Press.

Deloria, Vine, Jr. 1969. *Custer Died for Your Sins: An Indian Manifesto*. New York: Avon.

Emmons, George T. 1991. *The Tlingit Indians*. Edited by Frederica de Laguna. Seattle: University of Washington Press.

Grinev, Andrei V. 1991. *Indeitsy Tlinkity v Period Russkoi Ameriki, 1741–1867* (Tlingit Indians during the Russian American Era, 1741–1867). Novosibirsk: Nauka.

Hope, Andy. 1990. Review of *Symbolic Immortality: Tlingit Potlatch of the 19th Century*, by Sergei Kan. *Before Columbus Review* 1(3–4): 25–26.

Jackson, Sheldon. 1880. *Alaska and the Missions on the North Pacific Coast*. New York: Dodd, Mead.

Kamenskii, Anatolii. 1985 [1906]. *Tlingit Indians of Alaska*. Translated by Sergei Kan. Fairbanks: University of Alaska Press.

Kan, Sergei. 1979–97. Ethnographic notes on the Tlingit. Manuscript and audio tapes in author's possession.

———. 1982. "Wrap Your Father's Brothers in Kind Words": An Analysis of the 19th-Century Tlingit Mortuary and Memorial Rites. Ph.D. diss., University of Chicago.

———. 1985. Russian Orthodox Brotherhoods among the Tlingit: Missionary Goals and Native Response. *Ethnohistory* 32(3):196–223.

———. 1987. Memory Eternal: Russian Orthodoxy and the Tlingit Mortuary Complex. *Arctic Anthropology* 24(1):32–55.

———. 1989a. Cohorts, Generations, and Their Culture: The Tlingit Potlatch in the 1980s. *Anthropos* 84:405–422.

———. 1989b. *Symbolic Immortality: The Tlingit Potlatch of the 19th Century*. Washington DC: Smithsonian Institution Press.

———. 1991a. Russian Orthodox Missionaries and the Tlingit Indians of Alaska, 1880–1890. In *New Dimensions in Ethnohistory: Papers of the Second Laurier Conference on Ethnohistory and Ethnology*, ed. B. M. Gough and L. Christie, 127–160. National Museum of Man, Mercury Series, Canadian Ethnology Service, paper no. 120. Ottawa: Canadian Museum of Civilization.

———. 1991b. Shamanism and Christianity: Modern-Day Tlingit Elders Look at the Past. *Ethnohistory* 38(4):363–387.

———. 1996. From Clan Mothers to Godmothers: Tlingit Women and Russian Orthodox Christianity, 1840–1940. In *Native American Women's Responses to Christianity*, ed. Michael Harkin and Sergei Kan. *Ethnohistory* 43(4):613–641.

———. 1999. *Memory Eternal: Tlingit Culture and Russian Orthodox Christianity Through Two Centuries*. Seattle: University of Washington Press.

Krause, Aurel. 1993. *To the Chukchi Peninsula and to the Tlingit Indians, 1881/1882: Journals and Letters by Aurel and Arthur Krause*. Translated by Margot Krause McCaffrey. Fairbanks: University of Alaska Press.

Low, Jean. 1991. Lieutenant George Thornton Emmons, USN, 1852–1945. In *The Tlingit Indians*, by George T. Emmons, xxvii–xl. Edited by Frederica de Laguna. Seattle: University of Washington Press.

Muir, John. 1988 [1915]. *Travels in Alaska*. San Francisco: Sierra Club Books.

Olson, Ronald L. 1967. *Social Structure and Social Life of the Tlingit Indians in Alaska*. University of California Anthropological Records 26. Berkeley.

Scott, James C., Jr. 1953. Race and Culture Contact in Southeastern Alaska: A Study of the Assimilation and Acculturation of the Wrangell Tlingit and Whites. Ph.D. diss., University of Chicago.

Shwatka, Frederick. 1900. Report on a Military Reconnaissance Made in Alaska in 1883. In *Compilations of Narratives of Explorations in Alaska*, 282–362. Washington DC: Government Printing Office.

Swanton, John R. 1908. Social Conditions, Beliefs, and Linguistic Relationship of the Tlingit Indians. In *26th Annual Report of the Bureau of American Ethnology for the Years 1904–1905*, 391–512. Washington DC: Government Printing Office.

Veniaminov, Ivan. 1984 [1840]. *Notes on the Islands of the Unalashka District*. Translated by Lydia Black and R. H. Geoghegan. Kingston, Ontario: Limestone Press.

10

What's in a Name?

Becoming a Real Person
in a Yup'ik Community

Ann Fienup-Riordan

Naming is like the tide; it's always a little bit different, but if you watch it, you see how it works.

Billy Lincoln, Toksook Bay, 1977

Adoption was historically, and continues today to be, widespread in southwestern Alaska.[1] During the year I spent in Toksook Bay on Nelson Island in 1976 and 1977, 10 percent of the population had been adopted out of their families of generation, 62 percent of these by matrilateral relatives. In 1990, 40 percent of the households in Toksook Bay either had given a child up for adoption, adopted a child, or both.

Although there are no earlier figures for Nelson Island, reports from nearby Nunivak Island indicate that during the first half of the 20th century (a period of epidemic disease and population relocation) the frequency of adoption was even greater. During his visit to Nunivak in 1936–1937, German observer Hans Himmelheber wrote that 8 out of 18 children in a Nunivak village were not living with their biological parents (Fienup-Riordan 1999:9). Three years later, Margaret Lantis (1946:159–160) spent a year on the island, noting that of 31 families at Ellikarrmiut and Mekoryuk, 21 contained foster children or stepchildren. Moreover, several families included two or more adopted youngsters of different origins. Lantis attributed the high adoption rate both to high mortality and frequent marital separation, as marriages were traditionally weak and serial marriages common. Although these were certainly contributing factors, declines in mortality and marital separation levels have not resulted in a comparable drop in the rate of adoption, which continues to play an important role in Yup'ik community life.[2]

Most adoptions today come about not because a child needs a family but because someone wants a child. Adoption usually takes place between related families, most often by grandparents or same-generation consanguines (that is, a woman taking the child of either her daughter, son, or sister). As Lantis (1946:233) points out, although marriages were traditionally weak, bonds between grandparents, parents, siblings, and children continue to be strong. This is true in temporary as well as permanent adoption. The verb *alartuq* (literally, "mixed up") is sometimes applied to a child who gets attached to its grandmother or mother's sister when its mother has been gone and her parent or sibling is acting as caregiver in her absence.

Children come from relatives living as far away as Anchorage. In the early 1980s I received a call from a close Toksook Bay friend who had just arrived in Anchorage and wanted me to pick her up at the airport, which I did. We drove to an old apartment complex, rang the doorbell, entered, visited for ten minutes, and left with a three-month-old girl. My friend returned to Toksook the next morning. Ten years later, the same birth mother—a 30-year-old Yup'ik woman with a non-Native boyfriend—gave the family another child, bringing to six the number of that family's adopted children.

This particular Toksook family could not have children of their own, and to my knowledge infertility has not prevented any contemporary Nelson Island couple from raising children. Infertility, however, is perhaps the least common reason for adopting a child. Children most often are adopted both to spread out child-care responsibilities and to provide older relatives with companionship and the help of younger hands around the house.

Half-a-dozen terms commonly are applied to an adopted child, a testimony to its widespread practice: *anglicaraq*, or "someone raised," from *angli-* ("to grow or become big"); *aqumkengaq*, or "something that makes one sit down," from the root *aqume-* ("to sit down"), perhaps relating to the adopted child letting its parents sit down by working for them (Morrow and Pete 1996); *kitugtaq*, or "something straightened," from *kitugte-* ("to repair," "to fix," or "to straighten out a person's behavior"); *teguaq*, or "something taken," from *tegu-* ("to take"); and *yuliaq*, literally "a made person," from *yuk* ("person").

The Yup'ik words for adoption are *ilaksagute-* (literally, "to become related"; from *ilake-*, "to be related to," *yagute-*, "to reach the state of") and *yuksagute-* ("to become a person"; from *yuk*, "person," "human being"). If fed and clothed by the adoptive parents, the adopted child becomes like the parents' own. Yet unlike legal adoption in the United States, which usually severs the child's ties with its biological parents, the adopted child does not lose ties to its family of generation. Rather, the relationship between an adopted child and its natal parents and siblings is often maintained at the same time new ones are forged.[3] The adopted child has not only two sets of parents but two overlapping relational networks. Rather than being stigmatized as someone lacking the support of biological relations, adopted children have special standing as people rich in relatives. How this dual family membership is played out varies tremendously, ranging from close ties and daily visits with biological parents to more distant relations and infrequent face-to-face contact.

Neither Yup'ik nor Iñupiaq adoptions were marked by ritual distribution or ceremonial acts. Lantis (1946:233) said that this was because adoption, like divorce (another unmarked change in social status), did not affect the food supply: "Hence there were no taboos, and the community did not have any official part in these changes of status. . . . The indifference of the supernatural, absence of opportunity for social advancement by giving presents and feasts, and lack of other emotion-reinforcing acts and situations would keep these personal events from seeming overwhelmingly important even to the principals."

Extending kinship ties through adoption as well as other means served to extend one's support network and access to a variety of resources. The incidence of widespread adoption, even today, functions to extend families broadly within and between adjoining communities. As Maggie Smith put it, "There is *aata* [father] and *aana* [mother] going down the generations, forever and ever. Bobby . . . calls me mom, and he is not my own" (Fienup-Riordan 1983:165).

Given the frequency of adoption, its informality, and the broad, inclusive terms used to designate the adoption process, one might imagine easy adoption of anthropologists and others who come to live among Yup'ik families, now and in the past. During my 25 years living and visiting in southwestern Alaska, however, no Yup'ik family has adopted me. Yup'ik friends have told me (in Yup'ik and in English) that I am like one of the family, yet I have never heard them use the terms *ilaksagute-* or *yuksagute-* to describe our relationship.

Nelson Islanders have, however, given form to our long-standing relationship in uniquely Yup'ik terms that bring me into their families in essential ways. They have given me food and given me names, and I have reciprocated in kind. The reasons why I have not been adopted by a particular family but have been meaningfully incorporated into many families shed light on the Yup'ik understanding of adoption, naming, sharing, and what it means to be related.

When I arrived on Nelson Island in the early 1970s, people gave me two things readily and repeatedly—food and names. The food usually took the form of soup or dried fish shared at the kitchen table. This meant acceptance as well as a full stomach, as I had little money and no skills or equipment to catch my dinner. Later, when I got my own small house, gifts included fresh fish or meat for me to cook and share in my turn with those eating at my table. Over the years friends have marked my comings and goings with gifts of fish, berries, and birds. And if it is known that I have run out of a staple like seal oil, I soon receive a clean Clorox bottle full of fresh oil.

These gifts are not always from the families I knew best when I lived on Nelson Island. My relatedness now extends to the whole community. My relationship with many Toksook families has deepened, and I regularly go back to Nelson Island with my children so that they, too, can get to know their "relatives." I reciprocate by sending fruit at Christmas, boxes of clothes that my children have outgrown, gifts to distribute to guests at winter dances, and books and photographs. Families I know best can and do make requests for specific big-ticket items, such as tents, tape recorders, or cases of food from Costco. Most important, we share meals when people come into Anchorage. This style of giving—open-ended and unspecified—is similar to that between adopted children and their biological parents as well as other relatives. Ties of all kinds are maintained by giving gifts and sharing food. The extent of this largess varies greatly, depending on peoples' means and inclinations.

In recent years I have probably given more than I have received, reflecting my feeling of indebtedness for the things given freely and abundantly by Toksook families since the beginning of our relationship. By giving what I can, when I can, sometimes when asked and sometimes spontaneously, I realize in a small way the Yup'iks view of material wealth as something to be shared rather than possessed.

The names my family and I have been given provide another link with the Yup'ik community as well as a window on that relationship. As I've written elsewhere (Fienup-Riordan 1983:xvii), I came to Nelson Island with few expectations and no particular desire or ambition to be adopted. After I had lived at Toksook for several months, however, I did want to be named, although at that point I was almost entirely ignorant of what receiving a name implied.

During my first year on Nelson Island I received a name from a Chefornak family with whom I lived during berry-picking season. They called me Uqpak (literally, "big piece of seal blubber"). The name was not descriptive, as I was not so very heavy, but was bestowed because of something I had in common with a young Chefornak woman. Although a bit older than I, she was childlike in all her actions. When she was very young, her mother had died at the Bethel hospital, and for years Uqpak went to the airport to meet every plane, checking for her mother. The community watched over, humored, and cared for her. Her name certainly suited my comparably dependent and childlike state and rarely failed to elicit a smile or laugh during introductions.

Uqpak was not the first name I was offered. But I hesitated to accept what I thought might be an exclusive tie with one family. During that first year I did not know enough to understand that accepting one name did not preclude accepting another or that multiple names were the rule, not the exception. Since then, close Yup'ik friends have given me other names that I cherish. One woman recently told me that her mother, who died in 1993, had never liked that they called me Uqpak. She wanted me to be Nalukaq, the name of her husband's mother. The daughter gave me Nalukaq as another name, which I always use with her family. In fact, all my names come from the givers' close kin, and in a very real sense with each name I become a family member.

Not only have I received Yup'ik names, but my own *kass'aq* (non-Native) name has been "Yup'ified." Everyone in Toksook calls me Anna. Ann is not in the Toksook repertoire, but they have many Annas, alive and dead, and I have joined their number. Others call me in relation to my children, that is "Jimmy's mom" or "Frances's parent," and I sign Christmas cards accordingly.

My children have also been named, each one in a different way. Our eldest was given her Yup'ik name at six weeks of age on her first visit to Toksook. There, just weeks before, a male cousin of Frances Usugan, the woman who had taught me and helped me the most during my year on Nelson Island, had drowned during a storm. As soon as Frances Usugan entered her daughter's house, where we were staying, she gave my daughter her cousin's name, Qevlialria, "one who sparkles." Soon after, Qevlialria's widow and children visited us, bringing gifts and "oooing" and "ahhing" over their tiny "husband" and "father."

My daughter's naming first brought home to me the meaning that names carry. People asked my baby's name everywhere we visited over the next week and, when I told them, commented, "Oh, he's come back a *kass'aq* [white person]!" or "He always *did* want to learn English" or "And to think that now he has red hair!" This verbal play on her name was a way of welcoming my daughter into their midst. These endearments were also wonderfully explicit expressions of the belief that some aspect of the recently dead appears again in the newborn child. In the Yup'ik world, no one ever passes out of existence. Rather, through naming, the essence of being human is passed on from one generation to the next. My daughter had not only Toksook "relatives" in a general sense but a wife, children, and cousins. Qevlialria had been born again.

THE RELATIONSHIP BETWEEN THE LIVING NAMESAKE AND THE DEAD

The traditional Yup'ik concept of soul was complex and did not correspond to a simple distinction between mind and body. The human person comprised a number of spiritual components. At death at least one of these, in some accounts the *tarneq* (possibly related to *taru* or *taruq*, rarely used words for "human being" or "person"), left the human body and went to live in the land of the dead. From then on, its physical link with the human world was the namesake who reincarnated some essential part of the deceased.

Mather (1985:105–108) and Morrow (1984:128) record that the terms *anerneq* ("breath"), *avneq* ("felt presence," "ghostly humming"), *yuuciq* ("life," "lifeline"), and *puqlii* ("its warmth," "heat") were used to designate distinct aspects of the human person. Nelson Islanders also referred to a person's *umyuara* ("one's mind"), *unguvii* ("one's life spirit, or soul"), and *yuucian unguvii* ("one's living spirit"). Some people held that a person's "mind," "heat," and "breath" did not survive death. Others identified a person's *anerneq* or *yuucian unguvii* as capable of rebirth when a newborn received the person's name. But as with a person's *tarneq*, all agreed that loss of either one's breath or heat brought death, just as their possession was essential to living (Fienup-Riordan 1994:212).

As vital to life as one's thought, breath, heat, vision, voice, and visible image was the possession of an *ateq* ("name"). A nameless person was a contradiction in terms. When a child received a name, that aspect of the dead destined for rebirth transferred across the boundary between worlds and entered the child's body. As the part recalled the whole, the dead were reborn through the gift of the name. The name of the deceased was not, however, always or even usually bestowed on a single person. More than one child might be named after the same person (depending on the extent of the deceased's kin group and personal reputation), and most children received more than one name. An *atellgun* (from *ateq*, "name," plus *-llgute-*, "fellow") was a person having both name and namesake in common with another (Fienup-Riordan 1983:149–158).

Essential aspects of a person, like the *tarneq*, separated from the human body at death and began to follow the path to the underworld. However, it appears that the name, like the seal's *yua* ("its person" or "owner"), was destined for rebirth in human form. Edward Nelson (1899:437) observed that the human hunter both propitiated and to some extent controlled the *yuit* ("persons") of sea mammals by keeping them with their bladders and later returning them to their watery world. In this way he produced more animals than if he let them wander freely or go to the land of the dead. The same belief extended to inanimate objects (furs, food, parkas, and so on) of which a small part could retain the essence of the entire article. By retaining the name of the deceased, a part of the dead was reborn at the same time a channel was created between the world of the living and that of the dead.

Although no ritual accompanied adoption, naming was often marked by offering gifts to the living and food to the dead. At birth a child was named in a ceremony designated *kangiliriyaraq* (literally, "to provide with a beginning"; from *kangiq*, meaning "beginning," "source"). The essence of the dead destined for rebirth entered the newborn at this time. Children were most often named for a recently deceased relative or community member. The person naming the child dropped water at the "four corners" of the child's head but not on the head itself (*merrluku*, from *merte-*, "to sprinkle water"). While doing so they would say that the one whose name the child was receiving had come.

In the past the annual feast for the dead, known in some areas as *merqiyaraq* (the process of providing a human with *meq* ["fresh water"]), reaffirmed the original relationship between the living child and the dead person for whom he or she was named. Relatives gave gifts to the living namesakes to provision the deceased. Donors sprinkled pinches of food and small amounts of water in the fire pit or on the ground, being careful to recall who had gathered the food and helped in its preparation. As in food placed beside a grave, people believed the dead received these morsels as large stores. People always included fresh water to supply the needs of the "thirsty" dead.

People continue to believe that a part of the dead enters those named after them and in the process bestows something of themselves. *Kangiliriyaraq* still takes place both informally in the home and, in some Catholic communities, as a formal part of the baptismal service. As the part recalls the whole, the gift of the name constitutes the rebirth of the dead.

Sometimes a child became ill after someone died, and people attributed this to the child's desire to acquire the name of the deceased. It was said that the child was *kangingyugluni*, literally, "wanting to get a (new) beginning or source." Alternately, the deceased might want to enter a particular child and would hover around, making the child sick until it was properly named. Then the child would recover. If a couple had several children die at an early age, they might deduce that the infants' namesakes were requesting different parents. To avoid having discontented namesakes, the parents might name a subsequent child Atrilnguq ("No Name") or relinquish the child to their kin to raise to satisfy the dead's request (Morrow and Pete 1996:246). Parents also avoided punishing small children out of respect for the elder who may have taken up residence in the child. If they treated the child harshly, the shade would forsake the child, causing illness or death. The treatment of my own children by Toksook friends and relatives certainly followed this pattern.

Many Yup'ik men and women continue to place great importance on the fit between the child and the name. They believe that illness and even death can result if the match is not acceptable. When I was ill with cancer in 1992, I was given several new names as part of the healing process, gaining strength and support from an active network of new relatives. Not only does the deceased seek out a particular child, but the child desires a particular name. A newborn cries because it wants its name and will not be complete without it.

As in the case of my daughter's naming, the relatives of the deceased person for whom the child was named present the child with gifts of food and water. According to the late Billy Lincoln (April 1986) of Toksook Bay, "They give food to the namesakes remembering one's dead baby, father, or mother. They fill a bowl with good food and also include water in it. That is the way they give food. They also talk with him/her.[4] And then the one being given things drinks the water. And the rest of the food in the bowl is buried in the ground, *aviukarrluki* ["making a food offering to the dead"]. It is said that the food goes to the ones they are thinking about when they do that." Mary Worm (May 13, 1989) of Kongiganak continued, "When people die, they say what they call *kangiliriyaraq* ["to provide with a beginning"]; they give them names. It is said that their namesakes, when they get clothes, [the dead] also get clothes. When these people with the same names are given those things, the things do not go to any place else. But it all goes to that person who has died."

As with my daughter, relatives of the deceased later may give the child clothes or other small gifts. Frances Usugan made sure that my daughter Frances had a beautiful fur parka for her first winter, and many small *qaspeqs* (cotton dresses) and hand-knit mittens and socks came her way over the years. Although I was given the name Nalukaq secondhand and over the phone, in the weeks that followed, Nalukaq's granddaughter sent me two beautiful *qaspeqs*. These gifts supplied both the needs of the namesake in the human world and the needs of the dead. Relatives of the deceased both refer to and address the child with *tuqluutet* (relational terms appropriate to the dead namesake). In the past this treatment included rigorously avoiding the use of the proper name, although the public use of one's Yup'ik name today is more often a point of pride.[5]

Even today people say that the actions of very young children mirror those of their namesakes. The child's behavior and abilities, more than appearance, make it apparent who the child is. This is especially true during the first years of life. My third child, Nicky, was born with a lung condition, and during his first week he was very ill. Elena Charles of Bethel subsequently gave him the name of her brother Ellaq'aq, who had been sickly all his life and had recently passed away. Sometime later she called me on the phone and immediately asked after the baby's health. Assuming she was checking on my mothering, I assured her that her "brother" was fine. In fact, he had a bad cold. When we met Elena the next day, she warmly greeted her baby brother, and he responded by coughing in her face. Tears came to her eyes, and she exclaimed, "Now I really know him!" Since then, she has fondly called me Ellaq'am Arnaan, the mother of Ellaq'aq.

Yup'ik names are sexually undifferentiated—neither male nor female—and are gendered by reference to the namesake. Thus our daughter has a man's Yup'ik name, and one of our sons carries the name of a woman. Parents still sometimes dress their young children according to the gender of the one for whom they were named.

In the Yup'ik view of the world, procreation is not the addition of new persons to the inventory of the universe. Rather, it is the substitution of one for another. Some spiritual essence passes with the name, and in an important way the dead are believed to live again through their namesakes. With the gift of a name, one becomes more than a relative. One gains not only social connections but a distinct social identity, becoming a unique "real person." Each ancestral name, passed on through generations of men and women, has a life of its own. Although human beings come and go, the names of the "real people" remain the same.[6]

Through the ruled behavior surrounding death, childbirth, and naming, the Yup'ik people transformed the biological opposition between life and death into a cosmological cycling between birth and rebirth. The gift of a name following a human death ensured human life in perpetuity. Rather than a grand finale, the death of an individual was an instance of cosmological reproduction (Fienup-Riordan 1983:189–248).[7]

As a namegiver Frances Usugan recognized and gave voice to a connection between her dead cousin and our newborn child. She saw aspects of her cousin in our daughter at the time she gave her his name. Our daughter did not become generically Yup'ik with this gift; rather, she became a specific "real person" with a unique personality and family tree. I also became a particular person with the gift of the name Uqpak and again with the name Nalukaq. Moreover, while each individual name connects me to a specific person and kindred, no one has my particular combination of names.

Naming an infant for someone who has recently passed away is often more formal and deliberate and carries more weight than naming a non-Native adult after a long-dead or living community member. Phyllis Morrow told me that, like many other non-Natives living in Bethel, she received her Yup'ik name in a class in conversational Yup'ik given at the local community college. Yet having a Yup'ik name is significant no matter how it is acquired. How important a name becomes for someone depends not only on how the name was received but also, like Yup'ik kin relations more generally, on how one "acts on one's name" in the future.

From the Yup'ik point of view, the essence of what it means to be human passes through the name, not as in American culture "through the blood" (Schneider 1968; Bodenhorn 1995:15). This view of personhood, created through cosmological rather than biological reproduction, is simultaneously why adoption is so easy and casual and why naming is so important. Biological birth sets the stage, creating a person but not personhood. Relatedness is based on the long-term actions that follow the birth, not the sexual act that engendered it.[8] Our physical parentage did not create our daughter's character as a "real person." Rather, the gift of a name supersedes her *kass'aq* "bloodline" and gives her a concrete Yup'ik identity. Adoption into a Yup'ik family (that is, changing her residence from our Anchorage home to the household of one of her Toksook relatives) is not necessary to make her a full community member, nor would our legal adoption of a Yup'ik child automatically diminish that child's Yup'ik personhood.

In the past, proper names were never used in direct address or indirect reference, both out of respect for the namesakes and because of the names' power. They were replaced by variations on kin terms, such as Macungaq ("little grandmother") or Alaq ("older sister"). In address and reference, children might be referred to as so-and-so's son or daughter, while adults were called "oldest child's parent." Pet names like Akutaq (literally, "a mixture") also were used.

The original respectful avoidance of proper names still engenders a complex web of "calling names" within and between communities. Just as my family and I have received names that place us in overlapping kin groups, we have been given unique Yup'ik names that add to our special identity within the Yup'ik community. These "calling names" are not ancestral, that is, defining a person's position within a particular genealogy. Many are teasing names, comparable to English nicknames, and often they are widely known and used. For example, my children have animal nicknames, given them in jest because of their parents' incompetence at harvesting, and most people at Toksook know them. Frances is Iqalluarpak ("herring fish," the staple food of Nelson Island, which always evaded my net), Jimmy is Amirkaq (the young bearded seal my husband never caught), and Nick is Naternaq ("flounder," the lone flatfish I retrieved from a 30-foot setnet). By extension, I am also "mother of Herring" or "Herring" for short.

Until he entered grade school, Jimmy was known in Anchorage as well as southwestern Alaska as "Jimmy boy," another village-English name that an Alakanuk friend had given him that stuck. How much a part of our lives this "calling name" became was made clear one day when I went to pick him up from his Anchorage preschool. The caregiver told me that one of his playmates' parents was planning a party and had asked for the phone number of "Mrs. Boy."

My husband, Dick, also has the "calling name" of Nukalpiaq ("great hunter and provider"), received within our first months on Nelson Island. I made it a habit to study Yup'ik grammar on Tuesday and Thursday afternoons, when many in the community were busy playing bingo. During one such session I memorized the word *nukalpiaq*, defining it incorrectly as "husband." I compounded my error in the days to come by referring to Dick (a lawyer, not a hunter) as "my *nukalpiaq*." I thought I was being descriptive, but everyone else took my error as an opportunity for friendly teasing. Since then, young and old alike at Toksook hail Dick as Nukalpiaq, or Nukall' for short.

No discussion of relatedness in a Yup'ik community would be complete without mention of this gentle (and sometimes not so gentle) teasing, marking a comical feature or flaw with humor. Some teasing names, like Dick's designation Nukalpiaq, are widely known and broadly used. Others mark a teasing relationship between two people and regularly preface personal encounters between them. For instance, I nicknamed one young boy Kaugpak ("walrus") after the two streaks of mucus that regularly ran from his nose when he was a child. The boy is now grown, but the name remains. Twenty-five years ago, his father had the job of answering the one-and-only village phone with the greeting, "Toksook Bay." I've called him Mr. Toksook Bay ever since, and he calls me Anna Banana in return.

Kinship terms may also be used in reference and address in a less-than-serious manner. The terms for cross-gender cross-cousin, *uicungaq* ("dear little husband") and *nuliacungaq* ("dear little wife"), are particularly prone to such use, as the relationship between cross-cousins (mother's brother's and father's sister's children) is rife with teasing and sexual innuendo. Once I went looking for a woman friend in the steam bath and instead found half-a-dozen men. One old fellow took the occasion to call me his *nuliacungaq*, and he teased me with both word and deed for the rest of his life. Only when I was in my forties was I brave enough to reciprocate, which I did several times by publicly presenting him with little steam bath presents. Names, gifts, and lots of laughs all contributed to an ongoing teasing relationship and quasi "cousinship," which I've continued with his children since his death. Webs of many such strands weave each person inextricably and uniquely into the community.

Thus, at birth a person enters into a relationship with the dead based on shared name and a relationship with the living through both terminological skewing and an elaborate system of "calling names." Later, when people have their own offspring, they enter into a relationship with the living child through shared names (teknonomy), while simultaneously entering into a relationship with the dead by way of terminological skewing in reference to the child. A man may speak of his "father" when referring to his newborn son, and later laugh when the baby calls him "son." Thus a man becomes father to his father and offspring of his own child, standing Wordsworth's immortal phrase on its head in ways the poet could not have imagined. Alternate generations are equated. More than a relationship between the living and the dead, a cycling occurs between them. Continuity is emphasized, and death is denied (Fienup-Riordan 1983:153–158).

Just as more than one child may be named after a person (especially a well-loved and respected elder), children (and anthropologists) usually receive more than one name. I am both Uqpak and Nalukaq. My daughter is Qevlialria and Cikayak (after a Chefornak woman who also died before she was born). This multiplicity of names does not negate the cycling between generations but rather deepens and enriches it. Most people have many names, continuing to receive new ones throughout their lives. This is also true among many contemporary Iñupiat (Bodenhorn 1995). These multiple names can have negative repercussions in Yup'ik dealings with the non-Native world. In 1997 the U.S. Passport Agency initially denied requests for passports for four Yup'ik elders traveling to Berlin and finally only issued them on a limited basis because the elders' written records—baptismal and birth certificates, government enrollment forms, and so on—were issued in different names. Government agencies like the U.S. Passport Agency require a single fixed name and give no quarter to people who employ a more complex system.

Two of the three *kass'aq* names my husband and I chose for our children also come from Yup'ik families. Unlike Yup'ik personal names, which carry on the names of departed relatives, we named Frances and Nick after beloved living elders Frances Usugan and Nick Charles. Naming after living elders is not traditional, but in this expansive and infinitely creative system, it is a recognizable and acceptable variation on a theme, adding to our daughter's and son's unique personhood. Like the gift of a Yup'ik name from a Yup'ik friend to us, our use of two respected elders' English names adds depth to relationships already in place.

In all their permutations, these Yup'ik names are not just things my family and I possess but relationships we act upon with Yup'ik friends in many contexts. In all cases, in fact, acting like kin preceded our being named like kin. We shared berry picking, child care, ice fishing, and work in the herring pits, not to mention all manner of fun, food, and jokes. We were given both nicknames and real ancestral names accordingly, a process that will probably continue as long as our relationships with members of that community.

When I meet a Yup'ik person, I establish an immediate link by speaking their language. Usually they first ask where I am from. I often answer "Qaluyaarmiunguunga" ("I am a Nelson Island person"). Many then ask if I was a teacher there, and I explain that I first went to Toksook to learn their language and that I'm still learning. When they know where I am from and what I do, they may also ask my name and I ask theirs. After that link has been established, we know how we are related and we may greet each other accordingly whenever we meet.

People, especially those from Toksook, often ask after my children by one of their Yup'ik names, and newer acquaintances also begin to place me by asking what my children's names are. The children know their names and who their relatives are. We make these relations real with both small and large gifts, depending on the occasion. With the birth of our first child, my husband and I became subject to gift-giving requirements in her names. These we began to discharge when I brought her to a midwinter dance (*Kevgiruaq*, "Pretend Messenger Feast") and contributed canned goods, cloth, and tobacco as gifts in her name. We continue to remember her "wife" and "children" in small ways. Relatives of the deceased also have given small gifts to honor both their dead relative and the namesake child.

A child's first culturally significant accomplishments—such as first bird harvested, first dance, first berries gathered, or first fish caught—continue to provide the occasion for elaborate distributions on Nelson Island. These distributions may occur during annual dance distributions or as separate events accompanied by gifts of food to community elders. The seal party (*uqiquq*), a distribution of seal meat, oil, and gifts given annually by a man's wife or mother to celebrate his first seal of the season, is also appropriate (Fienup-Riordan 1983:190–201). When my children and I visited Toksook Bay in the summer of 1990, we brought several hundred dollars worth of store goods (cloth, diapers, candy, tea, yarn, plastic cups, and potholders) to give away for Jimmy (then nine), who had caught his first fish. Women from all over the village gathered in front of the house where we were staying to take part in the fun. My daughter and I helped distribute the gifts, while Jimmy and Nicky watched from the bedroom window. A month of preparation, and in less than 15 minutes the giveaway was done.

At all major ceremonies, even today, people distribute the most valuable gifts in the name of young children who are, by name, their ancestors incarnate. When guests gather in the community hall to receive their shares in the distribution, the hosts give out gifts to the eldest first on down to the youngest. At the head of the receiving line are parents with babes in arms who receive special gifts in the name of their offspring. At the same midwinter dance in which we gave gifts for our daughter, I was both embarrassed and proud to be singled out as Qevlialria's mother, receiving handmade quilts and a bolt of cloth in his name.

WHAT'S IN A NAME

A Yup'ik poet might well rewrite Shakespeare's famous phrase, "What's in a name? A rose by any other name would smell as sweet." For my Yup'ik friends, a person by any other name would be an entirely different person with a different set of relatives. For many Yupiit, it is not their parents (either natal or adoptive) but their names that distinguish who they are. Although biological birth sets the stage, it is not determinant in the creation and expression of Yup'ik person-hood. In the Yup'ik view of the world, shared names are what "shared substances" are in other peoples' understandings of what it means to be related: for example, blood in American kinship (Schneider 1968), semen among the Burmese (Spiro 1977), and breast milk among the people of Langkawi in Malaysia (Carsten 1997). Biological generation is necessary but not sufficient for cosmological regeneration by people who view relatedness as cyclical and creative rather than chronological and predetermined.

Anthropologists are far from the only ones to experience this naming and integration into Yup'ik community. Just as the namesake relationship is central to the fabric of Yup'ik life and what it means to be a "real person," so it is central in relations with outsiders. Teachers, health professionals, missionaries and priests, traders, collectors, in fact, any and all strangers to the region continue to be routinely named, fed, and teased (not necessarily in that order), some with their knowledge and some without. For example, a Moravian missionary in the Bethel area was given the name Qakineq, the white driftwood with the skin peeling off. According to John Active of Bethel, that was a good name for him because "*qakineqs* always burn really well in a steam bath." Usiyuq was a name given to a white trader who always said, "Oh, see you!" when he parted company with others. Another non-Native with wrinkly skin was called Puqliq (from *puqla*, "warmth," "heat"), while yet another was nicknamed Paraluruaq ("grain of rice"; literally, "imitation maggot"). The list goes on and on.

These nicknames, often bestowed in fun but integrative nonetheless, do not carry the same weight as ancestral names, which are usually accompanied by rights as well as duties. Whereas most outsiders, whether aware of it or not, receive descriptive nicknames that relate them to the entire community, not all non-Natives receive an ancestral name, a gift that simultaneously enacts and extends that person's social relations and obligations within a particular family. Yet even non-Natives working in the region who have never been named may be meaningfully integrated with the birth of a child who, as in the case of my daughter, will likely receive one or more ancestral names.

The longer one stays, and the more willing one is to share food and friendship, the richer and more complex one's web of connectedness becomes. In the same way that Yup'ik men and women receive a multitude of names and decide which among them to actualize, so too outsiders may be given many names, some of which they acknowledge and some of which they don't. Some non-Natives become so much a part of Yup'ik community life that they not only receive Yup'ik names but, when they die, their *kass'aq* names are passed on to succeeding generations of Yup'ik children. Father Frank Fallert, a priest who was a longtime worker in coastal communities, passed away in 1990, and numerous baby Franks were born soon after.

Incorporation into Yup'ik, Iñupiaq, and Inuit community life is extraordinarily complex and varied all across the Arctic, for anthropologists as well as others. In my case, the act of naming conferred personhood and status as a "real person," both giving form to and extending my relatedness to Yup'ik family and community. But I had to act in certain ways before I received these names, and accepting them has entailed both rights and obligations in return.

Personally, receiving Yup'ik names has meant a great deal to me. It has been both a sign of acceptance as a "real person" and an expression of fellow feeling already established. When I was sick, calls from Yup'ik friends saying that the village was praying for Uqpak in church gave me as strong a feeling of love and support as calls from my own *kass'aq* family. Many Yup'ik friends know what I do, that I am not perfect, and that I make mistakes. Continuing to "name-call" voices their willingness to accept me as I am, warts and all.

Like most of my contemporaries working in Yup'ik communities since the 1970s, my children and I were named but not adopted. Adoption of anthropologists in the Arctic is, I think, as rare as naming is common, and when it does occur it is—like naming—an ongoing, creative process, realized in many forms. Yup'ik adoption is, first and foremost, defined as taking responsibility and caring for someone, as opposed to ownership, as in "having a baby." It may be significant that the only two Arctic anthropologists I know who have experienced something close to adoption are two unmarried women, Jean Briggs and Barbara Bodenhorn, neither of whom have children. Although neither initially sought adoption, both have continued long-term relationships with Inuit families as "daughters." Each speaks of her incorporation into kinship relations as a complicated process, not an act or a fact, susceptible to change as long as they and their "kin" live.

Working in the Central Canadian Arctic in the early 1960s, Jean Briggs (1970:20–21) was absorbed into an Utkuhikhalingmiut family but not named. Briggs did not ask to be adopted, but her Inuit hosts interpreted her desire to be incorporated into a family in this way. When she said she wanted to live with a family, her initial contact (the Inuit Anglican minister's wife) responded, "There are several men looking for wives." When Briggs demurred, the woman suggested, "Then you should be a daughter," and sent a letter to that effect to the Utkuhikhalingmiuts.

A genuine sense of belonging developed between Briggs and the Inuit family with whom she lived so closely during 17 months of fieldwork. Briggs (personal communication) recalled her own surprise at the continued depth and complexity of this relationship. She remembered many occasions on which the kinlike character of their relationship was called into play, and she was referred to in a variety of ways, including *paniksaq* (literally, "daughter material"), *tiguaq* ("adoptee"), and "that *qaallunaaq* Yiini" ("that white person Jean"). Yet during one of many visits with her Inuit family, Briggs referred to herself as "Allaq's daughter," and Allaq corrected her, saying simply, "I take care of her." The adoptive relationship is a delicate one. While in some contexts it might be recognized, in others it presumed too much.

Barbara Bodenhorn, who has worked in Barrow since the early 1980s, also speaks of her incorporation into Iñupiaq society as a situated and flexible relationship, rather than a formal event. As she continued to act like a daughter, she was more and more often referred to as such. In response to my queries about her experiences, she wrote:

> What happened during my 1997 fieldwork is that I am more frequently identified in a specific relationship. In Barrow, Raymond Neakok often introduces me as *panin* [my daughter]. In Wainwright, one of Mattie Bodfish's sons teasingly introduces me to his kids as his sister. When I've overheard Raymond and Mattie telling others about my relationship to them, it's more often because I used to "go *aullaq* [camping]" with them. I was named in Raymond's adoptive folks' house—after a long discussion by several elders around the table. The *fact* that I was named was very important. The relationship that has grown and strengthened is my *atiq* [name] relationship. Mattie is the only one who calls me the name with any regularity, and once (to my knowledge) explained behavior in terms of my name (she had been chuckling over the fact that I'd brought her *maktak* [whale skin] from Barrow, and then said, "But of course, you're that one"). I expect that yours and my incorporation into various family systems has been somewhat parallel in that I probably wouldn't characterize it as "real adoption" but would probably be happy with "real kinship." (Bodenhorn, personal communication)

Jean Briggs, Barbara Bodenhorn, and I have had a variety of experiences. My family and I were given many names but never adopted, Jean Briggs was referred to with kin terms but not named, and Barbara Bodenhorn received a name as part of an ongoing process of acting like kin. These variations on a theme reflect Yup'ik, Iñupiaq, and Inuit differences as well as differences in the personal histories of those who came to work with them. Yet we all share the experience of being brought into family and community in meaningful ways over decades of work in the North.

I want to close with a point about the relationship between becoming a "real person," Yup'ik community membership, and access to information. Although I visit my "relatives" at Toksook more and more, I write about them less and less. Living with several families gives me access to personal information, but it has also made me reluctant to talk about them by name. They are friends, not subjects. What I learn from them helps me better understand what it means to be a Yup'ik person, but our relationship is private and personal. Although I do not choose to share the details of our friendship, I can and do share what they teach me. With their permission I can quote them. What I do not want to do is expose them. What I might do is encourage them to write their own books. But that is another story.

NOTES

Thanks to Barbara Bodenhorn, Jean Briggs, Tiger Burch, Sergei Kan, Susan McKinnen, and Phyllis Morrow for their helpful comments on an earlier draft of this essay. I dedicate the essay to the late David M. Schneider, who helped build the fire over which ideas like these continue to boil.

1. Adoption also has been and remains widespread among the Iñupiat and Inuit of northwestern Alaska and the Canadian Arctic (Bodenhorn 1995; Burch 1975:129; Gubser 1965:146; Guemple 1965, 1970, 1972; Heinrich 1955:149, 150; Jenness 1918:95; Murdoch 1892: 419; Spencer 1959:74, 91).

2. More than 20,000 Yup'ik Eskimos (or Yupiits) make their homes in Alaska, comprising nearly one-fourth of the total Native population of the state. While nearly 3,000 live in Anchorage, the majority live in the Yukon-Kuskokwim delta, scattered in 60 villages ranging in size from 150 to 800 people as well as in the regional center of Bethel. These modern villages each have elementary and secondary schools, a city government or traditional council, health clinic, church or churches, and airstrip. Each community supports a cash economy, and families have access to many pieces of Western technology, including television, snow machines, telephones, electricity, and, in some cases, running water and flush toilets. The

Yukon-Kuskokwim delta comprises one of the poorest and most economically depressed regions of the state. In part because of the beleaguered commercial economy and in part because of intense cultural preference, reliance on the harvest of the region's abundant natural resources—fish, seals, birds, moose, plants, and berries—continues to be strong.

Although monetarily impoverished, the Yup'ik people possess a rich cultural heritage, and they are among the most traditional Native American groups. Especially in coastal communities a primary occupation of men continues to be fishing and sea mammal hunting, and women devote weeks to processing the catch. Yup'ik dancing and traditional ritual distributions continue to be important parts of community life. Although most young and middle-aged community members are bilingual, Central Yup'ik is still a child's first language in coastal communities on Nelson Island and at the mouth of the Kuskokwim River as well as the primary language of village residents over age 50 (Fienup-Riordan 1996:33–42).

3. Legal adoptions are more and more common among Iñupiat and Yup'ik families today, although still far from universal. Some seek them while others avoid them because they do the culturally unthinkable—abolish the rights of the biological parents (Burch 1975:131; Morrow and Pete 1996:4). Conversely, mainstream adoption practices in the United States are increasingly approaching the Inuit recognition that biological ties need not be broken, in some cases allowing the adopted child freedom to choose whether or not to pursue the biological link.

4. Such talk can consist of endearments and instructions to act in certain ways. Jean Briggs (personal communication) was told that in the Canadian Arctic namesakes were instructed to do certain things that those for whom they were named had been unable to do in their lifetimes but hoped to accomplish in the next.

5. Today personal names may be used by Yup'ik men and women in public introductions because they are often speaking to people who do not know them. The first Alaska Natives whom I heard open public statements with their names and family connections were Tlingit speakers during Alaska Federation of Natives meetings in

Anchorage in 1978. The steady growth of intertribal contacts since then may have influenced Yup'ik speakers to do the same.

6. Compare the Krikati people of Brazil (Lave 1979:16–44) who also recycle a fixed universe of names in alternating generations, but in ways that have very different implications for relatedness in their communities. They, too, make a clear opposition between physical reproduction of the body, involving parenthood and kin relations, and the reproduction of social identity, involving name transmission, name relations, and ceremonial activities.

7. Mark Nuttall (1994:69) has found the same true among the Kallalit people of northwestern Greenland: "A recently deceased person will continue existing relationships through an *atsiaq* and will be linked to the namesharers and kin of the *atsiaq*. . . . Naming illustrates one of the most outstanding aspects of Inuit culture: the emphasis on continuity, rather than finality, of both person and community."

8. The downplaying of biology in Yup'ik conceptions of relatedness may partly explain why crossing the gender line is less problematic for many Yupiits (that is, naming an infant girl for a man and, in some cases, bringing her up accordingly until puberty).

REFERENCES

Bodenhorn, Barbara. 1995. Person, Place, and Parentage: Ecology, Identity, and Social Relations on the North Slope of Alaska. In *Arctic Ecology and Identity*, ed. S. A. Mousalimas, 103–132. Budapest: International Society for Trans-Oceanic Research.

Briggs, Jean. 1970. *Never in Anger: Portrait of an Eskimo Family*. Cambridge: Harvard University Press.

Burch, Ernest S., Jr. 1975. *Eskimo Kinsmen: Changing Family Relationships in Northwest Alaska*. American Ethnological Society, monograph 59. San Francisco: West.

Carsten, Janet. 1997. *The Heat of the Hearth*. Oxford: Oxford University Press.

Fienup-Riordan, Ann. 1983. *The Nelson Island Eskimo: Social Structure and Ritual Distribution*. Anchorage: Alaska Pacific University Press.

———. 1986. The Real People: The Concept of Personhood among the Yup'ik Eskimos of Western Alaska. *Etudes/Inuit/Studies* 10(1–2): 261–270.

———. 1994. *Boundaries and Passages: Rule and Ritual in Yup'ik Eskimo Oral Tradition*. Norman: University of Oklahoma Press.

———. 1996. *The Living Tradition of Yup'ik Masks: Agayuliyararput (Our Way of Making Prayer)*. Seattle: University of Washington Press.

———. 2000. *Hunting Tradition in a Changing World: Yup'ik Lives in Alaska Today*. New Brunswick: Rutgers University Press.

Fienup-Riordan, Ann, ed. 1999. *Where the Echo Began and Other Oral Traditions of Southwestern Alaska Recorded by Hans Himmelheber*. Fairbanks: University of Alaska Press.

Gubser, Nicholas J. 1965. *The Nunamiut Eskimos: Hunters of Caribou*. New Haven: Yale University Press.

Guemple, Lee. 1965. Saunik: Name Sharing as a Factor Governing Eskimo Kinship Terms. *Ethnology* 4(3):323–335.

———. 1970. Eskimo Adoption. Unpublished manuscript. Institute of Social and Economic Research, Memorial University of Newfoundland.

———. 1972. Kinship and Alliance in Belcher Island Eskimo Society. In *Alliance in Eskimo Society: Proceedings of the American Ethnological Society*, 1971 supplement, ed. Lee Guemple, 56–78. Seattle: University of Washington Press.

Heinrich, Albert Carl. 1955. An Outline of the Kinship System of the Bering Straits Eskimos. Master's thesis, University of Alaska.

Jacobson, Steven A. 1984. *Yup'ik Eskimo Dictionary*. Fairbanks: Alaska Native Language Center, University of Alaska.

Jenness, Diamond. 1918. The Eskimos of Northern Alaska: A Study in the Effects of Civilization. *Geographical Review* 5(2):89–101.

Lantis, Margaret. 1946. The Social Culture of the Nunivak Eskimo. *Transactions of the American Philosophical Society* (Philadelphia) 35: 153–323.

Lave, Jean. 1979. Cycles and Trends in Krikati Naming Practices. In *Dialectical Societies: The Ge and Bororo of Central Brazil*, ed. David Maybury-Lewis, 16–44. Cambridge: Harvard University Press.

Mather, Elsie P. 1985. *Cauyarnariuq [A Time for Drumming]*. Alaska Historical Commission Studies in History, no. 184. Bethel AK: Lower Kuskokwim School District Bilingual/Bicultural Department.

Morrow, Phyllis. 1984. It Is Time for Drumming: A Summary of Recent Research on Yup'ik Ceremonialism. In *The Central Yupik Eskimos*, ed. Ernest S. Burch Jr. Supplementary issue of *Etudes/Inuit/Studies* 8:113–140.

Morrow, Phyllis, and Mary Pete. 1996. Cultural Adoption on Trial: Cases from Southwestern Alaska. *Law and Anthropology* 8:243–259.

Murdoch, John. 1988 [1892]. *Ethnological Results of the Point Barrow Expedition*. Bureau of American Ethnology, annual report for 1887–88. Washington DC: Smithsonian Institution Press.

Nelson, Edward William. 1983 [1899]. *The Eskimo about Bering Strait*. Bureau of American Ethnology, annual report for 1896–97, vol. 18, pt. 1. Washington DC: Smithsonian Institution Press.

Nuttall, Mark. 1994. Names and Name-Sharing in a Greenlandic Community. *Musk-Ox* 40:66–69.

Schneider, David. 1968. *American Kinship: A Cultural Account*. Englewood Cliffs NJ: Prentice Hall.

Spencer, Robert. 1959. *The North Alaskan Eskimo: A Study in Ecology and Society*. Smithsonian Institution, Bureau of American Ethnology Bulletin 171. Washington DC: U.S. Government Printing Office.

Spiro, Melford. 1977. *Kinship and Marriage in Burma: A Cultural and Psychodynamic Analysis*. Berkeley: University of California Press.

Commentary

Raymond D. Fogelson

Over three years ago, the dean of social sciences at the University of Chicago asked me to serve on a committee for research on human subjects. I wrote him a rhetorical letter declining the invitation. I explained that in anthropology we didn't have human subjects (or, for that matter, human objects); if anything *we* were the subjects, or more scientistically, the dependent variables. Field research is only conducted with the approval and forbearance of the people "subjected" to the anthropologic gaze. What had once been an expected rite of passage in the training of an anthropologist has now become more of a privilege, as anthropologists increasingly retreat to the library or the navel-gazing safety of self-reflective study of their own society or closely related Western societies. I tried to convince the dean that the notion of human subjects was an inappropriate borrowing from the medical, biological, and psychological sciences. Anthropology, despite its intermittent claims to being a positivistic science, seems less wedded to the *naturwissenschaften* and more allied to the human sciences, the *geisteswissenschaften*.

The dean said he appreciated the substance of my letter, but he insisted that I serve on the committee anyway, since federal granting agencies were requiring stricter reviews of research projects. I have learned a few things since being coerced to join this committee. The criteria for informed consent are almost as vague and slippery as the vaunted anthropological method of participant observation, a kind of Caesarian triad—*veni, vidi, velcro* (I came, I saw, I stuck around).

Generally, anthropological proposals seek informant (or consultant, to be euphemistically correct) anonymity. However, a common source of contention involves the ultimate disposition of data. Do they belong to the anthropologist to whom the data were voluntarily given or acquired through purchase, or are these materials the intellectual property of tribal groups or individuals, not to be publicly disclosed without official approval?

Many of the issues regarding "human subjects" are directly and indirectly relevant to this unique collection of papers concerning the adoption and naming of anthropologists by Native Americans. As Sergei Kan points out in his introduction to this volume, adoption is a well established pattern, with many variants, that goes far back in the history of most Native American groups. Anthropologists had many predecessors as adoptees. Intra-group adoptions were common in most groups, reaching something of an apogee in the Arctic, as Ann Fienup-Riordan (chapter 10) and others document. Native adoption of captives individually or collectively was undoubtedly common long before the coming of Europeans. However, pressures occasioned by direct and indirect contact with Euro-Americans surely intensified adoption practices.

The advance guard of explorers, soldiers, traders, and missionaries were frequently given Indian names for purposes of reference as well as address. These indexical names often took the form of nicknames based on perceived peculiarities and distinctive identity markers; often these names were satirical and derisive. The idiom of kinship might also be invoked to express respect or degrees of closeness without any implication of formal or informal adoption. However, many times strangers were adopted by individuals and families for economic and political advantage or as a result of intermarriage and the birth of offspring.

Important proto-anthropologists were often adopted or intermarried into tribal societies and gained access to information denied more transitory observers. Such figures as James Adair, Mary Jemison, Louis Le Clerc Milford, John Heckewelder, John Dunn Hunter, Benjamin Arnsbard, and Henry Rowe Schoolcraft come readily to mind. As Elisabeth Tooker documents in her interesting essay, Lewis Henry Morgan requested that the Seneca formally adopt and provide names for him and three of his colleagues in their fraternal Grand Order of the Iroquois. Morgan used his personal contacts with the Parker family and considered adoption almost as something owed him for services rendered. The motives of the Senecas in complying with his request are unclear. On the surface, the Senecas looked forward to the feast that Morgan and his associates promised to provide. On another level, the Senecas were facing hard times and wished to present a favorable and sympathetic image to their white neighbors. Morgan seemed a suitable person to propagate such positive publicity. Retrospectively, Morgan's grandiose belief that his fraternal order would actually replace the venerable League of the Iroquois and keep alive its traditions may have seemed plausible at that moment. However, the League endured, while Morgan's Grand Order soon collapsed. Nevertheless, Morgan continued actively to support Iroquois causes throughout his life; but his adoption proved mostly honorary, as he didn't participate in ceremonies or otherwise engage in Seneca life.

William Fenton's adoption by the Seneca almost a century after Morgan was a gradual process driven by several generations of friendship between the Fenton family and the Snow family. The Snow family and relatives were his hosts, principal sources of information, and entry into the community when Fenton began fieldwork in the early 1930s. Although the Senecas already were suspicious of meddling anthropologists, Fenton's seriousness of purpose, respect for traditions, and eagerness to participate in religious "doin's" won the community over. Adoption for the Senecas seems to be based more on clanship than kinship; there was considerable discussion as to which clan or lineage would claim the young ethnographer. Part of the problem also involved the finite economy of available names. Eventually he was adopted into the Hawk clan and given the name He-lost-a-bet, the boyhood name of his sponsor, Jonas Snow.

Fenton's rich and detailed account of the adoption process is, in itself, a valuable contribution to Iroquois studies. The circulation of names among the Iroquois is epitomized in the names and titles of the hereditary chiefs of the League. These names have an existence of their own that transcends the life of a particular incumbent. Because names must be available for reassignment, the Iroquois seem chary about adopting outsiders. As Tooker notes, the adoption of Morgan and his fraternity brothers took place during a time of cultural crisis for the Iroquois; Fenton was only adopted because of transgenerational family ties and after considerable exposure to the community. The Iroquois are more likely to open their society and share cultural knowledge with outsiders during these times of crisis. This appears to have been the case in Morgan's time and in the late 19th and early 20th century when John Gibson and other ritual specialists recited sacred texts to Hewitt and Goldenweiser (see Kimura 1998); Fenton's adoption took place while the effects of the Great Depression were still rampant.

Michael Harkin's analysis of Northwest Coast patterns of adoption picks up a theme implicit in many of the other essays in this volume: that is, adoption as a means of socialization and control of the alien other as a way to reduce ambiguity and reassert structure. In Maussian terms, the bestowal of a name and a place in the social structure transforms an unconnected individual into a social person or, in the assumption of a ranked title, a personage. At once the society is augmented and renewed by this incorporation, or native colonization, if you will. The new title bearer is entitled to certain privileges and bodies of knowledge adhering to the title. There is a compromise between the internal individual identity and the more enduring external one, often personified in a characteristic mask. Harkin relates naming to cycles of birth and rebirth both with regard to the individual undergoing the transformation and the reincarnation of names or titles, which "have life of their own," although they may have been dormant for many years. The assumption of important titles requires public celebration, feasting, and gift exchange.

Harkin makes an interesting comment on the associations between ethnonyms and personal names. Collective and individual names are frequently constructed by Euro-Americans on the basis of personal characteristics, much like nicknames; Native terms for Euro-Americans often are constructed in similar fashion (see Alexander Chamberlain [1911] for a compilation of Native American names for Euro-Americans).

The adoption of anthropology's totemic ancestor, Franz Boas, by the Kwakwaka'wakw brings to light some new dimensions to naming processes. Harkin notes how Boas at different times provides alternate glosses on the name he was accorded, Heiltsakuls. First he mistakenly renders it as "the silent one," and later he more accurately translates it as "the one who says the right thing." About the same time that Boas was engaged in his fieldwork, Sigmund Freud was demonstrating how paraplexes or "slips of the tongue" were not accidental but determined, and in most instances overdetermined, by psychic processes. Perhaps "the silent one" represented Boas's idealized perception of himself as the neutral observer, the nonintervening objective scientist. Or maybe, as Harkin implies, the mistranslation was an overdetermined Native gloss intending to silence Boas and ensure that he wouldn't publicly broadcast the ceremonial secrets they were about to reveal to him. Many things are in a name.

The theme of secrecy continues in Harkin's revealing discussion of Thomas McIlwraith's exemplary ethnographic fieldwork among the Bella Coola. Again, adoption and naming are deployed as tribal defense mechanisms to control an investigator who was becoming privy to esoteric knowledge. Indeed, the effort at control and recognition of hierarchical status extended to Edward Sapir, McIlwraith's sponsor and superior, who also received a name, thus linking a remote Northwest Coast fishing fiord with the Canadian national seat of power in Ottawa.

These Northwest Coast adoptions presented by Harkin may represent metaphoric exocannibalism, or less atrociously reflect David Riesman's principle of rejection by partial incorporation. The marginality of the anthropological stranger is only temporarily overcome by fieldwork adoption, and with few exceptions the anthropologist is ultimately "redigested" and reassimilated into the academic community.

For Mary Black-Rogers, adoption is more than a temporary form of mutual adjustment to the ambiguities of fieldwork. She adopts the reportorial mode of "who, where, when, how, and why" to explicate her adoption among the Round Lake Ojibwas/Crees. The adoption was unsought by Black-Rogers, unmarked by any formal ritual, and only recognized when her adoptive mother, Meme, came to greet her new son-in-law, Mary's husband, the late Ed Rogers. Meme's unilateral move to adopt Black-Rogers appeared motivated by a desire to replace a daughter, also named Mary, who had died in infancy. Black-Rogers initially failed to acknowledge her adoption, wishing to preserve her anthropological objectivity and autonomy in the community. Her avoidance and ambivalence about her adoption reflected a strenuous effort to avoid the overrated anthropological sin of "going native."

The full significance of Black-Rogers's adoptive relationship deepened over the years through ongoing correspondence, regular trips to

Round Lake, and visits by her Indian relatives to California and To-ronto. Mary takes her kinship obligations seriously. For too many re-searchers, adoption becomes a manipulative field technique or a too soon forgotten romantic interlude rather than an abiding relationship of affection and trust; it's not surprising that many anthropologists are held in contempt by Native Americans for whom such relation-ships are far from "fictive." The death of Ed Rogers and his subsequent burial at Round Lake testify to the strength of the relationship that the Rogers have with their relatives. I know of only one other anthropolo-gist, James G. E. Smith, not coincidentally a close friend of Ed and Mary, who was also buried with his adoptive people, the Lubicon Lake Crees.

Mary Black-Rogers raises important theoretical issues in trying to distinguish adoption from fosterage. Northern Algonquians make some terminological distinctions between "raising someone" and full adoption as kin, but the sharp-edged differences get smoothed out in practice. She suggests the topic of fosterage needs more investigation.

Most anthropologists experience tension between trying to be ob-jective scientists while at the same time recognizing the profoundly humanistic aspects of their work. For Mary Black-Rogers this en-tailed a partial surrender of the sharply focused "white room/black box" character of her early research in favor of a more affective tone, a move from dispassionate distance to passionate proximity. Never-theless, through it all, Black-Rogers manages to remain a rigorous empiricist.

Bill and Marla Powers exemplify the virtues of long-term field-work, replete with its many obligations, minor vexations, and occa-sional conflict with anthropologic endeavors. They point up an im-portant Lakota distinction between naming and adoption. Naming can entail the creation of a new name based on physical features or idiosyncrasies of the individual being named. Names can also be transferred from living persons or the deceased. If a living person be-stows his or her name to someone else, he or she loses the use of that name; this is similar to the Iroquois practice discussed by Fenton. Among the Lakotas, naming is not the same as adoption, although the two events often coincide. Adoption may be informally based on "se-lection" and unmarked by ceremony, or it may entail a highly for-malized ritual ("making a relative") involving many participants and much gift exchange. Not only were the Powers adopted (twice each) and given names, but their two sons were similarly incorporated into the local kin group. As the Powers and other contributors assert, naming and adoption constitute social personhood and specify the necessity for knowledge of appropriate kin term usage and proper behavior. Their long exposure to the field and plural adoptions place the Powers in a complex web of kinship that allows alternate paths to defining relationships such that they can be active players in the system. Indeed, in good Lakota fashion, Bill and Marla Powers "know who they are; know what they are; and know where they come from."

Anne Straus's cogent essay on Northern Cheyenne adoption makes several points relevant to our discussion. Adoption of non-Indian others, including anthropologists, almost never involves official enrollment in the tribe. Such a legal status would entail important citizenship prerogatives: for example, voting in tribal elections, access to special treaty rights, and other exclusive benefits vis-à-vis federal, state, and local governments. However, this does not make adoption any less meaningful or emotionally charged for the adopted anthropologist. Straus mentions that most anthropologists working with contemporary Native Americans are conflicted over their scholarly intentions and their share of collective guilt over past and present mistreatment of Indians by members of the "dominant culture," including exploitative anthropologists. Being adopted, being "selected" in the Lakota sense, binds some of this anxiety and self-doubt about moral worthiness in the eyes of others.

Straus's own adoption by Josephine Sootkis came as a surprise when she was inferentially addressed as daughter. While skeptical of those who immediately experience adoption as a life-defining moment, Straus can retrospectively appreciate the profound and abiding changes that the adoption made in her own life. She has remained a loyal and dutiful daughter and sibling in her adopted family, and her own family has been affected in varying degrees by her adoption. She notes, as do others, that the adoption opens up possibilities for acquiring cultural knowledge through adopted kin while simultaneously limiting access to perspectives from other local families and sectors of the reservation community.

Anne Straus has subsequently established self-initiated kinship relations with members of the Chicago Indian community. Rather than representing a self-indulgent kind of double (or triple) dipping into the adoptive pool, these adoptions may better reflect her own bilocality and identification with multiple communities. She concludes by reminding us that adoption should not be regarded as a trophy of acceptance or a sine qua non for successful anthropological fieldwork.

Jay Miller goes Anne Straus one better by receiving four names from four very different Native American groups. One is reminded of Paul Radin's account of the overachieving Ojibwa boy who undertook multiple vision quests and obtained excessive spiritual power, which led to his self-destruction. Miller doesn't self-destruct or suffer identity diffusion; each situation he describes is distinctive and instructive.

Miller's first adoption among the Delawares seems to have been carefully programmed by his benefactor, the late Nora Dean. While his adoption is publicly celebrated, his new name remains private, as is customary in Delaware tradition. His Tsimshian adoption resembles a mutually agreed upon defense pact to protect against Jay's awkwardness and orotund improprieties. As such, it represented a responsibility assumed by his newly acquired kin, and it had the effect of constraining his fieldwork. He was not formally adopted by any members of the Federated Tribes on the Colville Reservation; rather, in a manner of treatment similar to other unattached outsiders residing among them, in particular the Jesuit missionaries, the elders took general responsibility for his well-being in the absence of other family.

I witnessed Miller's acquisition of a Muskogee name and also received a name myself on the same occasion. A name legitimizes membership in the local square ground or town, but provides no legal claim to tribal membership, nor does it secure a position in the kinship or clanship system. It might best be regarded as a ceremonial name limited to participation in square ground rites. The name itself was chosen by officials at the square ground on the basis of information gleaned from a brief interview and behavioral observation, an interesting instance of ethnoethnology.

I also was present when Jay Miller received his Tewa name during a conference at the Newberry Library. He was rewarded with a name by a Tewa musician who appreciated Jay's kindnesses. The name was more than a singular gift of thanks, since the relationship was reactivated on a subsequent visit Jay made to San Juan Pueblo.

It is interesting to note that among the Coast Salish with whom

Miller had experienced some of his most intense scholarly and legal advocacy involvement, he was neither named nor adopted. The occasional use of kinship terms was more a simplified form of address than terms of reference implying inclusion within the group. Thus adoption and naming are not a necessary outcome of long-term productive fieldwork and service to the host community.

Tim Buckley's paper on Yurok "In-laws and Outlaws" challenges us to rethink adoption as a mere form of kinship extension. He presents a four-generational account beginning with the efforts of Captain Spott to improve his status by obtaining wealth and traditional spiritual knowledge. Lacking an heir to inherit this esoteric knowledge, the Captain adopted his nephew (his sister's son) as his successor. The adopted nephew, Robert Frank, became Robert Spott and referred to the Captain as his father. Robert Spott underwent rigorous training and developed into a religious virtuoso. Because of his religious calling and sexual orientation, Robert Spott never married and chose to adopt a spiritually gifted white youth named Harry Roberts. Harry absorbed much Yurok esoteric knowledge, but he left the area and spent most of his adult life in San Francisco, where he held a variety of jobs and had several marriages. As an old man, Harry returned to the Yuroks to live out his days. He was estranged from his sons, and another young white man, Tim Buckley, became his intellectual heir to Yurok knowledge through informal adoption. Harry became Tim's anthropological midwife, not his fictive father or older brother.

This provocative essay reveals an intricate skein of inside and outside adoptions, ironically like interwoven strands of DNA or the imbrication on a Pomo basket. Yet Yurok transmission of sacred knowledge seems to transcend considerations of consanguineal kinship and folk genetics. Perhaps we have to think in terms of inheritance of acquired, as well as inherent, characteristics and construct models of heirship as well as kinship.

Ann Fienup-Riordan's richly embellished ethnographic paper on Yup'ik naming practices connects many points raised by the papers in this collection. Formal adoption, involving ritual announcement and official placement in the kinship system, is not highly elaborated in Eskimo society. Yet adoption *is* widely practiced and serves to unite communities internally and externally on many levels. Fienup-Riordan notes that most of today's adoptions take place because adults desire children, rather than because children require foster parents. However, this situation may not have always prevailed in the past, given the high rates of mortality and marital instability occasioned by Euro-American contact and conduct. The large Yup'ik vocabulary for adoption implies a variety of types and motivations, but perhaps the plurality of terms indicates a movement toward a less defined, unmarked category.

The Yup'ik naming system is quite complex. Not only are there various types of calling names (or nicknames) and teasing names (for example, Anna Banana), but proper names derive primarily from deceased kindred. Proper names may be shared by two or more people. While reminiscent of Northwest Coast inheritance of titles and the immortality of names, Yup'ik naming involves a closer interactive relationship between the living and the dead. This relationship represents reembodiment through revivified breath, lifelines, and claimed personhood. Material exchange between the living and the dead manifests itself through gift giving and food offerings: clothing and food received by a living person are shared with the dead personage. The deceased name donor and the living namesake both exercise volition vis-à-vis the name sharing. Illness or death can be interpreted as rejection of the shared name by either party.

Several other aspects of Yup'ik naming deserve comment. I found it interesting that the transmission of formal names ignored criteria of age and gender, such that a young girl might acquire the name of a living or deceased male elder, or an older man might inherit a younger woman's name. Since one received several names over the course of a lifetime, one's individual identity rested more in the unique configuration of names rather than in the distinctive features of the specific names themselves. The use of fresh water in the simple naming ceremony may only be an adaptation of Christian holy water rites, or, as I suspect, it may harken back to the effort to slake the thirst of the deceased, as is common elsewhere in the northern circum-Pacific area with bear ceremonialism, whale capture, and first salmon rites, where these beings are considered to be "persons." The use of teknonomy may reflect circumspection in using proper names directly as names of address. And finally the joking relationship between opposite-sexed cross-cousins may be a vestige of the former existence of preferential cross-cousin marriage.

Fienup-Riordan and her family acquired a diverse array of names that conferred personhood upon them and placed them within the Toksook community. Yet Fienup-Riordan, partly by preference, was never formally adopted. She compares her situation with that of two other female Arctic anthropologists, Barbara Bodenhorn and Jean Briggs. She notes that both women were unmarried and childless when in the field, factors that may have influenced their incorporation by making them less unconnected, vulnerable, and/or dangerous. Nevertheless, adoption or no, Ann Fienup-Riordan has clearly acquired Yup'ik personhood and has become enmeshed in the complex ties that constitute community life at Toksook. She privileges the information conveyed by her friends, who cannot be regarded as human subjects any more than Ann can assume the role of a neutral, if not neutralized, impersonal social scientist.

Sergei Kan's long-term Tlingit fieldwork is abetted by two formal adoptions that were more than honorary. Charlotte Young, a dedicated elder of the Russian Orthodox Church, befriended Kan and viewed him as a worthy replacement for a deceased male relative whose name was also kept in circulation by Charlotte's brother's son's son. The exclusive use of a name does not seem to hold for the Tlingits, unlike the situations we have seen elsewhere. Charlotte admired Sergei Kan's respect for Tlingit tradition, his Russian background and literacy, and his sense of proper behavior. Sergei's wife, Alla, was also adopted and appropriately assigned to a clan in the opposite moiety. With his newly acquired network of kith and kin afforded through Charlotte's web of affiliations, Kan was transformed from an outsider to an insider with access to privileged cultural data. He took his newly assumed obligations seriously by actively engaging in ceremonial performances, gift-giving, and maintaining regular correspondence when out of the field.

Mark Jacobs is an older Native intellectual into whose orbit Kan was increasingly drawn through shared interests in religious and cultural matters. Their friendship gradually matured into mutual respect and emotional empathy. While Sergei's relation with Charlotte tended to be more maternal and auntlike, the relationship with Mark was much closer and fraternal. In time, Mark carefully stage-managed Sergei's formal adoption into his clan and bestowed upon him the name of a deceased younger brother.

Being adopted into two different clans, albeit within the same moiety, is potentially problematic but not unprecedented. Thus far Kan has managed to avoid possible sources of conflict, but one can easily envision a time or situation when he will be forced to forsake one affiliation in favor of the other.

Sergei Kan is the only contributor in this volume to address directly the pandemic phenomenon of "anthro-bashing" that has become so prevalent in Indian Country today. He shows that this growing antagonism, while watered by the crocodile tears of Vine Deloria and others, is deeply rooted and that Native Americans have always been quick to point out misunderstandings, misappropriation, and other patronizing deficiencies in anthropological descriptions of their cultures. Indeed, Mark Jacobs is sharply critical of the accounts of Tlingit culture produced by previous anthropologists. In reaction, he not only became a skilled amateur anthropologist himself by collecting and collating traditional knowledge and posing significant questions about that knowledge, but Jacobs also adopted "his own anthropologist," Kan, as an alter ego with whom he could engage in ongoing productive dialogue.

Kan feels no conflict over his regard for his Tlingit relatives and his self-declared responsibilities as a professional anthropologist. He has little use for those who naively overromanticize their adoptions and, in their own minds at least, "go native." He feels that by remaining true to their mission, anthropologists have much to contribute, both intellectually and practically, not only to their academic audience but also to the people who adopted them. Indeed, genuine adoption is a continuing reciprocal process, not a onetime adventure to provide a temporary strategic advantage in field research.

In summary, this volume is not the last word on Native North American adoptions of anthropologists but a clear first call for more investigation of this crucial area of research where so many perspectives conjoin: for example, ethno-psychological definitions of self and personhood; cross-cultural dimensions of depth psychology and emotion; constructions of kinship and constrictions of social structure; and the moral career of the anthropologist's endeavor.

These diverse essays are provocative. One wonders why, or if, the adoption of anthropologists is so widespread in Native North America and seemingly less frequent in other parts of the world where anthropologists wander. Is this a legacy of the peculiar form of colonialism that has characterized historic Indian-white relations? Does shared marginality encourage adoption, or are democratic, assimilationist national policies influential?

These essays point to the need for a workable typology to capture the wide spectrum of adoptive forms and variable situations leading to adoption. But beyond classification, we need to be more sensitive to the nuanced pragmatics of adoption and to how emotions and ethics impact on both adopters and adoptees. Adoption and the attainment of a name need to be understood less as a certification of acceptance or as an instrumental fieldwork tactic by the anthropologist and less as a means of co-optation and exploitation by the adopters and more as a mutual moral commitment to honor and maintain, sometimes even beyond death. These essays eloquently emphasize the fact that adoption and naming are more than nominal acts.

REFERENCES

Chamberlain, Alexander F. 1911. Race Names. In *Handbook of American Indians North of Mexico*, ed. F. W. Hodge. Bureau of American Ethnology Bulletin 30, pt. 2, pp. 348–352.

Kimura, Takeshi. 1998. The Native Chiefs' Resistance Through Myth. Ph.D. diss., Divinity School, University of Chicago.

Contributors

Mary Black-Rogers, who received her Ph.D. in anthropology from Stanford in 1967, is currently adjunct professor of anthropology at the University of Alberta, Edmonton. She has published numerous articles on cognitive anthropology, Subarctic Algonquian ethnolinguistics, ethnohistory and social organization, and the ethnohistory of the fur trade and the Metis. She is currently preparing two books for publication: *Round Lake Study Database File* and *Treaty Gold: An Ethnographic History of the Treaty Period in Northern Ontario, 1900–1950*.

Thomas Buckley, who received his Ph.D. in anthropology from the University of Chicago in 1982, conducted fieldwork and practiced advocacy anthropology on the lower Klamath River between 1976 and 1990 and taught from 1980 until 2000 at the University of Massachusetts, Boston, where he was associate professor of anthropology and American studies. He is now an independent scholar focusing on the maritime world of the North Atlantic Basin. His major publications include the articles "Yurok Speech Registers and Ontology" and "'Pitiful History of Little Events': The Epistemological and Moral Contexts of Kroeber's California Ethnology." He also edited (with Alma Gottlieb) *Blood Magic: The Anthropology of Menstruation*. His monograph *Standing Ground: Yurok Indian Spirituality* will be published in 2002.

William N. Fenton began his career in Iroquois studies in 1933 as a graduate student at Yale, where he received his Ph.D. in anthropology in 1937. He is currently Distinguished Professor Emeritus at the State University of New York, Albany. In 1999, Yale Graduate School awarded him the Wilbur Cross Medal. He is the author of some two hundred publications on Iroquois culture and ethnohistory. His latest monograph, *The Great Law and the Longhouse*, published in 1998, was awarded the Rathbaum Prize.

Ann Fienup-Riordan, who received her Ph.D. in anthropology from the University of Chicago in 1980, is an independent scholar who has lived, worked, and taught anthropology in Alaska since 1973. She is the author of numerous articles and books, including *The Nelson Island Eskimo, Eskimo Essays, The Real People and the Children of Thunder: The Yup'ik Eskimo Encounter with Moravian Missionaries John and Edith Kilbuck, Boundaries and Passages: Rule and Ritual in Yup'ik Eskimo Oral Tradition, Freeze Frame: Alaska Eskimos at the Movies, The Living Tradition of Yup'ik Masks*, and, most recently, *Hunting Tradition in a Changing World*. She was named 1983 Humanist of the Year by the Alaska Humanities Forum and 1991 Historian of the Year by the Alaska Historical Society. At present she is working with Yup'ik elders, exploring museum collections in a project entitled *Elders in Museums: Fieldwork Turned on Its Head*.

Raymond D. Fogelson received his Ph.D. in anthropology from the University of Pennsylvania in 1962. He is currently professor of anthropology at the University of Chicago, where since the mid-1960s he has trained many specialists on North American Indian culture and ethnohistory. He has conducted ethnographic field research among the Eastern Cherokees as well as the Cherokees and Muskogees (Creeks) of Oklahoma. Besides the culture and ethnohistory of southeastern Indians, his research interests include American Indian ethnology and ethnohistory, psychological anthropology, anthropology of religion, and history of anthropology. He has published extensively on these topics and is the author and editor of several books, including *The Anthropology of Power* (with R. N. Adams), *Contributions to Anthropology: Selected Papers of A. Irving Hallowell*, and *The Cherokees: A Critical Bibliography*. He is currently editing the "Southeast" volume of the *Handbook of North American Indians*.

Michael E. Harkin, who received his Ph.D. in anthropology from the University of Chicago in 1988, is associate professor of anthropology at the University of Wyoming. He is the author of numerous journal articles and book chapters on semiotics, history of anthropological theory, gender, colonial and postcolonial discourse, and the culture and ethnohistory of Northwest Coast Indians, particularly the Heiltsuks. The latter are the subject of his book *The Heiltsuks: Dialogues of History and Culture on the Northwest Coast*. He is currently preparing *Between Mountains and Sea: Cultures and Histories of the Northwest Coast* for publication and is working on a project dealing with the mythopoetics of the Lost Colony.

Sergei Kan received his Ph.D. in anthropology from the University of Chicago in 1982 and is currently professor of anthropology and Native American studies at Dartmouth College. He has been conducting ethnographic and archival research in southeastern Alaska since 1979 and is the author of numerous articles and book chapters on the culture and history of the Tlingit Indians, the history of the Russian Orthodox mission in Siberia and Alaska, and the history of anthropology. His 1987 article "The Nineteenth-Century Tlingit Potlatch: A New Perspective" received the Robert F. Heizer Prize from the American Society for Ethnohistory, and his book *Symbolic Immortality: The Tlingit Potlatch of the Nineteenth Century* was given the 1990 American Book Award by the Before Columbus Foundation. His most recent publication is *Memory Eternal: Tlingit Culture and Russian Orthodox Christianity through Two Centuries*. He is currently editing (with Pauline Turner Strong) a collection of essays, *Native Peoples of North America: Cultures, Histories, and Representations*, and writing a biography of Lev Shternberg, a prominent Russian anthropologist.

Jay Miller received his Ph.D. in anthropology from Rutgers University, working in conjunction with the Princeton Anthropology Department, for his dissertation on Keresan Pueblos. He is an independent scholar who has taught Native Studies and anthropology at a number of universities in western Canada and the United States, and he is the former associate director of the D'Arcy McNickle Center for American Indian History. He has published extensively on the culture and history of the Native peoples of several regions of North America, particularly the Northeast, Southeast, Southwest, Plateau, Basin, and Northwest Coast. He is the editor of *Mourning Dove, a Salishan Autobiography* and a series of Native Washington autobiographies; he is also the author of several books, including *Tsimshian Culture: A Light through the Ages* and *Lushootseed Culture and the Shamanic Odyssey*.

Marla N. Powers received her Ph.D. in anthropology from Rutgers University in 1982 and has been on the faculty at Seton Hall University since 1989, where she is currently associate professor of anthropology. Between 1984 and 1994 she was a visiting research associate at the Institute for Research on Women and an associate member of the graduate faculty in anthropology at Rutgers. She is the author of *Oglala Women in Myth, Ritual, and Reality, Lakota Naming: A Modern-Day Hunka Ceremony, The Star Quilt: A Symbol of Lakota Identity*, and (with William K. Powers) *Sacred Foods of the Lakota*. She has written many articles for professional journals and has lectured widely in the United States and Europe. She is currently working on an ethnographic cookbook. She is also the editor and publisher of Lakota Books, which specializes in Lakota and Dakota culture-history and bilingual education.

William K. Powers received his Ph.D. in anthropology from the University of Pennsylvania in 1975 and was Distinguished Professor of Anthropology at Rutgers University. He is the author of numerous books and monographs on American Indians, including *Oglala Religion* and *Yuwipi: Vision and Experience in Oglala Ritual*. He has also published extensively in American and European journals of anthropology, history, and the humanities. His play *Collections* was produced at the Ice House Theater in St. Joseph, Missouri. He is currently the editor and publisher of Lakota Books, which specializes in Lakota and Dakota culture-history and bilingual education.

Anne S. Straus received her Ph.D. in anthropology in 1976 from the University of Chicago and is currently professorial lecturer in the Master of Arts Program in the Social Sciences at the University of Chicago. She has conducted ethnographic research on the Northern Cheyenne Reservation and has published a number of articles on Northern Cheyenne ethnopsychology, religion, ethnohistory, and contemporary politics. She considers herself an action anthropologist who engages in community-based research that seeks to serve the community as well as the academy. Her action anthropology work with Chicago's Native American community has resulted in a variety of journal articles on the urban Indians' experience and two books, *Native Chicago* and *Indians of the Chicago Area*. A collection of American Indian children's writing that she has edited is to be published in the near future.

Elisabeth Tooker received her Ph.D. in anthropology from Radcliffe College in 1958. She is currently professor emerita of anthropology at Temple University. She conducted field work on the Tonawanda Seneca Reservation and has published numerous articles and several books on the culture and history of the Northern Iroquoian peoples, including *An Ethnography of the Huron Indians, 1615–1649*, *The Iroquois Ceremonial of Midwinter*, and *Lewis H. Morgan on Iroquois Material Culture*.

Index

marriage with Nuxalks, 59; masks of, 60; names and naming among, 59–61

Herzog, George, 87

Hewitt, J. N. B., 93–94, 246

Heye, George, 83

Hunt, George, 10, 16 n.7, 62–65, 67, 69, 74 n.2, 75 n.7

Inuit: adoption among, 11–12, 18 n.25, 238 n.1, 239 n.4, 240 n.7; and naming whites, 235

Iñupiat (sing. Iñupiaq): adoption among, 221, 238 n.1; and contemporary legal adoption, 239 n.3; names and naming among, 232; and naming whites, 235

Iroquois: adoption of captives by, 4, 15 n.6, 51 n.7, 81; and anthropologists, 245–46; and ceremonial oratory, 38–39; Confederacy or League, 29, 32, 36, 47–48, 52 n.7, 81, 245; council house ceremonies of, 38–39; names and naming among, 52 n.7, 245; naming of colonial officials by, 52 n.7, 81. *See also* Cayugas; Mohawks; Oneidas; Onondagas; Senecas; Six Nations Grant River Reserve

Jackson, Michael, 73, 75 n.9

Jacobs, Harold, 203, 210 n.14, 213 n.42. *See also* Jacobs, Mark, Jr.

Jacobs, John, 88–89, 94

Jacobs, Mark, Jr., 10, 197–203, 206–7; adoption and naming of Sergei Kan by, 202–3; biography of, 197; Christian faith of, 197–98, 201–2, 211 n.27; and Jews and Judaism, 201–2; as Native political activist, 197, 211 n.29; as Sergei Kan's main consultant and teacher, 197–205, 212 n.30 n.32; as Tlingit clan elder and scholar, 197–200, 202, 212 n.32, 254

Jesuit missionaries: among Colvilles, 149–50; among Pine Ridge Lakotas, 121–22, 138 n.6 n.7

Jimerson, Avery, 89

Jimerson, John, 88–89

Jimerson, Johnson, 87–88

Johnson, Jemmy, 32–33, 36, 40, 49, 51 n.1

Jones, Albert, 85, 90–91

Jones, Horatio, 51 n.7

Kan, Alla, 192–93, 210 n.20. *See also* Kan, Sergei

Kan, Sergei: 1, 8, 244, 253–54, 259; adoption and naming by Daḵl'aweidí clan of, 202–3, 207, 253; adoption and naming by Ḵóokhittaan subclan of, 192–93, 195, 198, 203–5, 253–54; and Charlotte Young, 8, 190–95, 202, 253; childhood and education of, 188–89; effect of adoption on ethnographic research and writing by, 193–94, 203–5, 253–54; ethnographic research on and participation in ḵoo.éex' (memorial party, potlatch) by, 192–94, 195, 202–3; ethnographic research on Tlingit Orthodoxy by, 188–92, 194–95, 199–200; Jewish identity of, 188, 196, 201–2, 210 n.16, 212 n.34; and Littlefield family, 196; and Mark Jacobs Jr., 8, 10, 197–203, 205–7, 211 n.26, 212 n.31, 253; Russian identity of, 188, 191, 196; and Russian Orthodox Church, 188–91, 196, 210 n.16, 212 n.35; and Thomas Young Sr., 190, 193, 195, 210 n.17 n.20; and Young family, 193–96, 205, 211 n.24 n.25. *See also* Jacobs, Mark, Jr.

Kehoe, Alice, 113 n.8

Kiowa-Apaches, 3–4, 9

Kiowas, 4

kinship: American folk theory of, 13, 234. *See also* Native Americans

Kluckhohn, Clyde, 105

Kroeber, Alfred L., 170; and Robert Spott, 163, 167

Kroeber, Theodora: on Robert Spott, 163–64

Kwakiutl. *See* Kwakwaka'wakws

Kwakwaka'wakws, 16 n.7, 63; and Boas, 66–68; and Cannibal Dance, 63, 65; and ethnonym "Kwakiutl," 66; and naming Boas, 67–68, 246–47; and potlatch and Canadian legal system, 67; and Winter Ceremonial, 63–65, 68, 74 n.3

La Flesche, Francis, 17 n.13

Lakotas, 16 n.11; adoption among, 123, 126–28, 248–49; avoidance and respect among, 120; joking behavior of, 120, 134; kinship and social organization of, 126, 137 n.4; kinship terms used by

Lakotas (*continued*)
adoptees of, 126, 128; naming and naming ceremony of, 123, 127–28, 248–49; and oratory, 119; and sun dance, 122, 125, 134, 137 n.5

Lantis, Margaret, 238–39

Lenapes. *See* Delawares

Lévi-Strauss, Claude, 135, 189

Lurie, Nancy O., 9, 17 n.16 n.17, 18 n.24, 19 n.26

Lushootseeds. *See* Skagits

Mahikans, 144

Malinowski, Bronislaw, 73

Markowitz, Harvey: adoption by Lakotas of, 177–78

Mauss, Marcel, 60, 246

McAllister, Gilbert J., 3–4, 9

McIlwraith, Thomas F.: adoption by Nuxalks of, 58, 70; *The Bella Coola Indians*, 68; ethnographic research among Nuxalks by, 65, 68–71, 247; in Winter Ceremonial, 70–71. *See also* Nuxalks

Menominees, 18 n.23, 178–79

Mescalero Apaches, 5, 9, 17 n.15, 154

Miller, Jay, 4, 250–51, 259–60; adoption and naming by and ethnographic research among Tsimshians by, 145–48, 155 n.1, 250; on Colville Reservation, 149–50, 250; in Creek Green Corn Ceremony (*Busk*), 150–52; Delaware name given to, 144–45, 152, 250; Delaware research by, 143–45; Mohawk name given to, 142; Muskogee name given to, 150–52, 250; and Skagits (Lushootseeds), 153–54, 250; Tewa name given to, 5, 152, 155, 250

Mink, John, 17 n.17. *See also* Casagrande, Joseph B.

Minnesota Ojibwes, 107, 113 n.8

Mohawks, 52 n.7, 142, 144

Moody, Joshua: as McIlwraith's consultant, 69

Morgan, Lewis Henry, 2, 10, 12, 57–58, 73, 144; adoption and naming by Tonawanda Senecas of, 7, 38–47, 50, 81, 244–45; childhood and parents of, 30–31; and collection of items of Iroquois manufacture, 48, 52 n.8; earliest publications of, 31; education of, 31; field trip to Grand River Reserve by, 48;

field trips to Tonawanda Reservation by, 36, 38–47, 48; first encounter with Parker and other Senecas of, 32, 34; first ethnographic interviews and publications by, 34–36; and Gordian Knot society, 31; and Grand Order of the Iroquois, 7, 31–32, 34–37, 41, 44–46, 47–48, 50, 244–45; as the "Grand Tekarihogea of the Iroquois," 35, 37, 51 n.3; law practice of, 35, 49; marriage of, 49; as "Schenandoah," 31, 57; and Tonawanda Senecas' dispute with Ogden Land Company, 29, 37

—Works: *The American Beaver and His Works*, 31; *League of the Ho-dé-no-saunee, or Iroquois*, 29–30, 48–49, 52 n.8; "Letters on the Iroquois," 29–31, 38, 47, 49; "Notes on the Iroquois," 36; *Systems of Consanguinity and Affinity of the Human Family*, 49–50; "Vision of Kar-is-tagi-a, a Sachem of Cayuga," 34–35

Morrow, Phyllis: adoption by Yupiit of, 229

Muskogees (Mvskogis), 150–52; and adoption of anthropologists, 150–52, 156–57 n.2, 250; Christianity among, 151; and Green Corn Ceremony (*Busk*), 150–51, 156–57 n.2, 250; and *mikko* (chief), 151; names and naming among, 250; and removal to Oklahoma, 150; social structure of, 151, 250

The Mystic Warrior (film), 135

Nabokov, Peter, 19 n.27

National Park Service: and Wounded Knee National Memorial, 133, 135

Native Americans: adoption by whites of, 17 n.3; adoption and/or naming of anthropologists by, 8, 19 n.32, 72–73, 176–77, 206, 244, 249–50, 254–55; and adoption as turning strangers into relatives, 3–4, 14, 175–76, 246, 255; adoption of whites by, 4–5, 154, 244, 246, 248; American views on, 50, 58, 120, 136, 137 n.5, 188; autobiographies and biographies of, 18 n.26, 198, 213 n.41, 214 n.44; capture of whites by, 4–5, 16 n.9, 106, 244; as ethnographers and ethnographers' consultants (informants), 8, 10, 14, 16 n.7, 18 n.21, 69; hon-